1 8/00
x

RIVERSIDE
PUBLIC LIBRARY
1 BURLING ROAD
RIVERSIDE, ILLINOIS 60546

THE
WIZARDRY
OF
OZ

The Wizardry of Oz

The Artistry and Magic of the 1939 M-G-M Classic

JAY SCARFONE

WILLIAM STILLMAN

FOREWORD BY CHARLES SCHRAM

THE COWARDLY LION'S MAKE-UP MAN

Design by Rita Dubas

GRAMERCY BOOKS

NEW YORK

Overleaf: Deep in the Cowardly Lion's Forest, the Tin Woodman, Dorothy, and the Scarecrow proceed with trepidation in this Kodachrome publicity still.

Copyright © 1999 by Jay Scarfone and William Stillman.
The Wizard of Oz and all related characters and elements are trademarks of Turner Entertainment Co., © 1999.

All rights reserved under International and Pan-American Copyright Conventions.

No part of this book may be reproduced or transmitted in any form or by any means electronic or mechanical including photocopying and recording, or by any information storage and retrieval system, without permission in writing from the publisher.

This edition is published by Gramercy Books,™ a division of Random House Value Publishing, Inc., 201 East 50th Street, New York, New York 10022.

Gramercy Books™ and colophon are trademarks of Random House Value Publishing, Inc.

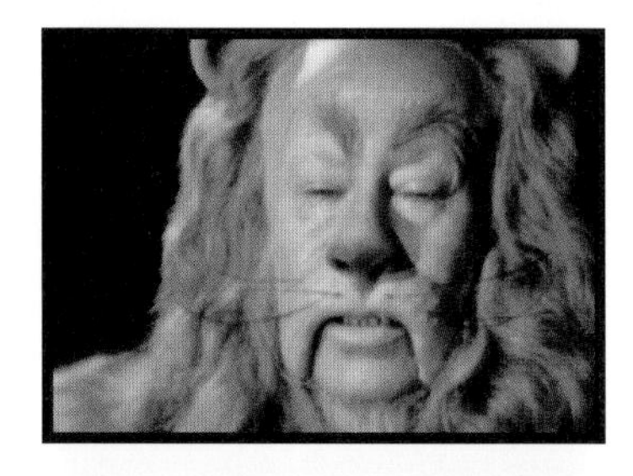

Random House
New York • Toronto • London • Sydney • Auckland
http://www.randomhouse.com/

Printed and bound in China

A CIP catalog record for this book is available from the Library of Congress.

The Wizardry of Oz / by Jay Scarfone and William Stillman
ISBN 0-517-20333-2

8 7 6 5 4 3 2 1

Publisher's Note. The language and terms used, particularly for descriptions of persons, that derive from archival sources, previously published material, and interviews, are quoted verbatim from these original sources, reflecting their original contexts/eras and satisfying scholarly criteria. Any offense to modern sensibilities is unintended.

CONTENTS

During a break in filming, Charles Schram kneels down to freshen the make-up of Olga Nardone, the tiniest member of the Munchkinland Lullaby League, December 21, 1938. To the left of Schram is Nita Krebs; to the right of Nardone are Yvonne Moray and Bobbie Koshay, Judy Garland's double. *Courtesy Charles Schram*

FOREWORD

More people have seen the 1998 re-release of *The Wizard of Oz* than saw the original issue sixty years ago. In 1939, motion picture studios gave very few screen credits on their pictures. Vast numbers of talented contributors were not given credit for their skills. At the same time, the Academy of Motion Picture Arts and Sciences recognized but few award categories. Make-up achievement was certainly one of those neglected categories, and one such overlooked individual was Jack Dawn, who created all of the make-ups for *Oz*. If the category of make-up for *The Wizard of Oz* was up for Academy Award consideration today, Jack Dawn would certainly receive an Oscar.

My own association with Jack Dawn began one afternoon in 1935. The dean of the College of Architecture and Fine Arts at USC (where I had recently received my degree) came to me and said he had just received a phone call from Jack Dawn at M-G-M Studios. Dawn, he said, was looking for a young man of my ability to train under him with the idea of developing some new processes in motion picture make-up. Dean Weatherhold told me he had made an appointment for me to go out and meet Jack Dawn the following afternoon. At that moment in my life, make-up was possibly the farthest interest in my mind for a career, but I went on the interview and started work the following Monday.

The apprenticeship training started with a dozen men of artistic ability working in the newly remodeled laboratory and a group of make-up rooms. Each room had a bank of overhead fluorescent lights with a barber's chair in the center and a counter with a large mirror against the wall. Jack Dawn's room was much larger, with plenty of space behind the make-up chair for us to stand and watch him work and give demonstrations. On his counter were rows of newly labeled brown bottles. A brush rack was against the bottom of the mirror, into which were stuck a long line of Windsor Newton red sable watercolor brushes in assorted sizes. Spread upon the counter were tubes and jars of Max Factor greasepaint make-up. Stacks of white hand towels and barber cloths to go over the actors were at one side. In all, the room was as neat and sterile looking as a surgeon's room before an operation.

This building was to be our school for many months. M-G-M was expanding rapidly from 1935 to 1940. Row after row of new sound stages were being built. New dressing rooms for the actors were being built as the old ones were torn down. New shops were added to the lumber mill where sections of the sets were built prior to assembly on the sound stages. There was a separate shop for almost every craft: paint, plumbing, electric, automotive, pattern-making, foundry, machine shop, printing, and upholstery.

As new pictures were being planned, screen tests of several actors for different roles were common. After the cast was set, many make-up, hairstyle, and wardrobe tests of each actor would be made. This brought a steady stream of actors into our building for make-up. Jack Dawn made up most of the "big stars" and, if we were quiet, we could stand behind them and watch in the mirror. As no rubber or plastic appliances were yet being used, changes in facial features had to be done by painting on shadows and highlights with dark and light greasepaint. This was then carefully blended together and make-up powder applied to set the make-up. Jack Dawn was a master at this technique—and a very demanding teacher. Watching him amazed us as he changed faces right before our eyes. It was like standing behind Rembrandt as he brought people to life on his canvases.

When all the actors had left, we would go to our rooms and practice putting make-up on each other. Later on the studio hired screen extras for us to practice putting make-up on. Part of our training was putting false hair on the face, such as beards, moustaches, and sideburns. This was done by painting a coat of spirit gum on the skin where hair was to be added. Then row after row of the matching false hair was pressed into the sticky gum with barber scissors and cut to the desired length, curled with small, hot curling irons, and made to blend into the actor's existing hair. This process took many months of practice to fool the camera that the added hair was really growing there.

Along with our daily make-up lessons, we began experimenting in the laboratory. Plaster of Paris forms of different-sized heads were made. They were coated with Vaseline, and then three coats of a thick liquid plastic was painted over them. When the liquid had dried to the touch, a heavy coat of talcum powder was applied and the bathing-cap-looking skin was peeled off the plaster form. The skin was then stretched over the hair of an actor and glued around the hairline with spirit gum. Then the bald cap and actor's face were covered with greasepaint and powdered. To all appearances, the actor had now shaved his head.

The next picture M-G-M was to make was *The Good Earth*. Paul Muni and sometimes one hundred or more extras were to wear these bald caps each day in lieu of shaving their heads. At that time they decided to use Caucasian actors to play Chinese characters. We made dental-like impressions of each of the actors' eyelids. Plaster models of each impression were altered with plastiline to change to an Asian-type eyelid. The final mold was made by pouring plaster over the altered eyelid, separating the two halves of the mold, cleaning out the plastiline, and using this mold to form the flexible plastic eyelids. Thus Paul Muni and the other actors "became" Asian.

The techniques developed for *The Good Earth* were next adapted to *The Wizard of Oz*. I think the most unique aspect of *The Wizard of Oz* was the use of the "midgets"—or little people, as they much prefer to be called.[1] Until that time, the only little people I had ever heard of were in newspaper publicity for Tom Thumb, and the posters for the circus. The M-G-M casting department scoured the world for those needed in the picture. There were a few scattered in the carnivals of the U.S., but most came from Europe. A man named Singer had troupes of them in many carnivals and circuses in Europe. A great many came from the district of Bavaria. Very few of those used in the picture could speak English.

This cast of little people brought us some new problems. Our barber chairs were too low for them to sit for the application of their make-up. We had to use boxes and pillows—and they sometimes had to stand up in the chairs so we could see what we were doing. Their size led to a further problem. If a small child comes to you to be made up, it is natural to bend down and lift the boy or girl into the chair. We tried this with some of the men and all hell broke loose. They would pull away and start swinging their arms and yelling in German, Spanish, or whatever.

After finishing the number with the little people, production was closed down to allow for rehearsals, tests, and final preparation for the remainder of the picture. In the first group of apprentices, Jack Dawn had picked a professional sculptor named Joe Norin. It was through his artistic skill that the cute forms of the rubber appliances used throughout the picture resulted.

I was very fortunate to have been selected by Dawn to do Bert Lahr's Cowardly Lion make-up. Bert was very enthusiastic and cooperative considering all he had to go through. He knew from the many tests we had made that his make-up would take about one hour to do. So each morning he would arrive at about quarter to seven, have his coffee, and stand in front of the mirror moaning about what hard work this picture was on him. He would watch the clock in the mirror until it reached seven o' clock. Only then would he sit in his chair for his make-up.

The dancing, running, and many physical antics Lahr had to perform on a sound stage lit by hundreds of 10,000-watt arc lights caused perspiration to soak his wig and the padding of his lion suit. They both had to be removed after each scene and dried. However, with Judy Garland and a cast made up of comedians, there were lots of laughs during rehearsals and between scenes.

After many months of work, *The Wizard of Oz* finally came to a finish. The many new make-up artists trained by Jack Dawn during the picture were lucky to have had this experience of working during one of the developmental periods of motion picture make-up. When I look back remembering all the fine artists, actors, and crew—few of whom are still living after all these years have gone by—I feel they all took pride in having contributed in making a picture that has delighted audiences the world over and has become an immortal classic.

Charles Schram

[1] Throughout this book, references to "midgets" have been reluctantly retained in the interest of scholarly accuracy in quoting the actual words of those interviewed and previously published and archival material. —The Editors

ACKNOWLEDGMENTS

Our journey in realizing *The Wizardry of Oz* as a published work dates back to 1993. We are most grateful to the following individuals for having helped us along the yellow brick road.

For sharing their personal memories of the making of *The Wizard of Oz*, reviewing our work, and giving our project their blessings, we thank: Beverly Allen; Del Armstrong; Stanton Baum; Florence Baum-Hurst; Betty Ann Bruno; Ruth Duccini; Buddy Ebsen; George Gibson; Mrs. William Horning; Marsha Hunt; Mrs. Henry Imus; Lois January; Donna Stewart-Hardway; Hedy Lamarr; Jerry Maren; Dona Massin; Margaret Pellegrini; Meinhardt Raabe; Bob Roberts; Mickey Rooney; James Roth; Ann Rutherford; Charles Schram; Marla Shelton-Gittleman; Karl Slover; Howard Smit; Duncan Spencer; Peter Stackpole; Clarence Swensen; and William Tuttle.

We thank Annemarie Bauer; Betty Chiniguy; Jeff Dawn; Sharon Dawn; Hango Dennison; Pierre Koshay; Tony Lane; Robin Dee LaVigne; Herbert Lahr; Hamilton Meserve; George Morgan; Hutzi Nickels; Linda Reyes; Del Roberts; Elmer Sheeley, Jr.; Clifford Shirpser, Jr.; and Carl Spitz, Jr., for adding detail around the respective work of their family members.

Woolsey Richard Ackerman was a tremendous resource in facilitating a variety of connections in the film-making and movie-memorabilia worlds.

For providing items from their personal collections, we thank James Comisar; Stephen Cox; Eric Daily; Rita Dubas; Charles Farrer; the Hufty family; Tod Machin; Joseph M. Maddalena (Profiles in History); Rudy Reyes; Debbie Reynolds (The Debbie Reynolds Hollywood Movie Museum); and Lee Speth.

Our esteemed group of photographers includes: George Anastassatos; Todd Bush; Timothy Costello; David Hardy; and Tim McGowan, the consumate gentleman and patience personified.

For their enthusiasm, support, and assistance, we are grateful to: Paula Allen (Warner Bros. Worldwide Publishing); Sam Antiput, who had the vision to champion our cause from the start; Ned Comstock (University of Southern California); Bob Cosenza (The Kobal Collection); John DeLuca; Amy Fischer (Max Factor archives); Todd Fisher and Michael Rennie (The Debbie Reynolds Hollywood Movie Museum); Katie and Jessica Grové for their friendship, and for arranging our New York accommodations; Beth Hergenhan (The Theater at Madison Square Garden) for arranging our interview with Mickey Rooney; Cindy Kellar; Timothy Luke (Christie's East); Ron Mandelbaum (Photofest) for his amazing expertise and attentiveness; Roland Parra; Allan Reuben (Culver Pictures); Charles Santore for the referral to Random House; Anthony Scarfone, Esq.; David Shayt (The Smithsonian Institution); Greg Suriano, our Random House editor; George E. Turner; and Jane Withers for her encouragement, and memories of Toto.

Deepest gratitude to our dear friend Rita Dubas for agreeing to design *The Wizardry of Oz*, and imbuing it with her warmth, care, and respect for the subject matter.

The collections of the following institutions were consulted in our research: The Academy of Motion Picture Arts and Sciences; The Alexander Mitchell Library, Aberdeen; The Beinecke Library, Yale University; The New York Public Library for the Performing Arts at Lincoln Center; The Library of Congress; The Lilly Library, Indiana University, Bloomington, Indiana; The Smithsonian Institution; The University of Southern California, Cinema Television Library and Archives of Performing Arts; and Walt Disney Productions.

The International Wizard of Oz Club was founded in 1957 to bring together all those interested in L. Frank Baum and Oz. The Club's "journal of Oz," The Baum Bugle, *is published three times a year. Membership in The International Wizard of Oz Club, which includes a subscription to* The Baum Bugle, *is open to all. Membership inquiries should be sent to: The International Wizard of Oz Club, P.O. Box 266, Kalamazoo, Michigan 49004-0266.*

FOR CHARLES SCHRAM

who endured more than five years of
continuous questioning about *The Wizard of Oz*
with grace, good humor, and unfailing support

INTRODUCTION

More than 165 arts and crafts were represented in the making of the picture, including workers never before used in a production. There were glass workers, color mixers, cellophane experts, flower makers, a sky writer, powder and fire men, magicians to invent new tricks, high voltage electrical experts, water tinters, beard dyers, wig makers, men who painted pictures with felt strips, lighting men, animal trainers, prospective artists, strange noise developers, hedge trimmers and dozens of others. . . .

For the picture a total of 3,210 costumes were designed and made, 8,428 separate make-ups were sketched in color and applied to faces, sixty-five fantastic settings built from 1,020 separate units, 212,180 individual sounds were placed in the picture and eighty-four different effects created for the unusual events of *Oz*.

And so began a 1939 press release heralding *The Wizard of Oz*.

It has been six decades since the release of Metro-Goldwyn-Mayer's film classic *The Wizard of Oz*. In the spring of 1938, the creative forces of this studio's art, costume, and make-up departments coalesced their unparalleled talents and ingenuity in the production of this unique and time-honored motion picture.

In retelling how *The Wizard of Oz* was made, our narrative's plot—by necessity—recounts a story that will be familiar to many. But while the plot may be familiar, our focus is unique. Other books that have documented the creation of *Oz* include *The Making of The Wizard of Oz* (Alfred A. Knopf, 1977) by Aljean Harmetz. This is a well-researched, technical treatise that is as much about studio hierarchy and film construction in the 1930s as it is about *Oz*. By all standards, Harmetz's account is considered the definitive compendium. However, much new visual material has since surfaced to warrant a closer examination of the various creative efforts that contributed to the look and style of the wardrobe, make-up, sets, and special effects that made *The Wizard of Oz* a milestone film, television classic, and video perennial.

The Wizardry of Oz is intended as a pictorial supplement to previously written works, providing never-before-seen visuals in conjunction with fresh anecdotal material. The territory covered largely skims the period of time from M-G-M's acquisition of *The Wonderful Wizard of Oz* as a book property in February 1938; through the March-to-October 1938 script drafts and revisions; to the August 1939 premiere of *The Wizard of Oz* and its subsequent foreign releases—much of which has previously been documented. The main cast of characters are known entities as well: ambitious and youthful producer Mervyn LeRoy; a succession of directors that culminated in Victor Fleming guiding *Oz* through most of its principal photography; the comedians and character actors in supporting roles; the young Judy Garland.

Where the Wizard implores us to pay no attention to what lies behind the curtain, *The Wizardry of Oz* draws back the curtain, exposing the wonderworks. Here for the first time in print is a detailed, step-by-step explanation of the procedures that allowed the *Oz* stars and extras to embody their respective parts, while their individual personalities shone through the greasepaint. Oz character wardrobe from design through fabrics, fittings, and alterations is juxtaposed with images

The Wizard of Oz (Frank Morgan) feigns indignation from the safety of his perch as the cast below points accusingly. *Courtesy the Kobal Collection*

of the actual costumes and props currently held in private collections. How the fairy tale world imagined by author L. Frank Baum was transformed into sketches and drafts, and realized in massive sets made of cellophane, plaster, and Masonite is documented. New facts related to the ingenious special effects in *The Wizard of Oz* are also revealed.

But our intent in presenting *The Wizardry of Oz* is also to acknowledge those men and women who worked behind the scenes—as much privy to the realities of conjuring artificial magic as is Dorothy once the Wizard's identity is revealed. At the time, these individuals went uncredited for their efforts, whether it be experimenting with rubber facial appliances; rigging special effects; grappling with scenic backings; or stitching costumes for small adults. (Throughout our research, we were continually impressed with the inordinate attention to detail that crafted *The Wizard of Oz.*)

The Hollywood press of 1939 was an accomplice of the studios, notorious for promulgating half-truths and falsehoods as fact. But M-G-M's surviving artists and craftsmen were profoundly accurate, honest, and forthright in their recollections—nearly sixty years later. Their memories guided our story. All still maintained a sense of devotion to M-G-M, and all possessed a quiet respect for the picture they helped create: *The Wizard of Oz*.

This book is as much for them as it is about them.

Jay Scarfone
William Stillman

A book poster by W. W. Denslow for L. Frank Baum's *The Wonderful Wizard of Oz* of 1900 illustrates the original concepts of the familiar Oz characters. *Courtesy Beinecke Rare Book and Manuscript Library, Yale University*

Prologue

OZ INFLUENCES

When M-G-M began work on *Oz*, a lot of folks said that such fantasy could be shown adequately only by the animated cartoon method. To which Producer Mervyn LeRoy replied, "If Disney can reproduce humans with cartoons, we can reproduce cartoons with humans."

— *Hollywood Screen Life*,
August 1939

Costume sketch for Dorothy (portrayed by Anna Laughlin), the darling of the 1902 stage show *The Wizard of Oz. Courtesy Performing Arts Research Center, The New York Public Library at Lincoln Center, Astor, Lenox, and Tilden Foundations*

After sixty years of entertaining generations of children, the popularity of M-G-M's *The Wizard of Oz* has eclipsed that of *The Wonderful Wizard of Oz*, the book on which it was founded. L. Frank Baum's original novel, published in 1900, is widely considered to be the first indigenous American fairy tale. Its boldly illustrative presentation set a standard that forever abolished the dark, crudely drawn ink sketches of traditional children's books. W. W. Denslow's countless decorative line drawings change hue with the shift in Oz topography; and are augmented with twenty-four color plates. The book's sprawling, fanciful layout with illustrations that spill across text and margins was as much responsible for its success as was its story. The book is not without its unsettling passages, but certainly nothing like the fearsome—and oftentimes gruesome—morality tales of Grimm and Andersen. The fabric of *The Wonderful Wizard* is stitched with heart and ingenuity—not retribution and angst.[1] Its narrative is punctuated with icons that are identified as uniquely American: the sparseness of the great plains; scarecrows; cornfields; and a man made of tin—not unlike turn-of-the-century merchant folk art.

Color plates from *The Wonderful Wizard of Oz* depict Dorothy and Toto being feted by the Munchkins, and the Scarecrow entangled by a fighting tree.

So well-received was Baum's tale that he eventually penned thirteen sequels about the land of Oz. Even his death in 1919 could not separate the nation's children from Baum's fabled utopia. Under Ruth Plumly Thompson's authorship, nineteen more titles appeared as the series flourished throughout the 1920s and '30s. During this golden age of Oz, the books became part and parcel of the modern child's library. Over the years several authors continued the Oz series; the fortieth and last official title was published in 1963.

Regrettably, the Oz books are now largely forgotten. However, any American child (or adult, for that matter) can instantly identify Judy Garland as Dorothy and her co-stars by their character names. Precocious toddlers can even recite lyrics and dialogue verbatim from repeated viewings of the M-G-M film on videocassette. Yet a surprising number of people don't realize that *The Wizard of Oz* is based on a book. Reveal that Dorothy's magic shoes were originally silver, and young and old alike will insist that they are indeed *ruby slippers*. In fact, *The Wizard of Oz* had a nearly forty-year history as popular entertainment prior to its 1939 screen adaptation. That history included interpretations of the tale in the forms of a

[1] Early versions of *Little Red Riding Hood* end with the young girl being attacked and eaten by the wolf. Likewise, Perrault's *Cinderella* sees the prince selecting the little scullery maid as his third choice after her two stepsisters each cut off portions of their feet to force the glass slipper to fit.

Broadway musical comedy, silent films, radio programs, comic strips, and assorted novelties. It was no coincidence that bits of this prior influence crept into the creation of M-G-M's *Oz*.

When M-G-M purchased the screen rights to L. Frank Baum's book from Samuel Goldwyn in 1938 for $75,000, the studio simultaneously secured the rights to all previous adaptations of the story. Metro wasted no time in accessing whatever was extant, pertinent, and of potential inspiration—scripts, photographs, films. The single greatest incarnation of *Oz* to date had been a highly successful 1902 stage musical. When the play moved from Chicago to Broadway in 1903, it ran for nearly 300 performances, and continued playing in roadshow companies into the next decade. So popular was the show's cast that tidbits about them appeared in the columns of newspaper music and theater sections. Foreshadowing the "Oz oddity" press the M-G-M picture would receive, little-known facts about the actors were revealed.

Lithographic poster for a national tour production of *The Wizard of Oz*. Pantomimist Arthur Hill personified the Cowardly Lion for the stage production. In 1902, the actor told the *Chicago Chronicle*, "This is the hardest animal role I have yet assumed because of the make-up . . . more of a strain than any other beast character I have ever played." *Courtesy Performing Arts Research Center, The New York Public Library at Lincoln Center, Astor, Lenox, and Tilden Foundations*

> It will be a distinct shock to many to learn that little Anna Laughlin, the dainty Dorothy Gale of *The Wizard of Oz*, is married. . . .
>
> Fred A. Stone is the only actor on the stage who admits to having baled hay in his possession. He . . . does have one bale in his dressing room all the time with which to replenish his wardrobe as the Scarecrow in *The Wizard of Oz* when it commences to bag at the knees. . . .
>
> The impersonations of animals on the stage has developed a class of actors who devote their whole attention to that style of work. The cowardly lion in *The Wizard of Oz* is portrayed by Arthur Hill, an English pantomimist.

In 1938, the show's players, songs, and spectacle were still fondly remembered by legions of theatergoers. Some critics felt Fred Stone should reprise his Scarecrow role in the M-G-M picture, or the play's song hits should be incorporated into the screenplay. Memories of the stage production's extravagant costumes, scenery,

The Munchkin Country of the early *Wizard of Oz* show was peopled with attractive chorus girls. Here, the Good Witch Locasta introduces Dorothy to Sir Dashemoff Daily, the play's romantic lead. The Gale farmhouse (far left), battered by the cyclone, served as the model for the crashed house in M-G-M's *Oz*. *Courtesy Performing Arts Research Center, The New York Public Library at Lincoln Center, Astor, Lenox, and Tilden Foundations*

and "transformation scenes" like the cyclone and poppy field were factors that underscored Metro's strive for opulence. Influences from the show on the film were ultimately few, but included the looks of the Scarecrow and Tin Woodman, the Good Witch using snow as an antidote to the poppies' poison, the use of farmhands (in *The Wonderful Wizard of Oz* there are none), and the disheveled appearance of the crashed Kansas farmhouse.

Other elements from previous Oz productions that inspired M-G-M's *Oz* included a brief bit of slapstick between Dorothy and the Scarecrow around the cornfield fence; and a dance of abandonment in Emerald City ("Union Rules/No Work After 12"), which likely gave rise to the lyrics of "The Merry Old Land of Oz," from a 1910 Selig Oz film. The Kansas farmhands reappearing in Oz and the story as a little girl's dream came from the 1925 silent

In 1925, comic Larry Semon interpreted *The Wizard of Oz* as a romantic comedy in a silent-film version of Baum's story. Though Semon cast himself as the Scarecrow, fiancée Dorothy Dwan as Dorothy of Kansas, and Oliver Hardy as the Tin Man, the film bore slim resemblance to the original novel. Pictured is a French-release poster. *Courtesy The International Wizard of Oz Club*

M. DeLange présente
ZIGOTO dans
LE SORCIER D'OZ
ZIGOTO
LE SORCIER
D'OZ
LE FILM COMIQUE LE PLUS FANTASTIQUE

Pictures from
THE WONDERFUL WIZARD OF OZ
The Scarecrow
The Tin Man
By W. W. DENSLOW
ILLUSTRATOR OF
DENSLOW'S NIGHT BEFORE CHRISTMAS — FATHER GOOSE.
SONGS OF FATHER GOOSE, etc. etc.

Pictures from The Wonderful Wizard of Oz (1903) capitalized on the success of the stage play by featuring Fred Stone as the Scarecrow and David Montgomery as the Tin Woodman on its front cover.

motion picture version. The switch from black and white to Technicolor, the "accidental" discovery of the Tin Woodman, and a carriage procession through the Emerald City were derived from an obscure 1933 *Wizard of Oz* cartoon short. Noel Langley, author of the first complete script for *The Wizard of Oz*, maintained that a bubble as Glinda's mode of transport was inspired by the sea witch in a silent film version of *The Little Mermaid*, but bubbles are also used as transportation in two books in the Oz series, *The Road to Oz* (1909) and *Handy Mandy in Oz* (1937).[2]

However, the single greatest influence in shaping M-G-M's screen adaptation of *The Wizard of Oz* did not have its roots in Oz history at all. The formulas Walt Disney used in creating *Snow White and the Seven Dwarfs*, the most successful motion picture of 1938, were a veritable textbook for producer Mervyn LeRoy and his staff. Not all the elements of Disney's cartoon feature were exclusive, but if *Oz* had turned out as originally planned, its likeness to *Snow White* would have been embarrassingly similar. Consider the following.

◆ *Snow White and the Seven Dwarfs* begins with a large storybook opening the film. A May 6, 1938, list of possible effects

[2] Interestingly, in *The Lost King of Oz* (1925), Dorothy briefly finds herself in Hollywood on location during a film shoot.

for *The Wizard of Oz* cites a "book opening routine" for the main title (although, at the time, the "book routine" was considered de rigueur when adapting classic novels to the screen).

◆ Large sections of dialogue from *Snow White* are scripted in rhyme. The same is true of the Munchkinland sequence in *Oz*. (Both films owed much to Gilbert and Sullivan.)

◆ The Seven Dwarfs are the comedic focal point of *Snow White*. In *Oz*, the Munchkins were originally intended to rival the appeal of the Disney Dwarfs. Early concepts sought to further define the roles of many Munchkins. The celebration in Munchkinland was to include the Munchkin Navy and Mother Goose Club, in addition to the Munchkin Fire Department, which was to reappear at the end of the film.

◆ The Seven Dwarfs' marching song, "Heigh Ho, Heigh Ho," gained immediate popularity with the release of *Snow White*. *Oz*'s equally popular "We're Off to See the Wizard," with its tongue-twisting lyrics, had tentatively been titled "The Marching Song."

◆ Snow White is awakened from "The Sleeping Death," a spell concocted by the Evil Queen, with a kiss. At least one script

From September 25, 1933, to March 23, 1934, NBC broadcast a *Wizard of Oz* radio program three days a week. In 1939, Nancy Kelly—the show's Dorothy—was just a year older than Judy Garland, but already too buxom and mature to reprise her *Oz* role. At the time though, the actress acknowledged that she was "very lucky, really, securing spots on the . . . *Wizard of Oz* [radio show]."

A scene still from the 1925 Chadwick Pictures film *The Wizard of Oz*. From left to right are: Oliver Hardy, G. Howe Black, Charlie Murray, and Larry Semon. Though already associated with Stan Laurel, Hardy would officially team with his famous sidekick the year after *Oz*. G. Howe Black had appeared with Semon in other pictures. *Courtesy Culver Pictures*

Animator Kenneth L. McLellan was keenly interested in the Oz stories and developed these character concepts as part of his proposed *Land of Oz* cartoon short. By 1938, he was using stop-motion animation puppets instead of painted cels. McLellan gained the trust and support of L. Frank Baum's widow, but was unable to secure the finances to produce Oz films. *Courtesy Lee Speth*

treatment for *Oz* was to have Dorothy awakened from the poppy field, a spell cast by the Wicked Witch, by the Tin Woodman's tears. (In Baum's *The Wonderful Wizard of Oz*, the poppy field is a naturally occurring phenomenon.)

◆ The poisoned apple is a pivotal plot device in *Snow White and the Seven Dwarfs*. There are no talking apple trees in the Baum book as there are in the film—only fighting trees encountered toward the end of the story. (In Disney's cartoon, however, there are trees that appear to come to life as Snow White flees into the forest.) Throughout the Tin Woodman's song, Dorothy prominently clutches a piece of the forbidden fruit retrieved from the apple trees. (In its synopsis of the *Oz* screenplay, the August 1939 issue of *Screen Romances* magazine went so far as to publish a still from the apple orchard scene with the caption, "The Scarecrow cried his warning just in the very nick of time. 'No, no Dorothy. Those apples are poisoned. Don't touch!'")

◆ Also as in *Snow White*, Dorothy was to have a blossoming love interest (in the Kansas farmhand who appears as the Scarecrow in Oz). Early drafts of the *Oz* script open with Dorothy fantasizing that she is being courted by a prince, as roleplayed by Toto. The only nuance of the romance remaining in the finished film is at the conclusion when Dorothy reveals to the Scarecrow, "I think I'll miss you most of all."

◆ In *The Wonderful Wizard of Oz*, the Wicked Witch of the West is a minor character, relegated to just two chapters of a twenty-four chapter book. Disney's Evil Queen/Wicked Witch character is an ever-present threat throughout the film. *Oz* producer Mervyn LeRoy (and scriptwriters Florence Ryerson and Edgar Allan Woolf) thought it only fitting that his witch be of comparable menace.

◆ The *Oz* Witch was originally slated to be a virtual copy of the Evil Queen in *Snow White*. The *Oz* script for July 27, 1938, includes a note to Mervyn LeRoy from the scriptwriters indicating a rewrite

Overleaf: Ken McLellan's concepts of the famous Scarecrow and Tin Woodman of Oz illustrate varied facial expressions as a guide for animators, circa late 1930s. *Courtesy Lee Speth*

The SCARECROW of OZ

TIN WOODMAN of OZ

Sorority of the broomstick: Walt Disney's Evil Queen (1937) and her apparent twin, Gale Sondergaard as *Oz's* Wicked Witch, September 22, 1938. *Image above © Walt Disney Productions; courtesy Photofest*

to make "the Witch match up to your new characterization." The Witch is described as "not the long-nosed, toothless 'old witch' of the fairy tales, but a woman with an eerie face, even a hint of evil beauty." Attired from head to toe in black sequins, Gale Sondergaard's Wicked Witch of the West was a glamorous imitation of Disney's antagonist. (Originally cast as the Witch, Sondergaard bowed out of the role before filming began, replaced by Margaret Hamilton.)

◆ One of the most horrifying scenes in *Snow White* occurs when the Evil Queen transforms into the Wicked Witch. A similar—though less intense—transformation occurs in *Oz* at the height of the cyclone's fury. For no apparent reason other than dramatic effect, Miss Gulch appears outside Dorothy's bedroom window. Peddling fervently on her bicycle, Miss Gulch dissolves into the personification of a shrieking witch, straddling a broomstick.

◆ Disney's Evil Queen has a decorative zodiac around her magic mirror—her oracle. Likewise, M-G-M's Wicked Witch of the West

A chart rendered by M-G-M make-up man George Lane depicts early concepts for the Munchkin characters in *The Wizard of Oz*. This approach bears striking similarity to the character model sheets used by Walt Disney, Max Fleischer, and other animators of the day. A number of Munchkins appear influenced by the Disney Dwarfs; still others resemble Denslow's drawings. The characters portrayed include 3 Sweet Children and 3 Sisters, who appear typical of the cartoon style of that period. Others are: Braggart, Deaf Old Man, 3 Tough Kids, and Town Crier. *Courtesy Tony Lane*

has a decorative zodiac on the floor around her crystal ball. (A May 4, 1938, "Temporary Set List and Effects" indicates a crystal *and* mirror for the *Oz* Witch in which appear the main characters "walking in the Black Forest"; the Cowardly Lion's face; and "Buggy on way to Witch's castle," presumably to rescue Dorothy.)

◆ The Wicked Witch in *Snow White* speaks to her raven when casting spells. *Oz*'s Wicked Witch confers with Nikko, the character specifically developed by M-G-M as her Winged Monkey familiar.

◆ Another sequence scripted for *Oz* parallels the scene in *Snow White* during which the Queen eavesdrops on Snow White filling her bucket at the well, singing "I'm Wishing." For *The Wizard of Oz*, it was to be Dorothy filling her scrub bucket at a fountain in the Witch's castle, reprising "Over the Rainbow." The Witch overhears the girl, consults an ancient spell, and brews a lethal rainbow bridge at her cauldron.

◆ Cartoon animation did make its way into *The Wizard of Oz* in two scenes that were cut from the final release version of the picture. The first scene occurred after the Witch threatens to use the Tin Man for a beehive. Immediately following her departure, bees flew from the Tin Man's mouth, ears, and funnel. The other scene took place in the Haunted Forest, and involved the jitterbug, first described as "pink spotted mosquito on Lion's neck." Another effect earmarked for Metro's animation department was that of the Witch flying away on her broom, as opposed to disappearing in a ball of smoke and flame. Make-up man Charles Schram believed that the disembodied Wizard's head was enhanced with animation.

◆ In both films, the Evil Queen and Wicked Witch of Oz have similar thrones. The *Oz* Witch looks like the *Snow White* Witch in at least one example of preproduction art. Adriana Caselotti, the voice of Disney's heroine, sings one line during the Tin Woodman's song; the *Oz* script identifies her as "the voice of Snow White." Likewise, Pinto Clovig, the voice of Disney cartoon character Goofy, as well as Sleepy and Grumpy from *Snow White*, provided dialogue for several Munchkin voices. And finally, to invite the ultimate comparison, the *Oz* campaign billed its extravaganza as "*Snow White* with living actors."

In constructing *The Wizard of Oz* from the ground up, M-G-M looked to a number of sources for inspiration. Film fantasy was clearly Disney's domain, and Metro approached *Oz* with the scheme of making a live-action feature containing elements proven popular in cartoons: comical characters, romance, slapstick, and exaggeration. Finally, after all was considered, the studio needed to look no further than its own backyard to pool the resources necessary for audience acceptance and success. *The Wizard of Oz* silenced those critics who asserted that flesh-and-blood fantasy could only result in disaster and disbelief. M-G-M's staff of artisans created original character make-ups, costumes, sets, and special effects from sheer invention. The finished film was Hollywood's updated version of a classic childhood fable; a glossy, decadent musical filled with burlesque and spectacle. But in the end, its wit and whimsy stemmed from the wisdom, heart, and courage that had been infused throughout L. Frank Baum's *The Wonderful Wizard of Oz* from the very beginning.

Opposite: Six *Little Wizard Stories* books, 1913, comprised brief Oz tales written by L. Frank Baum for readers too young for full-length Oz books. John R. Neill's illustrations indelibly defined the public's vision of the Oz characters from 1904 until his death in 1943. (Note the rare instance of the Cowardly Lion prancing upright on his hind legs.)

Three decades of the Tin Man and Scarecrow in like poses: David Montgomery and Fred Stone in *The Wizard of Oz* stage production (circa 1903); John R. Neill's ink drawing for the contents page of 1920's *Glinda of Oz* book; Jack Haley and Ray Bolger reenact the "over-the-top" fence routine in 1939.

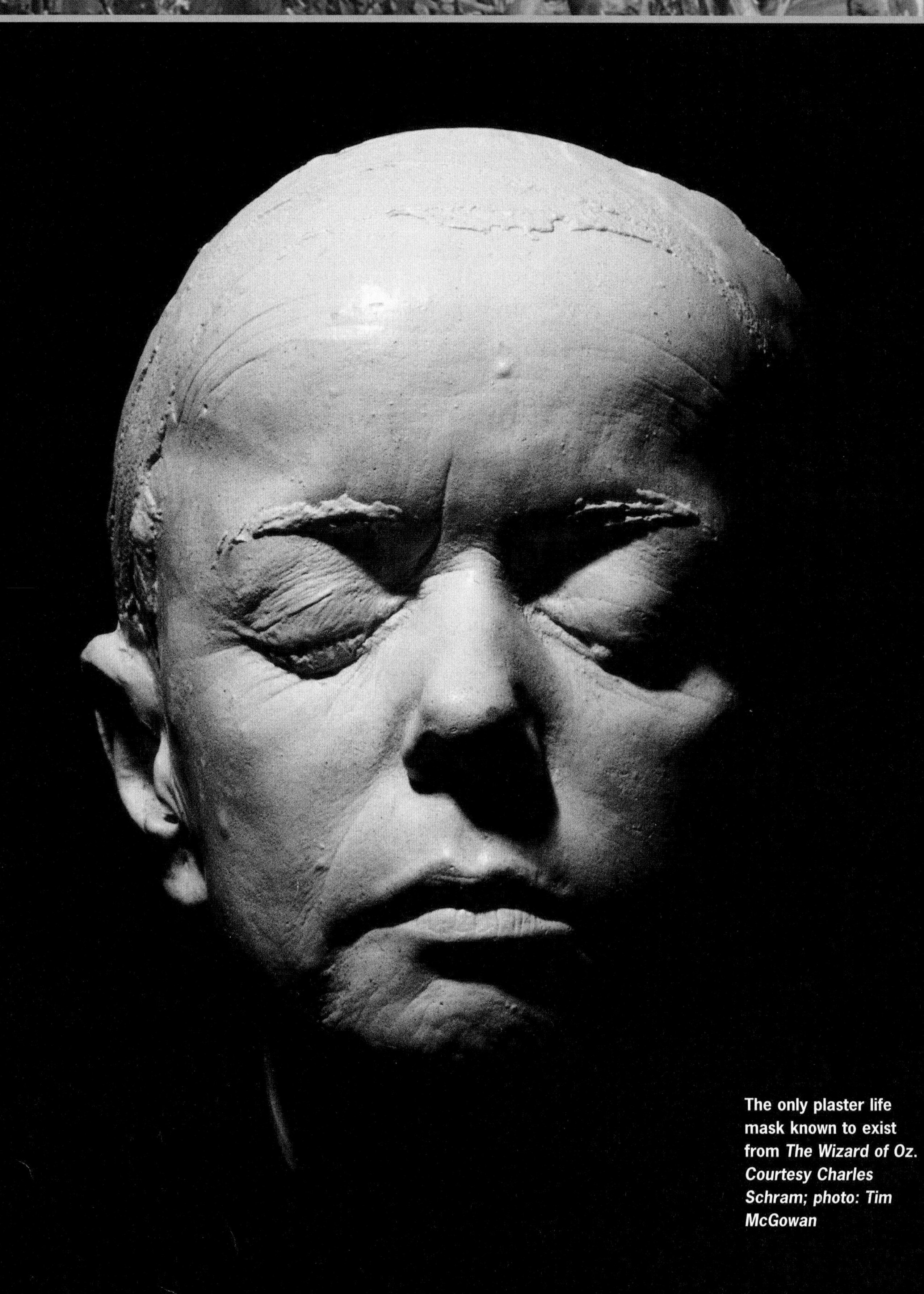

The only plaster life mask known to exist from *The Wizard of Oz*. *Courtesy Charles Schram; photo: Tim McGowan*

MAKE-UP

The Art of Transformation

HOW WAS HE TO KNOW

The casting director gave pause
On a set of The Wizard of Oz.
They were making some tests
Of a group of grotesques,
In masks made of rubber and gauze.

He stopped before one in surprise.
"Would you kindly remove your disguise?"
"Please—just take off your mask,
"Tho there's no need to ask:
"You are Gable, or Taylor—we're wise!"

Said the Shakespearean actor, "Begone!
"On me Broadway's lights have oft shone.
"Why, you poor low-browed pest,
"I am not in this test,
"Nor have I got any mask on."

— Robert Watson, *Hollywood Spectator*,
September 16, 1939

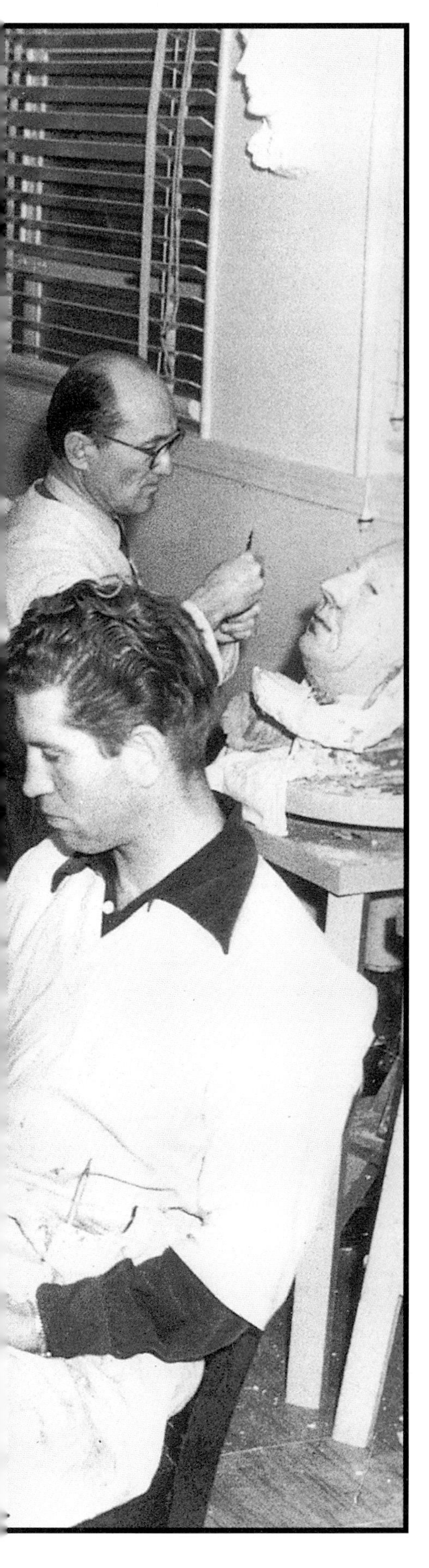

Jack Dawn was not a household name in 1938. But, as make-up artist to M-G-M's reigning film queens, his name was widely recognized by avid patrons of glamour. The attention Dawn and his exalted techniques received from fashion and beauty editors nationwide ranged from practical to silly. Typical features advised readers to "saturate your hands with olive oil before you go to bed; . . . in the morning your hands will glow," or "take Jack Dawn's Beauty Quiz." ("Does your lipstick leave embarrassing smears on handkerchiefs, napkins, or your beau's lips when you kiss him?")

Although Jack Dawn began his Hollywood career as an actor, his proclivity for painting and sculpture led to make-up artistry. After honing his craft throughout the 1930s at Fox Studios and Twentieth Century Pictures, Dawn progressed to Metro-Goldwyn-Mayer. There he eventually succeeded the brilliant Cecil Holland as director of the make-up department.

A rigid disciplinarian, Dawn devised an efficient system of recruiting young men with artistic leanings. Such apprentices were gleaned from USC or within the studio system. Daily classes instructed Dawn's protégés in the art of cinema make-up. Under his tutelage, and attired in mandatory white smocks, the novices practiced applying bald caps, make-ups, and wigs on each other. "He let you know if you weren't putting it on right!" recalled William Tuttle of Dawn's penchant for perfectionism. Others' memories had a more bitter edge. Jack

Opposite: The Bullpen, June 5, 1937. With Jack Dawn's apprenticeship program in full gear, an annex to the make-up department, nicknamed The Bullpen, was created. Here Dawn's budding make-up artists could refine their technique. Clockwise around the table are: Jack Kevan, Eddie Polo, Del Armstrong (standing), George Lane, Don Cash, and Jack Young. (The two men seated along the wall at right are unidentified sculptors.) These young men all contributed to the make-ups in *The Wizard of Oz*; Jack Young was assigned to re-create Margaret Hamilton's Wicked Witch make-up throughout the picture.

Young, another Dawn apprentice, remarked, "Jack Dawn was a tough bastard. The kids that fell under his lash were many, but the ones that survived came out as damned good artists."

Once satisfied that the requisite techniques had been mastered, Dawn assigned his pupils to work on actual film productions. This "assignment" status continued until a make-up artist completed his apprenticeship and was deemed "on staff." Through this tutorial process, many of the great make-up artists of the film industry learned their craft.

In 1936, this program was well established in preparation for *The Good Earth*, Dawn's first large-scale experience in effecting make-up suitable for mass production—and mass application. Filming Pearl S. Buck's novel about the plight of Chinese farmers necessitated the racial "transformation" of the lead actors and a small army of extras. It was during this production that Dawn employed extensive use of facial molds. In this manner, eye-tab appliances and bald caps could be exactingly reproduced with a consistency superseding daily re-creation by hand.

If *The Good Earth* presented Jack Dawn with challenges, *The Wizard of Oz* presented innumerable obstacles. Chief amongst these: How could humans be successfully disguised as Ozians? From the outset of preparation for *Oz* in the spring of 1938, Dawn experimented with methods to minimize the required character make-ups. Ideally, the actors would simultaneously resemble their Oz counterparts *and* themselves. Their individual personalities and facial characteristics could then transcend whatever external make-up had been applied. Of this, Dawn was particularly sensitive. In a 1939 interview in *Picturegoer* magazine, the craftsman was asked to comment on his work in making up Metro's glamour girls. He noted, "Of course it has always seemed to me that personality is more important than any amount of beauty. If a . . . woman is fortunate enough to have both, she is unbeatable. That is the combination one finds on the screen, the quality that makes great screen favorites. In spite of beauty . . . they all have an overabundance of personality."

Achieving this goal was the source of much trial and error. Still within recent memory was the failure of a comparable fantasy, Paramount's 1933 version of *Alice in Wonderland*. Boasting an all-star cast, any box-office appeal had been sufficiently squelched as Cary Grant, Gary Cooper, and W. C. Fields masqueraded beneath huge masks and headcoverings. Though elaborately costumed, the actors were unrecognizable, their performances discernible through voice alone.

For the *Oz* character make-ups, Jack Dawn began by rendering a reported two thousand watercolor sketches. Using black grease pencil, Dawn's fanciful concepts were next drawn directly onto stills of the actors' bare faces. The stills served as a guide in designing facial appliances compatible with each player, including extras. In attaining the end result, Dawn's strategy proved overwhelmingly successful. At least one bit of postrelease publicity noted: "The picture will feature a brilliant array of personalities; all faces will be visible." Amy H. Croughton, writing for *The Rochester* [New York] *Times-Union*, further praised Dawn's efforts.

> Jack Dawn, make-up man for *The Wizard of Oz*, should get a special award for his part in making the picture the splendid entertainment it is. If you remember the picture *Alice in Wonderland* you recall there was a certain irritation in hearing well-known voices of Hollywood stars issue from grotesque masks in which there was no semblance of humanity. It is different in *The Wizard*. The thin, delicate masks made for the three grotesque characters by Dawn allow a degree of their personality to peep through.

The transformation process was as strenuous for the actors as it was for the make-up artists. According to Charles Schram, casts were initially made of the actors' faces. A thin coat of warm Negacol, a gelatinous product, was painted over each actor's face with a brush. The Negacol held the shape of the face while a layer of plaster of Paris was next applied and allowed to harden. (The process had the unflattering distinction of capturing every pore and scar in detail.) Each cast took about forty-five minutes to complete. From the shell-like impression made, plaster busts could be created that produced a snow-white life mask of each actor's face.

Swedish father-son duo, Josef and Gustaf Norin, were among the make-up department's most talented sculptors. For *Oz*, the Norins used the plaster busts to test the construction of the character appliances, which were initially sculpted in a modeling clay called plastiline. The sculpted pieces were then converted to molds, into which was poured an exclusive sponge-rubber mixture developed by the Firestone Tire & Rubber Company.[1] This material was then

The make-up department made plaster casts of Metro's actors in order to randomly experiment with rubber facial appliances. Thirty-three-year-old Nita Krebs sat for this mask, and appeared on film as a Munchkin ballerina and villager. The mask was made in late August 1938—early on in production—before it was determined that only the male Munchkins would wear such appliances. *Courtesy Charles Schram; photo: Tim McGowan*

[1] Using the trade name Foamex, Firestone began advertising the impending multitude of uses for a variant of the foam-rubber latex. Progress was curtailed by World War II, and the public was advised, "All of our rubber is required for the armed forces and for essential civilian needs. But after victory, Firestone is prepared to start making Foamex quickly. Foamex will be widely used after the war in . . . America's finest automobiles; in living room chairs; mattresses [and] seats in theaters . . ."

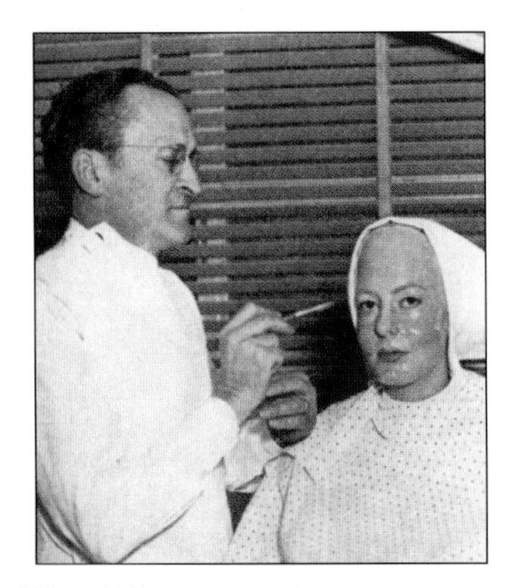

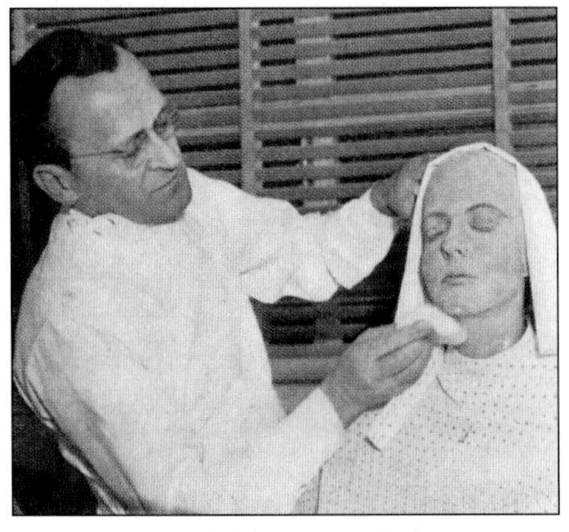

This series of photos taken for *Modern Woman* magazine are the only pictures known to show Jack Dawn making up an Oz character. Here, Dawn transforms reporter Sue Clark into an Emerald City ingenue. In the March 1939 issue of *Motion Picture*, the make-up artist confessed that *Oz* was his "biggest and most difficult assignment to date." *Courtesy Sharon Dawn*

baked in a process that is still employed in today's films. Jack Young remembered: "The big oven in the lab was going day and night turning out foam pieces; . . . molds were stacked everywhere." In 1938, however, baking sponge rubber was not a reliable process. Achieving success was a random experiment as the molded pieces could cure, crumble, or collapse.

The numerous bald caps used for the denizens of Oz were likewise constructed on facial-cast molds. This concept of creating bald caps had all but been perfected by Jack Dawn during *The Good Earth*. The caps were made, recalled Charles Schram, not of vinyl (as they are today) but of used Nitrate motion picture film dissolved in acetone, a solvent similar to lacquer thinner. The mixture was then plasticized with castor oil. This gooey liquid was painted directly on the actors' plaster busts. As they had a tendency to creep and shrink, the caps were formed heavier on the crown and thinner around the edges. Once dry, the caps could be peeled off the busts with reasonable ease.

After their construction, the bald caps and facial appliances needed to be convincingly adhered to the actors themselves. The spirit gum used for these applications consisted of gum arabic dissolved in ether. Such a concoction was exemplary of the limited resources in those days; however, it served the purpose, dried fast, and could be painted over. Prior to applying the bald caps, the actors' hair would be slicked down with either wax or bandolene, a viscous substance. Liquid rubber latex was painted over the edges of the caps and appliances to blend them to the skin. (Not surprisingly, the caps easily filled with perspiration and would run during filming. It was Charles Schram's responsibility to watch from out of camera range and advise director Victor Fleming if wigs slipped or skin was showing.) Once everything was affixed to the head and face (approximately thirty to forty-five minutes), the actual make-up was painted on. This entire process became basic in the creation of many of the main characters in *The Wizard of Oz* as well as a reported 26 Winkies, 36 flying monkeys, 124 Munchkins, and 350 other people of Oz.

Writing for *Modern Woman* magazine in 1939, reporter Sue Clark told of a recent trip to the M-G-M make-up department, which was in the midst of experimenting with character wardrobes and make-ups for *The Wizard of Oz*. "There were shoe-button noses, pointed chins and droll little elfin costumes all over the place," she commented. "I was fascinated."

In her article entitled "How Make-up Made Me into an Emerald

Empress," Clark went on to tell how Jack Dawn used her as a model for one of the citizens of Emerald City.

> He combed my hair straight back and placed a rubberlike cap over my head. This cap was drawn over my forehead and fastened in place with spirit-gum.
>
> As he applied layer after layer of make-up, Mr. Dawn told me many interesting things about cosmetics as they apply to women in every-day life. . . . As he talked my face began to feel like it was in a mud pack. Cheek pieces and a false chin, of plastic inlay material, were plastered on. Mr. Dawn explained that with plastic inlays—an invention of his—any person's appearance can be changed completely.
>
> The assistants spread on a final coating of grease paint to cover my false chin, dusted on more powder and, to make my Emerald Empress make-up complete, I donned flowing green robes and a sequin turban. This . . . whole process hadn't taken more than twenty minutes.

While enhanced to display Dawn's aptitude, this process was typical of the daily regimen required to move several hundred *Oz* extras through the make-up department in a timely manner. Dawn's cadre of apprentices and assistants was expected to work six to seven days a week from 6:30 a.m. to 6:30 p.m.—and sometimes later—in order to maintain Dawn's standards of excellence and preparedness. Despite the efficiency of the regimen, the make-up procedures were no less grueling for the more complicated character make-ups—or the actors who had to endure them. But reports of *Oz* make-up applications lasting hours are greatly exaggerated; Jack Dawn would never have tolerated such ineptitude.

In addition to making up the star doubles, Munchkins, and Winkies, Charles Schram was exclusively assigned to effect Bert Lahr's Cowardly Lion make-up throughout the duration of *The Wizard of Oz*. It was a process Lahr would quickly come to loathe, and eventually he would allow for no more than an hour in the make-up chair. Schram remembered Lahr as "a gruff sort of guy; he had a funny eccentricity." Arriving shortly before his 7 a.m. start-time, Lahr would crack jokes with the make-up men over his morning coffee. However, he was adamant

A Technicolor test of Bert Lahr's make-up. Lahr's expert performance caused his son Herbert a twinge of embarrassment. "I was eleven years old [at the time]," the younger Lahr reflected, "and for years I was called the Cowardly Cub! Almost all the kids in junior high school saw the picture! I had mixed feelings—on the other hand, I was very proud of Dad." ***Courtesy Charles Schram***

Bert Lahr's Cowardly Lion mane consisted of a full-length wig with rubber ears sewn into the top, augmented with a separate beard that closed shut under the actor's chin. A second version of the wig was needed after the Cowardly Lion receives his permanent wave in the Emerald City beauty salon. The only example of the Cowardly Lion's wig known to exist is in the collection of The Academy of Motion Picture Arts and Sciences. *Courtesy Charles Schram*

about not giving Schram a minute more in the chair. Watching the make-up room clock in the mirror, Lahr would wait until exactly the last minute. "Then he'd say, 'okay,'" Schram recalled.

The Cowardly Lion make-up began with the standard bald cap. The pre-formed nose and jowl appliances were affixed with spirit gum, and carefully blended with Lahr's skin. Several black broom straws on either side of his muzzle served as the lion's curved whiskers. The actor's eyebrows were painted over with collodion, an ether-based liquid usually used over wounds. Once the appliances were in place, a medium-dull orange make-up was applied with a sponge. Adding to Lahr's chagrin, the make-up was sticky, hard to put on, and required heavy powdering to absorb the grease. With his own eyebrows slicked flat, Lahr's lion brows were attached with spirit gum. (The Cowardly Lion's eyebrows were made in the make-up department—the hair laced through fine netting by hand in a process known as "ventilating.")

Lahr humorlessly bemoaned the daily ritual to *New York Times* reporter Bosley Crowther, citing a vastly abbreviated version of his make-up: "They . . . plastered my face all up with goo. Took me an hour and a half to make-up each day. Had to eat my lunch through a straw. Twenty-six weeks of it. Tough job." Studio publicity further streamlined the tedious process to highlight Lahr's presumably leonine features, noting that the actor's "only facial make-up was a pair of slanting eyebrows and a stiff upper lip."

Wearing white long johns, Lahr would leave make-up and walk onto the set "looking like a chicken," remembered Charles Schram. There, Schram helped Lahr put on his wig and a fur neckpiece that snapped shut under his chin. Sewn into the top of the wig were two sponge-rubber ears, colored with a special paint make-up to match the color of Lahr's face. Once the wig was adjusted, Lahr was ready to whimper, cower, and project mock valor as the comical Cowardly Lion. When the camera stopped, however, Lahr's wig immediately came off, drenched with perspiration. This necessitated two hairpieces, which could alternate under a dryer between shots.

Fortunately for Lahr, a man plagued by neuroses, his make-up was at least tolerable compared to the claustrophobic cowl wrapped around Ray Bolger's head. Interestingly, Dawn struggled most with creating Bolger's Scarecrow make-up. When it was determined that a light make-up resembling Fred Stone (the Scarecrow of the 1902 *Wizard of Oz* stage production) wasn't effective enough, Dawn devised a sponge-rubber mask that covered Bolger's head but was thin enough around the actor's facial features to be pliable. The result was that Bolger's head appeared to be a realistically textured burlap sack, stuffed with straw and tied with a rope at his neck. If removed carefully, each rubber sack could be used more than once.

Adhered with spirit gum, the edges of the mask were expertly blended with make-up at Bolger's eyes, nose, and mouth by Norbert Miles, Bolger's make-up man. His head encased in a sheath of sponge rubber for long hours at a time, Bolger would occasionally feel faint while strenuously dancing and pratfalling during filming. A cocky young trouper in his mid-thirties, Bolger's lightheadedness was not a reflection of his stamina. The rubber mask had effectively sealed off all the pores in his face and, as the actor remarked in interviews in later years, he simply couldn't breathe. For longer breaks in filming, the seam on the back of Bolger's headpiece could be split open to allow for some ventilation and respite from his stifling condition.

Silver Screen magazine reported that Bolger took precautions to protect his skin against the wear and tear of the make-up. The fan magazine described Bolger's nightly ritual in which the dancer "applied lemon cream to his face, followed it with warm water, an application of turtle oil, another application of warm water, then a layer of special ointment to wear overnight." Bolger's skin care likely received some editorial embellishment; he drove home at the end of each day exhausted, with little time to unwind except for cocktails before dinner.

Jack Haley's own exhaustion during *The Wizard of Oz* was literal. Working on *Oz* by day and furiously preparing for his weekly radio show after hours, Haley's predicament was compounded by his cumbersome Tin Woodman costume and an exacting make-up. (Make-up man Emile LaVigne contended that a double was used for Haley whenever possible.) Trivia fans of the M-G-M film are well aware that the production began filming in October 1938 with hoofer Buddy Ebsen as the Tin Man. Ebsen recalled the make-up's prime ingredient: "It was aluminum; . . . it was *powdered* on me." Ebsen suffered a near-fatal reaction to the metallic dust used to silver his face because he inhaled the powder with each application, "which coated my lungs like paint," he said. He was replaced in the role by Jack Haley, who was on loan to M-G-M from his home studio, Twentieth Century-Fox. Using a physician-approved aluminum *paste* to cover his face (and to avoid accidental ingestion), Haley's make-up was equally as painstaking as that of his co-stars.

On October 8, 1938, Ray Bolger tested the thin, sacklike rubber mask that would serve as his make-up. Effective blending of the mask's edges with his own skin and the addition of a broad-brimmed black hat allowed the actor to step before the cameras under Richard Thorpe's direction. When interim director George Cukor replaced Thorpe later that month, only minor make-up changes transformed Bolger into the Scarecrow as he appears in the finished film.

Ray Bolger in full make-up, shown in this Kodachrome publicity still.

Like the Scarecrow, original concepts of the Tin Man were reminiscent of David Montgomery's portrayal of the character in the early stage musical. The make-up was light but without fantasy character to it. Emile LaVigne and another young make-up man, Lee Stanfield, alternated making up Haley and his double. In the book *Making a Monster*, LaVigne described the specifics of creating the final version of the Tin Woodman.

> The Tin Man's face and head consisted of three appliances. The funnel formed the top of his head and went down the back of his neck—behind his ears and below his collar. This gave his neck a straight, stiff look and covered his hair, fitting the contour of Jack Haley's head. . . .
>
> The nose extended slightly into a funnel shape. The third appliance, which was the jaw piece, extended from above his

A Technicolor test frame of Jack Haley as the Tin Woodman during the actor's first three days of filming, early November 1938. When it was realized that the Tin Man should be rusty—not polished—when Dorothy discovers him, Haley's make-up was appropriately adjusted. ***Courtesy Charles Schram***

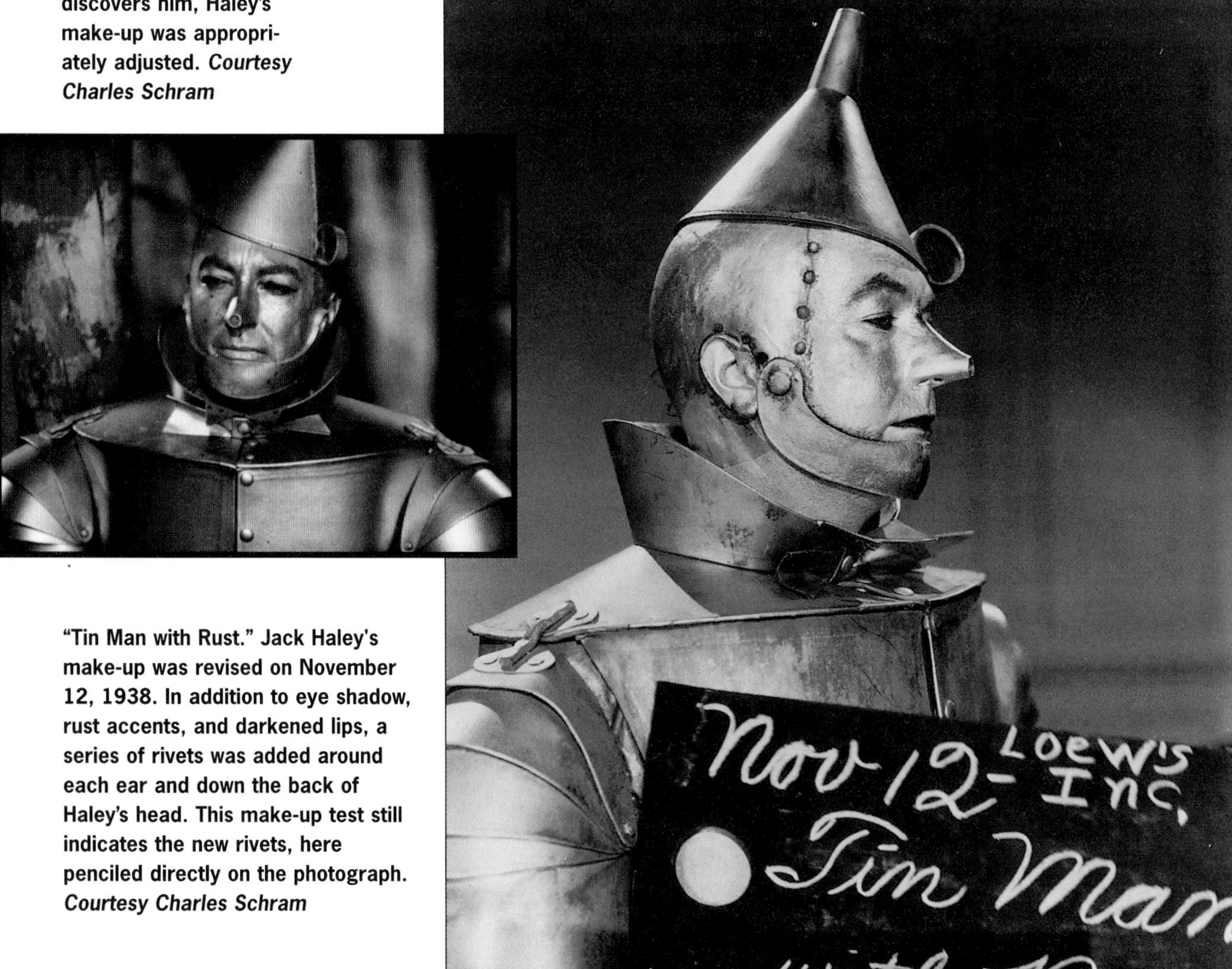

"Tin Man with Rust." Jack Haley's make-up was revised on November 12, 1938. In addition to eye shadow, rust accents, and darkened lips, a series of rivets was added around each ear and down the back of Haley's head. This make-up test still indicates the new rivets, here penciled directly on the photograph. ***Courtesy Charles Schram***

ears, down around his jaw, and moved when he spoke, as if hinged. . . .

We then put a thick layer of pancake on the exposed skin before applying the silver paint over the appliance and his face. The pancake was used as an undercoat to protect Haley's skin as constant use of the silver paint directly on his skin proved irritating. Talcum powder was used to set the make-up, and a soft powder brush removed the surplus powder.

The Tin Woodman suitably polished for a Kodachrome publicity portrait.

Like his co-stars' make-ups, Haley's Tin Woodman visage was briefly tested on film while in the make-up department to ensure an effective translation to the screen. However, Haley's first several days of actual on-set Technicolor film was scrapped because it was realized that the Tin Man was supposed to be rusty—not polished—at that point in the story. On November 12, 1938, Haley's make-up underwent minor revision. In addition to the requisite "rust" accents, eye shadow was added and his lips were darkened. A series

adhered around his ears and down

n film, Metro claimed, "Jack Haley as
its worth of powdered metallic silver
r looks more silvery with a slight tinge
Haley's make-up . . . contained a trace
n its pulverized silver face powder."
ff is to be believed, Haley's make-up
polisher" or "polished with a soft cloth

abricated an unlikely tale about
: "Margaret Hamilton as the Wicked
e which she carried in her purse one
movie. A purse snatcher got the purse,
a note: 'Wow! So this is Hollywood!'"
n nose not made of metal but, the
ped like my nose; most of it was my
ke-up department kept changing and
pecially my nose. One wanted the nose
n less of a bump. So I tried on several
il they decided which was best." In
l pointed chin (replete with a wart
air) were made of the same baked
other actors' appliances.

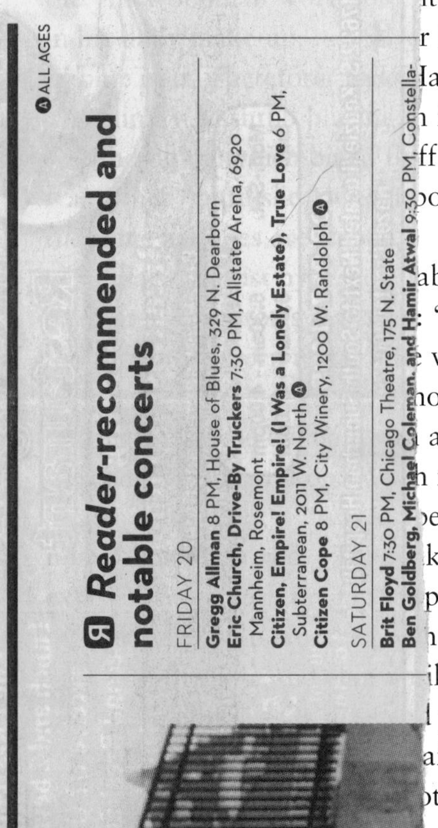

Я Reader-recommended and notable concerts
ALL AGES
FRIDAY 20
Gregg Allman 8 PM, House of Blues, 329 N. Dearborn
Eric Church, Drive-By Truckers 7:30 PM, Allstate Arena, 6920 Mannheim, Rosemont
Citizen, Empire! Empire! (I Was a Lonely Estate), True Love 6 PM, Subterranean, 2011 W. North
Citizen Cope 8 PM, City Winery, 1200 W. Randolph
SATURDAY 21
Brit Floyd 7:30 PM, Chicago Theatre, 175 N. State
Ben Goldberg, Michael Coleman, and Hamir Atwal 9:30 PM, Constella-

According to Hamilton, "[I spent] two hours [in] make-up, getting my hair back. The base had copper in it to make it green." Jack Young, the make-up man assigned to work with Hamilton throughout *Oz*, began the actress's ghastly transformation using the same formula that created the other characters. Once Hamilton's face was properly augmented, varying shades of green make-up were applied to effect highlights and shadows. The same greasy make-up also covered her neck and hands. Additionally, Hamilton's lips were painted and her teeth were yellowed, causing the reviewer for *Young America* to quip that "the Wicked Witch is very ugly with . . . a red tongue that she keeps sticking out to show her anger." A hairdresser finished by arranging the Witch's wig.

Because of the toxicity of the copper make-up, Hamilton's face was meticulously cleaned before she left the studio at the end of the day. She recalled:

Margaret Hamilton's green-complexioned Witch make-up, as seen in a Technicolor test on the Munchkinland set. Max Factor provided Metro's make-up department with any unusual color make-ups free of extra charge. *Courtesy Charles Schram*

> M-G-M made several tests in color of different shades of green. They tested me in make-up and costume against backgrounds. Every time they applied this make-up, they used these not-too-soft pieces of cloth. And it *hurt* when they took the make-up off. By the time I got through with that, I was a wreck. During the production I told them, 'If I'm not needed on certain days, I don't want to come in! I want to give my poor face a rest!' It was so sore and it felt like they rubbed sandpaper over it. Finally, I had to go to a doctor.

Max Factor supplied M-G-M with its cache of make-up supplies in various pigments, including Margaret Hamilton's copper green make-up. The make-up was specially developed at the Max Factor laboratories with a castor-oil base needed to adhere to foam rubber. (Previous trials using mineral-oil-based products only discolored and rotted the foam.) To her amusement, Hamilton's evil countenance had a lingering effect. Hamilton reminisced in an interview published in the April 1989 issue of *Hollywood Studio Magazine*.

> I didn't expect it, but my skin had a faint green to it for weeks and weeks afterwards. And a funny thing happened to me later on. I was at a friend's house shortly after the picture was finished. My friend asked me if I felt alright. I said "Yes,

A near-final make-up test still for Margaret Hamilton as the Wicked Witch of the West, circa late October/early November 1938. Jack Young has taken a pencil to the photo, and shaded the foam-rubber appliances on the actress's nose and chin to indicate how these pieces would blend with her facial make-up. The spectacles dangling from Hamilton's witch costume were intended to mirror those used by Miss Gulch, her Kansas counterpart, but were discarded before filming resumed under director Victor Fleming.

I'm fine." She said, "You don't look fine!" So we both went over to her big mirror. I couldn't see anything wrong. My friend turned on the overhead light. "Now, have a look at your face. You look green!" I said, "Don't be silly!" But when I looked very closely at my face, I noticed it. I said, "My Lord, I do look green!" And I roared with laughter because I hadn't noticed it before.

Make-up man William Tuttle remembered that the same green make-up (and a similarly hooked nose) was used on the more than two dozen men recruited to play the Witch's Winkie guards. While Tuttle was intensively involved in preparation for *The Wizard of Oz*, he wasn't assigned to work exclusively on the picture. The artist recalled, "I would be doing Lana Turner, Hedy Lamarr and a Winkie all in one morning." Sluggishly piling into make-up in their street clothes, the would-be Winkies still presented dilemmas. "The challenge was taking a roomful of men who looked nothing alike and making them all look alike," said Tuttle. (Many years later, Tuttle

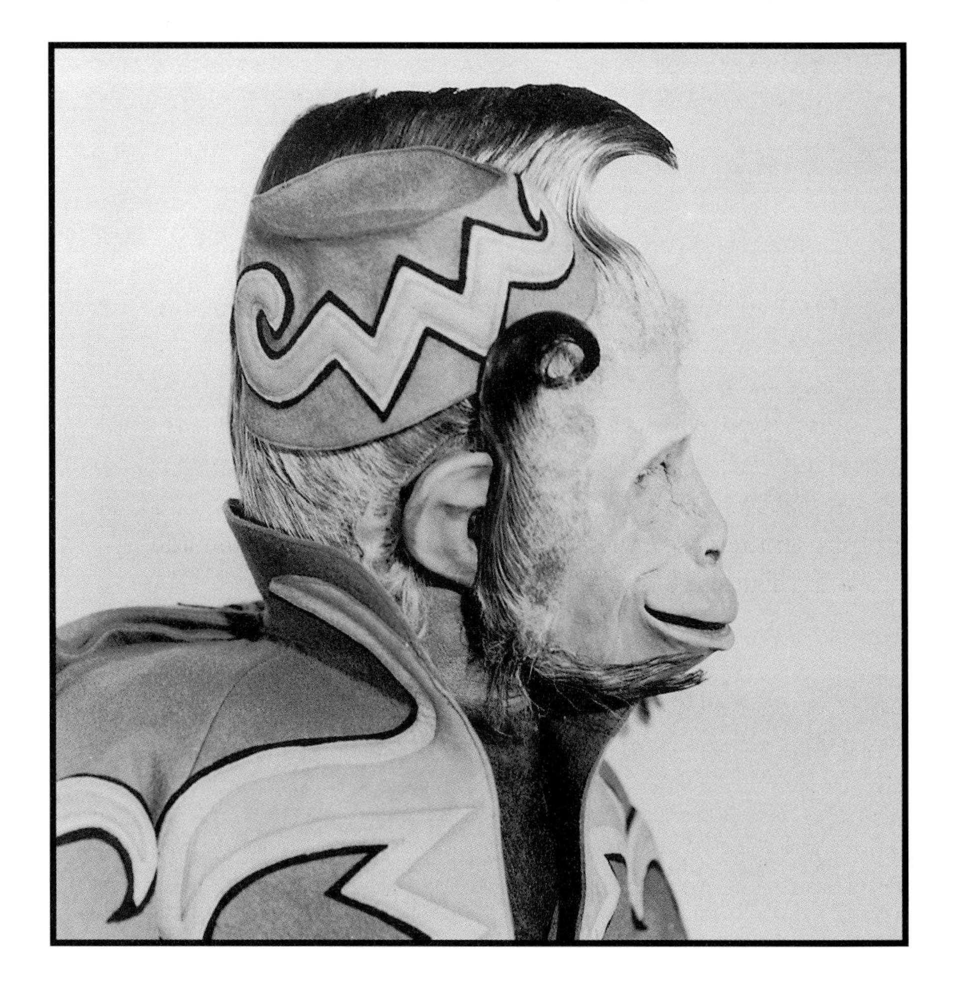

Make-up test for Pat Walshe as the Witch's monkey servant, Nikko. Jack Dawn's concept of the Winged Monkeys transformed Baum's mischievous chimps into grotesque hobgoblins with gray grimaces. M-G-M's monkeys likely owed their inspiration to the famed "spitting" gargoyle of the Notre Dame cathedral with its simian features, arched wings, and prominent crest.

received an assignment to create the make-ups for a bank commercial with an Oz theme. With only forty-eight hours notice and a 5 a.m. morning call, Tuttle longed for the prep time afforded him in his M-G-M days. "You learned to become resourceful," he mused.)

In addition to assisting with the Winkies, Tuttle made up flying monkeys and painted red spots on the cheeks of starlets appearing in the Emerald City sequences. Making up the extras playing Emerald City citizens was another exercise in consistency. Several actors were assigned specific roles for these scenes—The Minister, The Man Who Leads the Triumphal Procession, and so on. However, most others were grouped into varied categories of townspeople. True to Dorothy's Technicolor nightmare, the peasants were to resemble china dolls and toy soldiers, probably in concession to "The Dainty China Country" chapter in *The Wonderful Wizard of Oz*.[2] Females received standard pancake make-up, which included false lashes and a large red circle on each cheek. Effecting the wooden soldier look, however, was more time-consuming. Each man received a bald cap and facial make-up, which might have included sideburns and a moustache. (Emerald City guards were also given Cyrano de Bergerac noses.) To create the enameled look of the townsmen's glossy hairlines, thick black paint was simply brushed directly onto the bald caps.

Jack Young recalled the days when a seemingly infinite number of extras required make-up:

> Office boys were borrowed for the early start and were given trays that, to the layman, looked like trays of hors d'oeuvres. Piled with different appliances, the kids would go along the make-up line and the make-up men would take whatever appliances they would need for that particular make-up. The different steps were assigned to different people. For instance, those who excelled in appliances would put on the noses; then the beard. Hairdressers would add wigs. The same procedures were used for the townspeople: caps, base, hairdress—a real mass production line.

Also on such days an open call was put out to the local make-up and hairdressing union for freelance make-up men to work on *Oz* per diem.

[2] In L. Frank Baum's original book, the journey through the Dainty China Country was an anticlimactic adventure not considered for the screenplay. The miniature citizens of the country were delicate, doll-like, and extremely fragile. By contrast, inhabitants of the Emerald City were described as having "greenish skins."

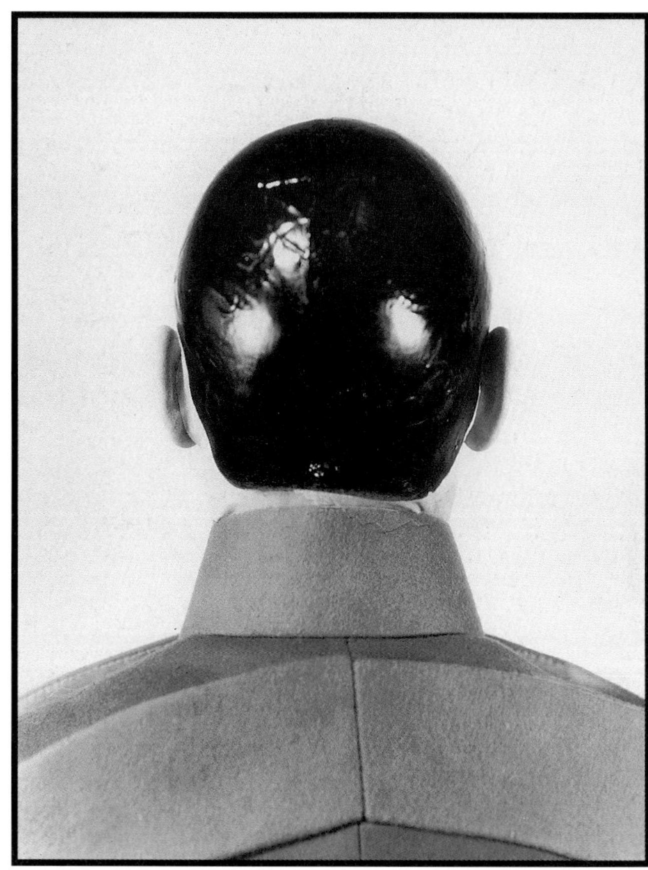

Two views of an Emerald City extra's make-up. A Kodachrome make-up test for a soldier, taken by Charles Schram in the M-G-M make-up lab (left), and the black-and-white test still (dated November 11, 1938) illustrate the effective use of a bald cap (with a black painted hairline), facial appliances, and a false moustache and goatee.

The efficiency, patience, and good humor of the make-up crew was universally tested by the male performers playing Munchkins. Those surviving make-up artists, and even the families of those deceased, still remembered that these actors "were difficult to work with," as Robin Dee LaVigne recalled from her father Emile's anecdotes. Any conflicts between the little people and the young assistants were likely the result of cultural impasse than anything else. Many of the little people were not English-speaking, and most felt the need to assert their adulthood to diffuse any stereotype of childlike behavior. Creating an atmosphere of mutual understanding was muddied by the pressures of making up this large group of actors in assembly-line fashion.[3] Robin Dee LaVigne recalled her father relating a tale of alleged retaliation: on one occasion, the bald caps were intentionally adhered to the hair of several male little people. This compounded an already problematic situation for the

[3] Stage mothers who could tend to their little girls playing Munchkins in long shots were permitted to do so without a qualm. Donna Stewart-Hardway recalled, "My mother made me up. . . . The smell of real heavy pancake make-up smelled like tallow. The abalone cream [used to remove it] also smelled rancid." Betty Ann Bruno wasn't sure if her mother did her make-up, but was certain that "we would not have been made up at the same place as the midgets. The children were always segregated from the midgets."

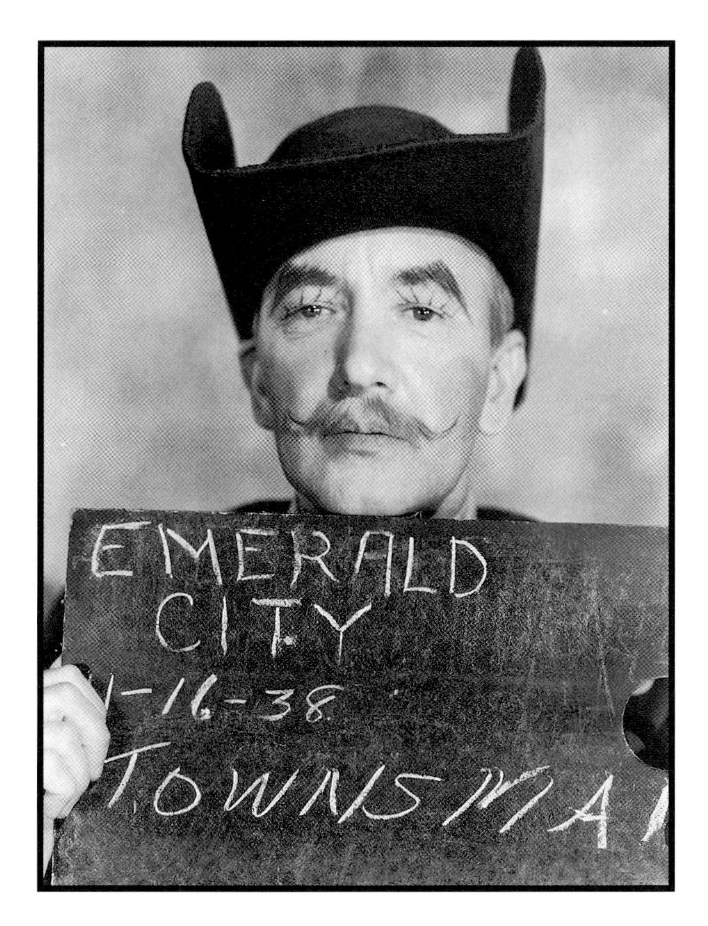

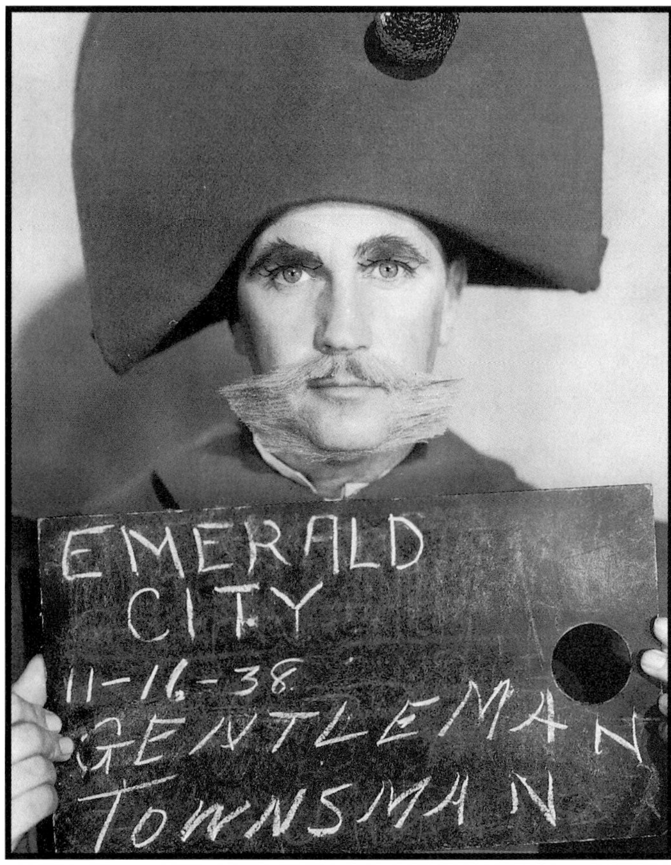

Make-up test stills for an Emerald City Townsman and Gentleman Townsman, November 16, 1938. The severe whiskers of the Gentleman Townsman were not applied in the completed picture.

actors. Charles Schram remembered that these actors in general had skin that "was delicate, like a child's." Removing the make-ups could be very painful, and certainly didn't bode well toward bonding with the make-up artists. Often the little men would come in to be made up with red welts on their faces from the day before.

The make-up department was not without its lighter moments, though. As the Munchkins would line up each morning for make-up, they would be selected, one at a time, by Dawn's crew. The make-up men would ask them their names or the parts they played in order to match their appearance with stills. For years afterward, Emile LaVigne would regale friends and relatives with the story of one small actor who looked up at LaVigne's name above the door to his make-up room and blurted out, "Oh, Jew à la mode!"

The outlandish look of the Munchkin make-ups was primarily achieved using bald caps and hairpieces. (The female Munchkins only suffered standard Technicolor cosmetics.) William Tuttle distinctly recalled that the wigs for the male Munchkins were made in the make-up department by people "good at laying on hair." Bleached white yak hair was used for its coarseness and ease in handling. The hair was dyed a rainbow of hues before being laced, a

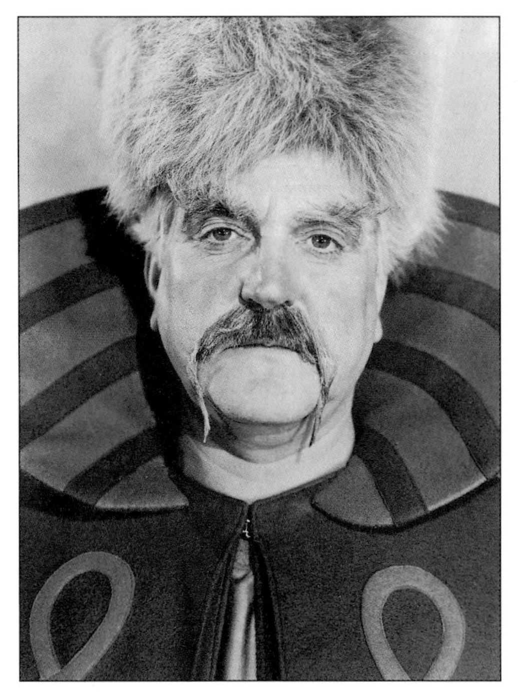

On November 16, 1938, make-up photos were taken of Frank Morgan for two of the five characters he portrays in *The Wizard of Oz.* At right, Morgan poses as the doorman to the gates of Emerald City; at left, he is seen as the guard to the Wizard's throne room. With the exception of exaggerated moustaches and eye-brows, both make-up treatments were fairly light—and both were changed prior to filming.

few hairs at a time, into netting. Beard dyers were reportedly hired to keep the beards of the Munchkins "freshly colored with pink, green, and blue dyes." The hair was then sprayed with lacquer to form a variety of points and peaks. The lacquer kept the hair stiff and held its shape. A liquid-rubber adhesive, squeezed from tubes, affixed the wigs to bald caps. To Jack Young, the wigs were "more of a helmet than a wig, but the visual effect was that whatever it was grew out of [the Munchkins'] heads."

All manner of bald caps and hairpieces were tested for Frank Morgan, not only for his role as the Wizard, but for the four other parts the veteran actor portrayed in *Oz*. Given Morgan's star status and top billing in the picture, he was personally made up by Jack Dawn himself. Despite a battery of make-up tests, the final results were deceptively subtle. Studio publicity related, "Morgan . . . plays the Wizard role without any make-up excepting for white hair. However he does don various beards and whiskers because, in the story, the Wizard poses as doorman, cab driver, guard, and various other persons in the Emerald City." Only *Minicam* magazine noted, "The Wizard's accentuated make-up gave shiny cheek bones to battle with. This was solved by adjusting the position of the lights."

Like many preproduction aspects of *Oz*, the on-screen portrayal of Dorothy initially strayed from the original source. In *The Wonderful Wizard of Oz*, W. W. Denslow pictured a young, stocky child with thick brunette braids. In succeeding Oz books, however, illustrator John R. Neill had envisioned Dorothy as slightly older, slender, and blonde. To fans of the book series, this had been the accepted image of the Kansas heroine for more than thirty years.

It would seem that early make-up tests for Judy Garland were attempts at capturing an amalgam of different ideas, through which only indecision prevailed. Should Dorothy be brunette and dainty like Snow White, or blond and childish like Alice or even Shirley Temple? In the end, so much emphasis had been placed on perfecting the quintessential storybook heroine, that the results were disastrous. Immobilized in long blond curls and heavy make-up, Garland's appearance was neatly obliterated from that of the sparkling screen teenager. Under Richard Thorpe's direction, she acted accordingly; her resultant performance affectedly precious and coy.

When interim director George Cukor replaced Thorpe on October 25, 1938, he was appalled by both Garland's acting and appearance. The next day, an urgent interoffice memo was quickly circulated from producer Mervyn LeRoy to production manager Keith Weeks. It implicitly stated that Cukor had ordered "new hair and wardrobe tests on Judy Garland . . . immediately." While Garland endured another round of wig and make-up tests, Cukor coached her into simplifying her delivery. Her former blonde self was appropriate to the fantasy world of Oz but was ludicrous in 1938 Kansas. And, as Cukor told her to remember, "she was just a little girl from Kansas."

Final make-up tests for Dorothy returned to a look similar to Denslow's illustrations. Garland's revised appearance was more typical of mainstream America, although her polished coiffure still echoed Hollywood glamour. Her own hair was reddened and matching falls were woven daily onto the back of her head. In concession to the discarded blonde curls, a similar ringlet style was scripted into the second half of the film. False eyelashes, eye shadow, and a subtle rouge were applied by Garland's make-up man, Webb Overlander; liberal body make-up completed the effect.[4] Interestingly enough, this all occurred every morning before Garland ever set foot on the M-G-M lot. Because Judy was sixteen, the studio was mandated to comply with child labor laws. Metro's loophole was to

[4] "In those days, men did the [facial] make-up," recalled Betty Chiniguy, whose mother, Edith Wilson, was Jack Dawn's sister. Edith worked on *The Wizard of Oz*, applying "any make-up from the jaws down. Hands, feet, arms, throat." As Technicolor was especially sensitive to variations in skin tone, particularly reds, body make-up was a necessity. Without it, skin would photograph orange, brick red, or even blue.

Frank Morgan's Wizard make-up would need some refining, but essentially remained unchanged from its appearance in this Technicolor make-up test. Morgan stands before the backing of the mountains and cliffs seen outside the Witch's tower-room window. As the backing was painted to Technicolor specifications, it was ideal for comparison against test footage such as this. *Courtesy Charles Schram*

Overleaf: Judy Garland began testing wardrobe and make-up for *The Wizard of Oz* while still before the cameras for her film *Listen, Darling*. Here she is shown (in both portrait and profile) modeling one of at least three Dorothy dresses tested on August 27, 1938, along with blonde Wig 1. Although the costume was rejected, Judy would wear the wig during the initial days of (discarded) footage shot by director Richard Thorpe, October 13 through October 24.

WIG 1

WIG

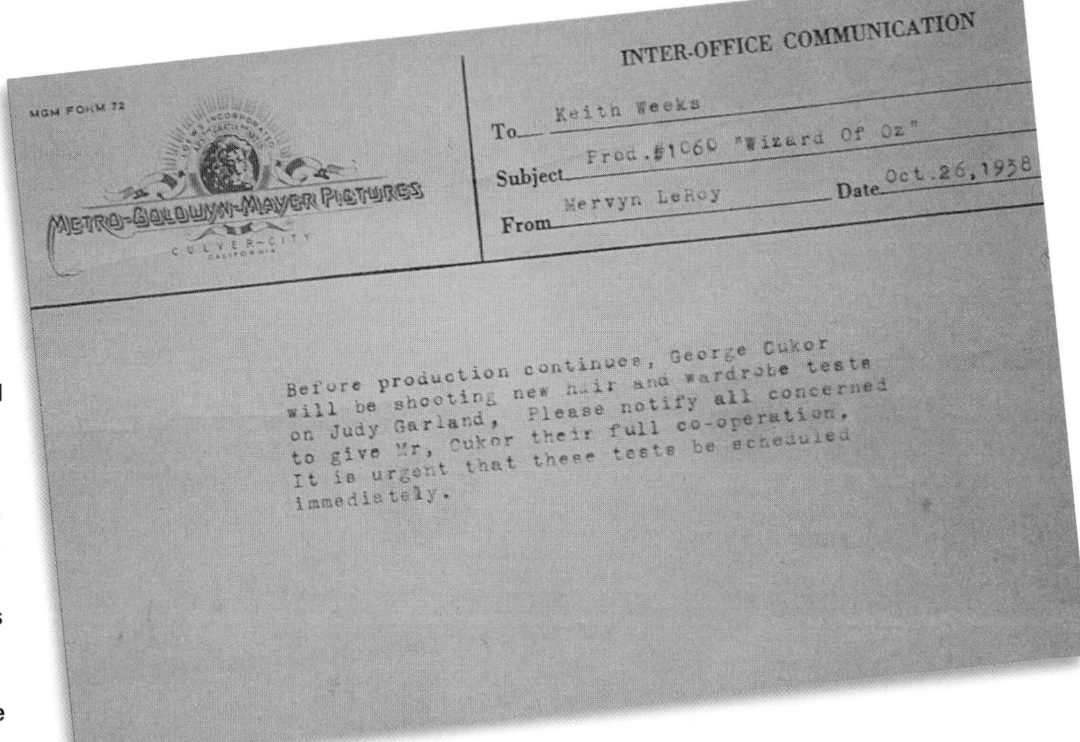
INTER-OFFICE COMMUNICATION

MGM FORM 72

METRO-GOLDWYN-MAYER PICTURES
CULVER-CITY
CALIFORNIA

To Keith Weeks
Subject Prod. #1060 "Wizard Of Oz"
From Mervyn LeRoy Date Oct. 26, 1938

Before production continues, George Cukor will be shooting new hair and wardrobe tests on Judy Garland, Please notify all concerned to give Mr, Cukor their full co-operation. It is urgent that these tests be scheduled immediately.

The memo that altered the course of film history: George Cukor orders immediate hair and wardrobe tests for Judy Garland, October 26, 1938. Though assigned to *Oz* for less than a week, Cukor's direction of Garland's acting and appearance contributed to the actress effecting a simpler, more natural Dorothy. Judy wrote her tutor's daughter, "Playing the part of Dorothy was such fun, and so realistic, that I feel as if I'm not Judy at all, but Dorothy Gale from Kansas." *Courtesy Eric Daily; photo: George Anastassatos*

send Overlander, a hairdresser, and wardrobe girl out to Garland's West L.A. home each morning *after* they punched in at the studio. The team could then prepare the actress for the day, be in compliance with the law for minors, and have Judy to the studio ready to begin filming. Garland's workday officially began once the studio's Packard sedan returned her through the front gate.[5] (With breaks for lunch and schooling, the youngster could work at least until 6 p.m. six days a week.)

Motion Picture magazine apprised its readers of Garland's appearance "Have you seen Judy in *The Wizard of Oz*? Then you know her hair is red." The article noted, "It's that way naturally" but the actress had to "use a henna rinse to make it even redder for Technicolor." *Modern Screen* reporter Robert McIlwaine raved about Garland's Technicolor auburn locks. "As for her personal appearance these days, she's bordering dangerously near being glamorous. Her hair is a little lighter with just the right touch of gold to enhance those lovely eyes that feature dark curling lashes." The actress, however, was reported to have magnanimously explained, "And just look at my hair! They had to change it for

5 Such measures were not necessary for Garland's double, Barbara "Bobbie" Koshay, who was twenty-nine at the time of *The Wizard of Oz*. Koshay was an Olympic-caliber swimmer and movie stuntwoman.

the color sequences in *The Wizard of Oz*. Now my friends kid me about that, too."

Typical of most prestigious films of the day, the "better" wigs used in *The Wizard of Oz* were created by wigmakers at Max Factor's cosmetics facilities. It was there that eighteen-year-old designer Bob Roberts made what is known as a "seven-eighths wig" for Judy's Dorothy. (Roberts also participated in designing the wigs used by Vivien Leigh and other actresses in *Gone With the Wind*.) Garland's wig, as he recalled, had a "lace center part" and comprised a "skull cap with a silk net that fitted to her head." Constructed in such a manner, it allowed use of the actress's own hair for the front of the hairstyle. In preparation for creating the wig, designer Fred Frederick had gone out to M-G-M in order to take measurements of Judy's head. From those measurements, a wooden block the size of her head was made, on which to construct the wig. Samples were also taken of Garland's own hair in order to match the texture and color.

In 1996, Roberts didn't remember anything about dyeing Judy's hair or making the wig "red." He instead recalled the wig color as being a "warm brown," which he described as a natural-type, medium chestnut color—"but not so flat, having some lighter or redder highlights." Likewise, he didn't remember going through any blonde or other test wigs prior to the final version. According to Roberts, he was simply provided with sketches of exactly what was wanted for Dorothy and specific instructions to "keep her simple and natural like any schoolgirl of that time." Once designed, he distinctly recalled making the wigs in duplicate. "At least three of them, maybe more. Perspiration gets on the wigs and they need time to dry out."

Judy Garland during a break in shooting her first scenes as the "new" Dorothy. (Note the assistant walking off-frame to the left.) With Judy's hair dyed auburn and her pinafore changed to blue gingham, filming resumed November 4, 1938, on the Scarecrow's cornfield set. This is how Garland appeared in the final film; however, her make-up would be a bit lighter and the length of her curls a bit tighter throughout the remaining scenes. *Courtesy Charles Schram*

Unlike the greater press disregard of Buddy Ebsen and Richard Thorpe's departures from *The Wizard of Oz*, a number of papers and magazine features did mention Garland's false start. The *Des Moines Sunday Register* reported, "For a while, M-G-M executives toyed with the idea of making Judy a blonde, but an experiment with a wig proved that light hair changed her personality. That wouldn't do—Dorothy must be Dorothy to the fans who know the book from cover to cover—and back again."

Though not a major star, Billie Burke nonetheless exuded celebrity on the *Wizard of Oz* set. A former stage beauty, silent film veteran, and widow of showman Florenz Ziegfeld, Burke maintained a regal air. Jack Dawn's brother, Lyle Wesley Dawn, worked with the matronly actress to achieve a make-up for Glinda, the Good Witch, that prompted gossip columnist Louella O. Parsons to pen, "Burke looks like a twenty-year-old . . ." Burke's youthful appearance owed as much to cosmetic lifts as it did to any make-up man's brush. Lifts were small pieces of fine silk glued with spirit gum in front of each ear, and pulled taut with a secured thread to correct "sagging flesh." The edges of the lifts were serrated for ease in blending with make-up. A full-length wig manufactured by Max Factor realistically completed the ethereal effect (and disguised the lifts). *Photoplay* magazine was duly impressed, and remarked, "The famous Burke red-gold hair rippling loosely about her shoulders shimmered with diamond dust and infinitesimal stars." Bob Roberts recalled the wig for Billie Burke's Good Witch as "a full wig with a hair-lace front edge" that could be invisibly adhered to the front of the hairline.[6]

A Technicolor close-up of Judy Garland's make-up on the Witch's-castle set not only tests the lighting and hue of her hair and skin, but also captures her tears immediately following an emotional scene. Here, Judy is shown in her ringlet-style wig, after Dorothy's visit to the Emerald City beauty parlor. *Courtesy Charles Schram*

On at least two occasions, Dawn's apprentices were required to reprise the *Oz* character make-ups outside of the studio. Jack Young had befriended Munchkin actor Billy Curtis and recalled both instances (which involved Curtis) with humorous anecdotes.

> M-G-M had a *Wizard of Oz* float in the Rose Bowl Parade on New Year's Day [January 1, 1939], and I was assigned to accompany Billy and a couple of other midgets made up as Munchkins. We started about two in the morning and by the time the parade started, we were really sleepy. Billy saved the day. He had a jug. The kids went wild as we went by. I was buried in the depths of the float, and between the scent of the flowers and the engine fumes, I thought I would never make it. I was starting to fall asleep

[6] As late as June 1996, a replica of Burke's *Oz* wig was displayed with other movie artifacts at the now-defunct Max Factor Museum of Beauty in Hollywood.

Charles Schram was Judy Garland's make-up man for the actress's films prior to *The Wizard of Oz*. He remembered that the child star "wasn't serious about much of anything" and "had a laugh you could hear a block away." Both attributes appear apparent in this Technicolor test, which illustrates the final-version wigs for both Garland and Billie Burke. *Courtesy Charles Schram*

> and Billy, waving and smiling to the crowd, would stretch down and kick me in the back of the head. It was a long parade. . . .
>
> The premiere of *The Wizard of Oz* was at the Chinese Theatre in Hollywood [August 15, 1939]. It was a smashing success. The Munchkins were in the foyer and some stupid mothers with their kids would come up to them. I was standing next to Billy when one of them came up to him. He swiftly put his cigar behind his back. The mother asked, "Would you please tell my little Percy why you didn't grow any taller?" Smiling sweetly, Billy pitched his voice to a high level and said, "Delighted. I never ate my vegetables when I was a kid." The mother walked away, saying to little Percy, "I told you so." Billy turned around, jammed the cigar back in his mouth, muttering, "Hope the little bastard chokes on them."

It may have been more than coincidental that *The Wizard of Oz* completed its shooting schedule with the Kansas scenes in February 1939. The previous four months of Technicolor filming had been inordinately taxing on cast and crew alike. With the exception of a few retakes, wrapping up the film unencumbered by extensive make-ups and costumes created a welcome reprieve for the actors. Black-and-white-film make-up only necessitated toning the white of the skin using a very orange make-up. Without the intense arc lighting required for Technicolor, the cast could finish the last several scenes of *The Wizard of Oz* in reasonable comfort.

As originally designed, the ruby slippers were heavily jeweled and ornate with a curled toe. *Courtesy The Debbie Reynolds Hollywood Movie Museum; photo: David Hardy*

Two

COSTUMES AND PROPS

Adrian's Style Behind the Seams

THE TIN WOODMAN
(JACK HALEY)

The woodman with his blade so trusty
Must yield to oiling daily
For when he weeps his joints get rusty,
Oh, Jeeper Weeper Haley!

— "Lion's Roar" column,
Country Home, July 1939

M-G-M's premier costume designer, Adrian, in a pensive pose taken August 17, 1938. At this time the artist was engrossed in finalizing many of his concepts for the *Oz* character wardrobes. Of his association with Adrian, Ray Bolger remarked, "I always had a deep admiration for his artistic ability and knowledge that every costume should be practical. People had to work inside them." *Courtesy Photofest*

When two creative forces attempt to collaborate, the process can become chaotic. Each artist is deeply vested in his individual insights. Any affront to such impressions can be met with passionate volatility. But film is a collaborative art. At Metro-Goldwyn-Mayer, the working philosophy instilled in all departments was one of unity. Not only was it disrespectful to assume personal credit for one's contributions, it was disloyal. This was edict. It stemmed from the ethics of the studio's vice-president and reigning patriarch, Louis B. Mayer, and filtered down to all personnel. Fortunately for the evolving

Overleaf: An Adrian sketch for the Munchkin heralds, and the completed wardrobe modeled by Karl Kosiczky.

Adrian saved only a handful of costume sketches for *The Wizard of Oz*—all of them Munchkins. Presented here is a rejected sketch for the Munchkin ballerinas, signed in the lower right corner. Also shown is an outtake of the three Munchkin ballerinas wearing the final costumes. (According to a June 13, 1938, script draft, the Lullaby League ballerinas hand Dorothy a huge floral safety pin following their welcome.) *Courtesy Charles Schram*

3 Heralds –
Trumpeters.

Photo 8 – 9 Queen

WARDROBE STILLS
PROD 1060
HERALD

production of *The Wizard of Oz*, the two artisans who would work most closely together shared similar ideals.

Jack Dawn's counterpart in the wardrobe department was Gilbert Adrian—known simply by his surname. Like Dawn, Adrian had developed a national reputation as Hollywood's purveyor to the stars. Irving Berlin discovered Adrian studying art in Paris and brought him to New York to create costumes for the Music Box Revue. Cecil B. DeMille hired him as style creator and Adrian went to M-G-M with DeMille in 1930. During the next decade, the designer gained recognition (and subsequent demand) as official couturier to the likes of Greta Garbo, Joan Crawford, Norma Shearer, and Janet Gaynor (whom Adrian married in August 1939). He was said to have "long been one of Garbo's closest confidants and has never betrayed that confidence. He could tell you enough about Shearer, Crawford, MacDonald, Loy, or any of the other Metro darlings to fill a book." He also subscribed to Dawn's beliefs about the importance of projecting one's personality in unison with attitude and appearance. An article about the Adrian-Gaynor union in *Film Weekly* magazine revealed, "Adrian works on the principle that a designer should 'dress the mind,' and he seeks to reflect in the clothes the personality of the woman who is wearing them."

Examples of Adrian's colorful and whimsical Munchkin attire. During a Technicolor test, Judy Garland is flanked by Meinhardt Raabe as the Coroner (left) and Charley Becker as the Mayor (right). ***Courtesy Charles Schram***

Conspiring with Dawn to create the characters who would people the land of Oz was a process that Adrian reportedly relished. Designing costumes for pictures such as *Queen Christina*, *Romeo and Juliet*, and *Marie Antoinette* necessitated only researching and enhancing preexisting period fashions. The fantasy of *The Wizard of Oz* came with few boundaries. "Adrian . . . had been having an attack of costume pictures," related *Photoplay*, "and for a creative clothes designer, costume pictures, no matter how lavish, can be a bore."

The designer was allegedly familiar with the Baum stories, and the studio contended that Adrian was scanning the thirty Oz books for costume planning. Though imaginatively illustrated by John R. Neill, the Oz books offered little technical assistance. Much of the Ozian attire, such as the outfits traditionally worn by Munchkins, echoed their earliest incarnations in Oz books written more than three decades before, as in the following description from *The Patchwork Girl of Oz*.

[Ojo] wore blue silk stockings, blue knee-pants with gold buckles, a blue ruffled waist and a jacket of bright blue braided with gold. His shoes were of blue leather and turned up at the toes, which were pointed. His hat had a peaked crown with a flat brim, and around the brim was a row of tiny golden bells that tinkled when he moved. This was the native costume of those who inhabited the Munchkin Country of the Land of Oz.

The Munchkin Coroner's scrolled hat, worn by Meinhardt Raabe in the film. *Courtesy Eric Daily; photo: George Anastassatos*

These concepts were familiar to readers but lacked the modern flair and embellishment Adrian sought. A designer of great caliber, Adrian wouldn't be satisfied or challenged by merely recreating Neill's drawings. M-G-M reported Adrian's next course of action.

From the fly-leaves of Adrian's schoolbooks came the inspiration for the fantastic Munchkins and their fellow characters . . . in *The Wizard of Oz*. . . . This fact came to light when the designer dispatched a wire to his home town of Naugatuck, Connecticut, requesting that his box of old schoolbooks, in storage for many years, be shipped post haste to Hollywood. . . .

As a child, *The Wizard of Oz* was Adrian's favorite book. So clearly were the various characters impressed on his mind that a frequent occupation was sketching these imaginary personalities in the fly-leaves of his textbooks when class hours proved especially boring. . . .

"I remember the Munchkins all had long moustachios which shaded from yellow to blue green, and the Quadlings were extremely proud of the golden cages which grew from their head and contained strange animals," he declared. . . .

On these childish sketches, taken directly from the old schoolbooks, Adrian's costume designs for *The Wizard of Oz* were based.

"No Place Like Home" for the Holidays. To celebrate the 1939 holiday season, Judy Garland posed for this rarely seen M-G-M publicity photo. Although partially covered by her chef's apron, the young actress is wearing what is unmistakably her Dorothy costume from *The Wizard of Oz*.

Adrian was clearly enamored of the possibilities for the Munchkin costumes, and indeed, one of his favored sketches depicted such a character with a bird cage sprouting from his head.[1]

[1] After production of *The Wizard of Oz* and his subsequent retirement in 1941 (upon expiration of his studio contract with M-G-M), Adrian retained only six costume sketches for *Oz* — all of them Munchkin designs.

Adrian costume sketches for Munchkins, including the Mayor, were published as a *Photoplay* layout in 1939.

The premise for imagining the wardrobes of Munchkins and other Ozians began with a "Temporary List of People Requiring Costumes," which was distributed for circulation to producer Mervyn LeRoy's assistant, Bill Cannon, on July 12, 1938. The list was a comprehensive roster of any and all persons appearing in the film. For the "exterior of Munchkinland (number and atmosphere)," a caution was added lest Adrian become too ornate and impractical: "Following list of people will all be midgets (during the scenes the midgets will all have to fall to the ground as the Wicked Witch enters)."

The Munchkin costumes were critical from several standpoints. Being the first creatures encountered by Dorothy upon entering Oz, the fanciful nature of the Munchkin wardrobe would set the tone for the rest of the picture that followed. The Munchkin sequence was emphasized for the extravagant shift from black and white to three-strip color photography. The omnipotence of traditional blue attire was not a consideration for the expensive Technicolor film; and it was intolerable to envision the potentially brilliant hues of this scene reduced to a monochromatic wash. Additionally, individual Munchkin personalities were to have been defined in a manner that would rival the popularity of Walt Disney's Seven Dwarfs. These included a "Total of 35 Munchkins with Special Business," such as:

- 1 Man Braggart
- First Townsman
- Second Townsman
- Deaf Townsman (Ear Trumpet)
- 1 Mayor of Munchkinland
- 5 City Fathers (including First and Second)
- 1 Barrister
- 1 Coroner
- 1 Town Crier
- 1 Bearded Man
- 3 Little Tots (Girls)
- 3 Little Tough Boys
- 1 Munchkin General
- 6 Munchkin Soldiers
- 5 Little Munchkin Fiddlers

These characters were to be augmented by "58 Men Assorted Munchkin Townsmen," "31 Women Assorted Munchkin Townswomen," The Munchkin Navy, The Munchkin Fire

Department, and The Mother Goose Club, comprising a total of 124 little people.

The mutations and limitations of Technicolor photography were of little concern to Adrian as he began to effect the Lilliputian costumes. This mindset eventually led to a heated confrontation between Adrian and color director Henri Jaffa over the feasibility of colors for the Munchkin wear. Cinematographer Harold Rosson had to work out a list of "relative color values" that filled six typewritten pages to guide make-up and costumes, and it was reported that Adrian's sketches were hand-tinted to match Technicolor requirements.

Technicolor processing, though highly developed for the time, in particular curtailed the creative scope of costume designers. Hues and tints would translate to color film with frustrating inconsistency. The sensitive nature of the film required extensive planning and testing well in advance of photography. Depending upon color and lighting, pale blues faded to nothingness, bright blues were startlingly brilliant, and yellows could look green or orange. Pure white photographed as a bright blur and needed to be toned in a gray bath in a procedure known as teccing. Varying shades of grays were meticulously charted so that the resultant dye process achieved the desired accuracy.

Adrian began conceptualizing his ideas for *Oz* by filling countless sheets of 14-by-17-inch paper with pencil and watercolor pictures, to which he occasionally stapled material swatches. The sketches were

A fanciful Munchkin vest with ornamental pompom was part of actor Harry Monty's Technicolor ensemble. *Courtesy Stephen Cox; photo: George Anastassatos*

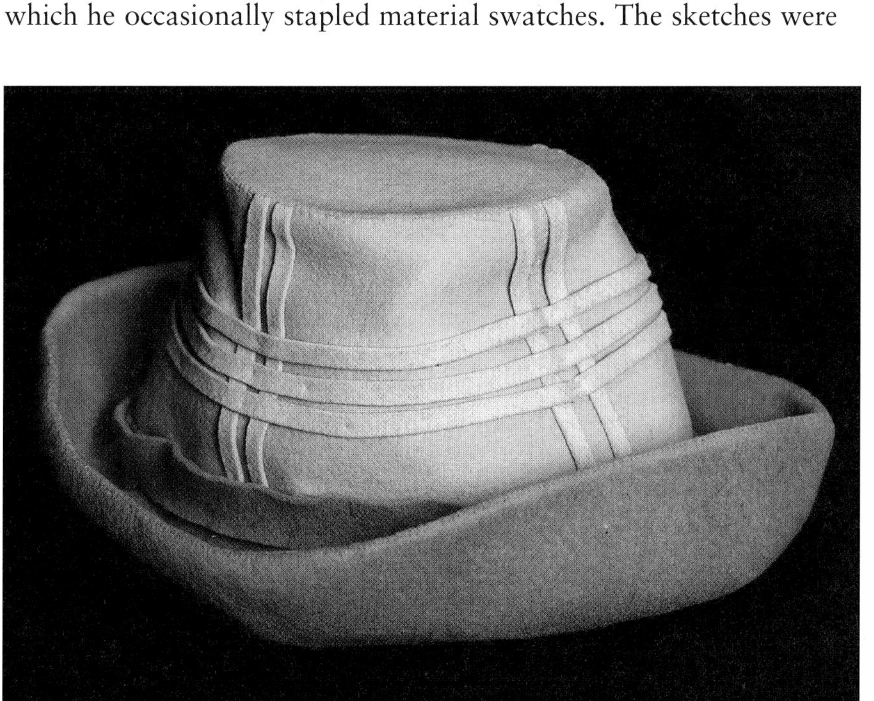

A sample Munchkin hat, stitched from heavy felt fabric, is labeled "Geo Ministery [*sic*]." Ministeri was also the Munchkin coachman. *Courtesy the Hufty family; photo: Todd Bush*

Completed jackets for Freddie Retter, one of five Munchkin fiddlers (left), and Joseph Herbst, a Munchkin soldier (right). Both costumes included lengthy coattails. The Herbst costume is also marked, "Length 45, Chest 32." ***Courtesy the Hufty family; photo: Todd Bush***

routed to Mervyn LeRoy for his signature of approval before being returned to the wardrobe department for exacting execution by seamstresses and tailors. (Once the picture's cast had been determined, each actor's measurements were carefully recorded, necessitating only followup fittings and alterations once the costumes had been constructed.) After Adrian okayed the completed costume, a film test of it was made on the actor (or a double, if the actor was unavailable). If the results were satisfactory, the costume was made in any number of duplicates.

Adrian determined to maximize the slight stature of *Oz*'s smallest actors by elaborating their proportions with voluminous sleeves, huge vests, and oversized jackets. The rationale for the design of each Munchkin costume was further described in the publicity-campaign book for *The Wizard of Oz*.

> [For the Munchkins] Adrian sought for the doll effect because when a girl enters a dream world as Dorothy does in Oz she imagines some people small like her own dolls. Hence,

Adrian used felt for them, exaggerated jewelry and thousands of individually made flowers. A full picture of Munchkinland with the actors in costume looks like a flower garden.

It seemed as though Adrian's goal was successfully achieved, as evidenced by the following account in *Modern Screen* magazine of the film's West Coast premiere.

> The premiere of *Wizard of Oz* was a high spot in the youngest movie set. . . . Joan Bennett had [daughters] Diane and Melinda along with her. It took all Joan's persuasion to get Melinda, the five-year-old, into the theatre to see the picture. She was too fascinated with the live dolls out in front. The "dolls" were the Singer Midgets who showed up [in costume] . . . as Munchkins.

Adrian supposedly felt the creative use of flowers, tassles, appliqué, capes, and cloth jewelry for Oz characters would start a new feminine mode of fashion. While realizing that none could be adaptable in its entirety, he believed that detail adaptation would be widespread, "particularly . . . in hats, gloves, shoes, boots, and aprons." However, neither *Vogue*, *Glamour*, nor *Harper's Bazaar* purported evidence of Adrian's prediction.[2] Less likely to be stylishly adapted were Munchkin flowerpot hats, cuckoo birds on springs, and daffodils budding from abdomens. If too cutting edge for the most fashionably elite, Adrian's Munchkin attire enhanced the fantasy of Oz, right down to the "ant feelers" curling from the toes of their miniature felt shoes. These and other accoutrements perfectly suited the little people who would initially camouflage themselves in flower beds. Still, Betty Ann Bruno felt a bit shortchanged. One of about a dozen children employed as background filler, Bruno recalled that her Munchkin costume wasn't on a par with her adult counterparts. "I was disappointed that it wasn't more colorful; my costume was gray felt! But it was beautifully made with muslin lining." Bruno's bonnet was not of the flowerpot variety either. "[It] was red and white . . . with a skinny little bud vase on it!"

Glinda, the Good Witch of the North, would also make her first appearance in Munchkinland. In condensing the plot of *The*

Adrian's flair for the ridiculous is evident in this charming flowerpot hat, worn by Joan Kenmore, a child actress. *Courtesy Charles Farrer; photo: Timothy Costello*

[2] Antebellum gowns and accessories inspired by *Gone With the Wind* did influence the fashion world in late 1939 through 1940.

"Glinda—the Beautiful Witch of the North." Billie Burke poses for Clarence Sinclair Bull's camera, October 30, 1939. The June 9, 1938, script describes Glinda as "a lovely vision—tall, sweet faced—graceful—in other words—a child's idea of 'the good fairy.'" Outside of her scripted lines, Burke concurred with this description, and referred to her character exclusively as a "fairy" rather than use the term "witch." (The June 15, 1938, script still distinguished the two good witches found in Baum, connoting the Witch of the North as a "Laura Hope Crews type." By June 27, the two characters had been merged.) *Courtesy Joseph M. Maddalena, Profiles in History*

Wonderful Wizard of Oz, scriptwriters had combined the *two* good witches who befriend Dorothy in the book. In Baum, the Good Witch of the North is "a little woman. . . . Her face was covered with wrinkles, her hair was nearly white. [She] wore a white gown that hung in pleats from her shoulders; over it were sprinkled little stars that glistened in the sun like diamonds." The other witch, Glinda, resides in the red Quadling Country in the southern region of Oz. She is described as "beautiful and young. . . . Her hair was a rich red color and fell in flowing ringlets over her shoulders."

In designing Billie Burke's Glinda costume, Adrian also merged the descriptions of Baum's sorceresses. Burke's gown was created of layers of delicate pink tulle sprinkled with stars and scattered snow crystals, denoting the Good Witch's northern origins.[3] To symbolize Glinda's gracefulness and ability of flight, Adrian also infused the gown with a butterfly motif, evident in jeweled decorations and pink tulle "wings" at the shoulders. The image of sheer fairy tale fantasy was completed with Burke's shimmering, starry headdress that routinely necessitated lighting adjustment to avoid glare.

At age fifty-three, Billie Burke's Glinda was a heavenly vision that prompted reviewers' raves. ("[Burke] appears almost like a being eternally young," praised the *Los Angeles Times*.) Six months after she completed her last takes for *The Wizard of Oz*, Burke was still tickled with her finished appearance. Encouraged by the picture's accolades, she arranged for Metro's top portrait photographer, Clarence Sinclair Bull, to capture her in all her glittering splendor as Glinda. Burke then had the best portrait of the sitting redrawn as a charcoal sketch and printed up as a Christmas card with the greeting, "May your dearest wish come true." In 1941, she was still using the card and inscribed to a fan, "This was my Christmas card two years ago when we did *The Wizard of Oz* and I played the Good Fairy with Judy Garland—so I didn't see why it still couldn't be sent for this year with the good wishes she brings . . . [signed] Glinda the Good Fairy." [4]

Billie Burke appears to float in this full-length view of Glinda's elaborate costume. (Burke holds her mark as Technicolor test footage is run following a take in which Glinda disappears.) This footage may have been shot as late as May 1939, when Burke and Judy Garland were called back to shoot some pick-up shots. Fortunately for Burke, a cast on her foot for a fracture suffered the previous March was concealed by the length of her gown. *Courtesy Charles Schram*

[3] Glinda's icy adornments would also foreshadow the snowstorm she creates to rouse Dorothy and her friends from the deadly poppy field.

[4] In her 1949 autobiography, *With a Feather on My Nose*, Burke declared: "My favorite role was in *The Wizard of Oz*, directed by the great Victor Fleming, in which I played Glinda, the Good Fairy."

After the concept of the glamorous Wicked Witch was abandoned, Gale Sondergaard continued to test less overt costumes and make-up. On October 3, 1938, Sondergaard was photographed in alternate wardrobe as an interim between the Disney Evil Queen look and a traditionally eerie witch. *Courtesy the Kobal Collection*

A test frame of Margaret Hamilton, Judy Garland, and Billie Burke in Munchkinland. Hamilton's black wardrobe proved especially difficult to capture on Technicolor film. To overcome this, extra lights were directed at the costume and (unlike this scene) the Witch was usually photographed against a gray background to avoid too great a contrast. *Courtesy Charles Schram*

Glinda's nemesis and Dorothy's tormentor, the Wicked Witch of the West, was originally intended to mirror the glamorous Evil Queen in *Snow White and the Seven Dwarfs*. Shrouded in a cowled gown and matching witch's hat made entirely of black sequins, Gale Sondergaard was a deliciously evil imitation of Disney's villainess. Though Sondergaard recalled the costume as "absolutely gorgeous," it was a concept ultimately at odds with the hateful Halloween witch of Oz book fame.

It would have been tempting to dress Sondergaard's replacement in a black hooded cloak like Disney's Wicked Witch. Indeed, Margaret Hamilton reported that she tested for the role wearing a shawl and some decrepit-looking rags. For Metro's witch, Adrian maintained the villainous black garb, which would contrast well with Hamilton's stark green face and hands. The actress recalled just one costume fitting for Adrian's approval before the design was duplicated. "There was *three* of everything," said Hamilton. "One model and two copies." The Witch's costume, with its flowing cape, bishop sleeves, and sleek medieval style, gave Hamilton a lean, spidery appearance that heightened her wrongdoing. A tassled satchel hung around the Witch's waist, and on her feet Hamilton wore high-button, high-laced shoes with low heels. Because of the intensity of her performance, Hamilton's costume required that comfort and wearability be paramount. "[It] had to be so," she affirmed. "The movements we *all* made were not easy and particularly the Witch, who swept around—up and down flights of stairways. . . . [The costumes] had to be loose *though* well-fitting and they were." The monotone color of the dress required direct lighting, and the actress was filmed against a gray background as often as possible.

Two Emerald City starlets compare costumes for a publicity still.

Copies of the dress were made not only for Technicolor, but also for black-and-white photography, as noted by the costume roster: "Black and White—One Costume for the Bad Witch (Up in Cyclone)." This version of the dress was duplicated in gray for effective translation to black-and-white film. Even so, it was described a bit incorrectly by *Photoplay Studies*: "When Miss Gulch changes into the witch, did you notice how her hat grows thin, then her dress elongates into a black robe, her sleeves begin to spread like the wings of a bat, and her bicycle becomes a witch's broomstick?"

Judy Garland and Emerald City extras pause for a Technicolor test on the Wash and Brush Up Company set. Standing to the right of Garland is radio singer Lois January, who shares a brief duet with Judy in this scene. In 1995, January remembered Garland affectionately: "She was just fabulous! She had heart! She concentrated on lyrics. As a singer, I've always lived the music. She lived the lyric." ***Courtesy Charles Schram***

Just as the Munchkins were defined by select characters, the citizens of the Emerald City were also assigned roles, although it was noted that the peasants were "All Actual Adult Size."[5] The extras required in the palace and in the "Principals' Triumphal Return after Killing The Witch" were to total "300 People for All the Scenes in the Emerald City." (During the triumphal procession, Dorothy and her friends were to have been escorted by Emerald City soldiers on either side of the carriage in which they initially toured the town.) This extensive number of performers kept the wardrobe department

[5] L. Frank Baum wrote in his text that the Emerald City citizens were "about the same size as the Munchkins."

working overtime, dyeing fabrics green en masse. Extras needed for "Background Atmosphere" included:

- 20 Men Shop Keepers
- 10 Street Vendors—Men
- 25 Townsmen Gentlemen
- 20 Shop Keepers Wives
- 25 Women Wives of the Gentlemen
- 25 Girls 18 to 25 Years
- 41 Women Assorted Townswomen
- 100 Assorted Townsmen

Also included in the crowd was the starlet who cradles the yowling Siamese cat that prompts Toto to give chase. Lois January has frequently been cited as that young woman; however, the former singer firmly asserted, "That's not me holding the cat." January auditioned for the role of a Wash and Brush Up Company attendant

An Emerald City peasant jacket, worn by one of the several hundred extras needed as "background atmosphere." ***Courtesy Eric Daily; photo: George Anastassatos***

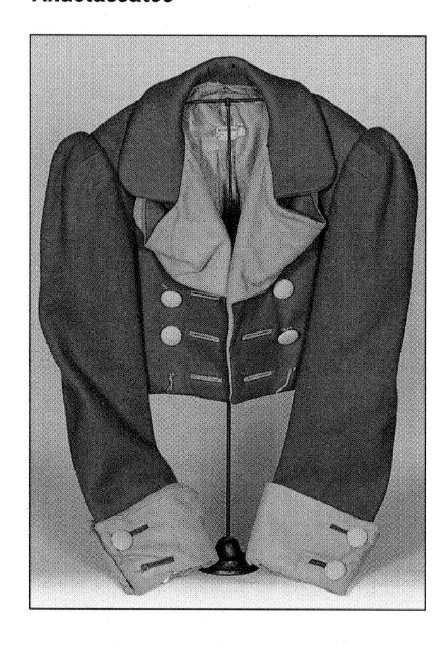

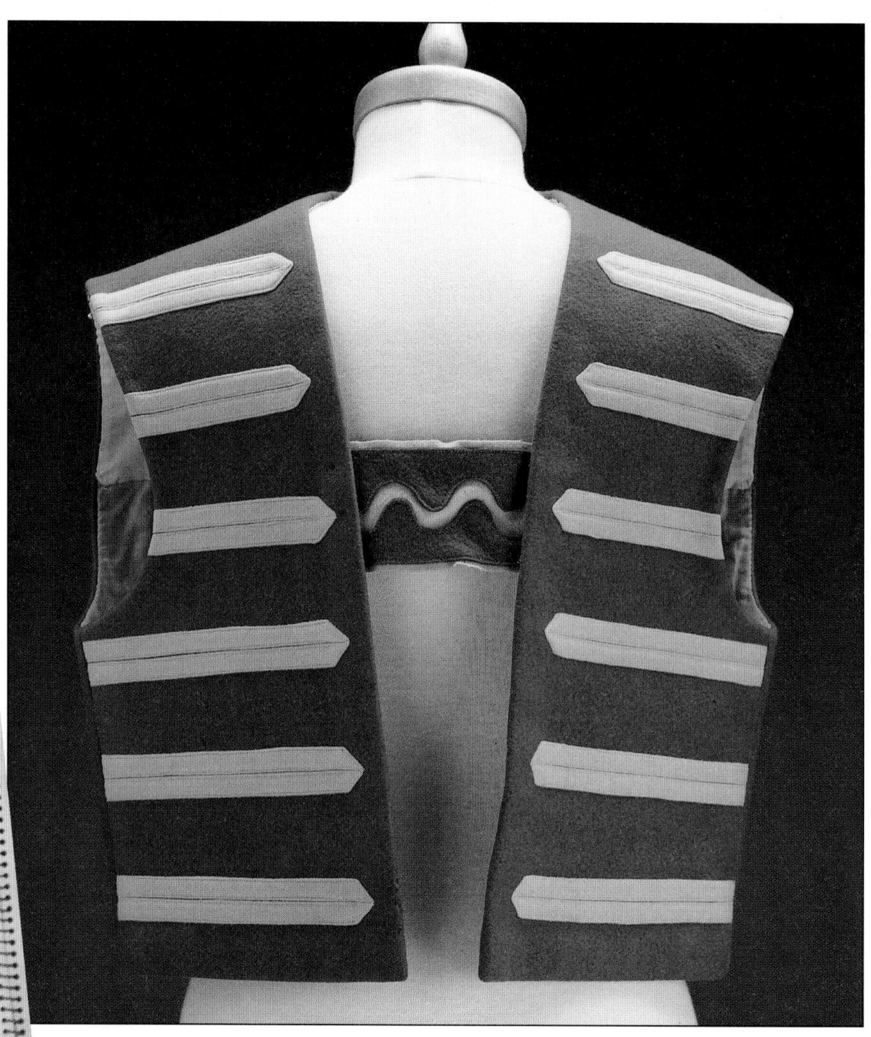

An Emerald City peasant vest, ornately constructed of green and white felt. The sewn-in studio tag reads: "Metro-Goldwyn-Mayer/ Shopkeeper/1060-40-7842." ***Courtesy Christie's East***
A page from a costume key book shows how the vest was to be worn. ***Courtesy Eric Daily; photo: George Anastassatos***

The Man Who Leads the Triumphal Procession, as sketched by Adrian, and his flared gloves with oriental appliqué. *Gloves courtesy the Hufty family; photo: Todd Bush*

This jacket, worn by an Emerald City townsman, was one of several made in this design. Other jackets were nearly identical, save for the direction of the loop pattern on the yoke. While identifiable in the film, the extras wearing these costumes were most prominently featured parading behind the principals in the deleted triumphal procession through Emerald City (after the Witch has been destroyed). *Photo: Tim McGowan*

in the fall of 1938. More than mere background atmosphere, the part called for her to share a musical couplet with Judy Garland: "We can make a dimpled smile out of a frown." "Can you even dye my eyes to match my gown?" January believed she got the role due to her experience as a radio singer, although her on-screen appearance wasn't exactly glamorous. "They had to make me look fat so my costume was heavily padded," said January. Characteristic of the studio's propensity for detail, the actress added, "They were so particular about being sure my padding didn't slip!"

The other actors in the same sequence had costumes specific to their parts as well, like the topical "Oz" T-shirts worn by the men who restuff the Scarecrow with straw. Wherever possible, though, groups of Emerald City extras with like measurements were categorized according to the costume roster. This approach lessened the wardrobe department's constraints, and is supported by existing men's coats bearing a Metro-Goldwyn-Mayer label and marked "40" and "42," indicating standard jacket sizes.

The appearance of the Witch's Winkie guards was that of menacing uniformity; however, the intricate design of the costumes required individualizing each garment. Made of a heavy wool felt, the Winkie costumes were of complicated construction but reflected

Pic magazine snapped this candid photo, taken in the M-G-M commissary, showing several Emerald City extras lunching while attired in full costume and make-up.

Adrian at his most whimsical. The hussarlike attire featured a layered kilt that flared from the waist, metallic accents, bold red tassles, and fur shoulders. This imposing presentation was in sharp contrast to the small, timid Winkies in Baum, whose dispositions matched their favorite color, yellow. Typical of distinct player costumes, the Winkie wardrobe was identified by each actor's name inked into the lining.

For consistency, the gray, black, ecru, and orange felts used for the Winkies were adapted to the jackets of the Winged Monkeys. Nikko, the Witch's familiar and confidant, would wear a similarly styled cap, as would the monkey captain that the Witch orders to abduct Dorothy. (W. W. Denslow hadn't illustrated the monkeys as wearing anything but did distinguish the monkey leader with a large, brimmed cap.) The full-body hair suits for the monkeys were reportedly made for the picture by Max Factor's artisans.

Over two dozen men portrayed Winkies, the Wicked Witch's menacing sentries. The uniforms were cumbersome, but allowed for the Winkies' military maneuvers. The completed wardrobe differs from the more ominous July 25, 1938, script description: "The Winkies are huge figures with grotesque and hideous headdresses like the death's head helmets in Japanese armor. They are absolutely inhuman." ***Photo: Tim McGowan***

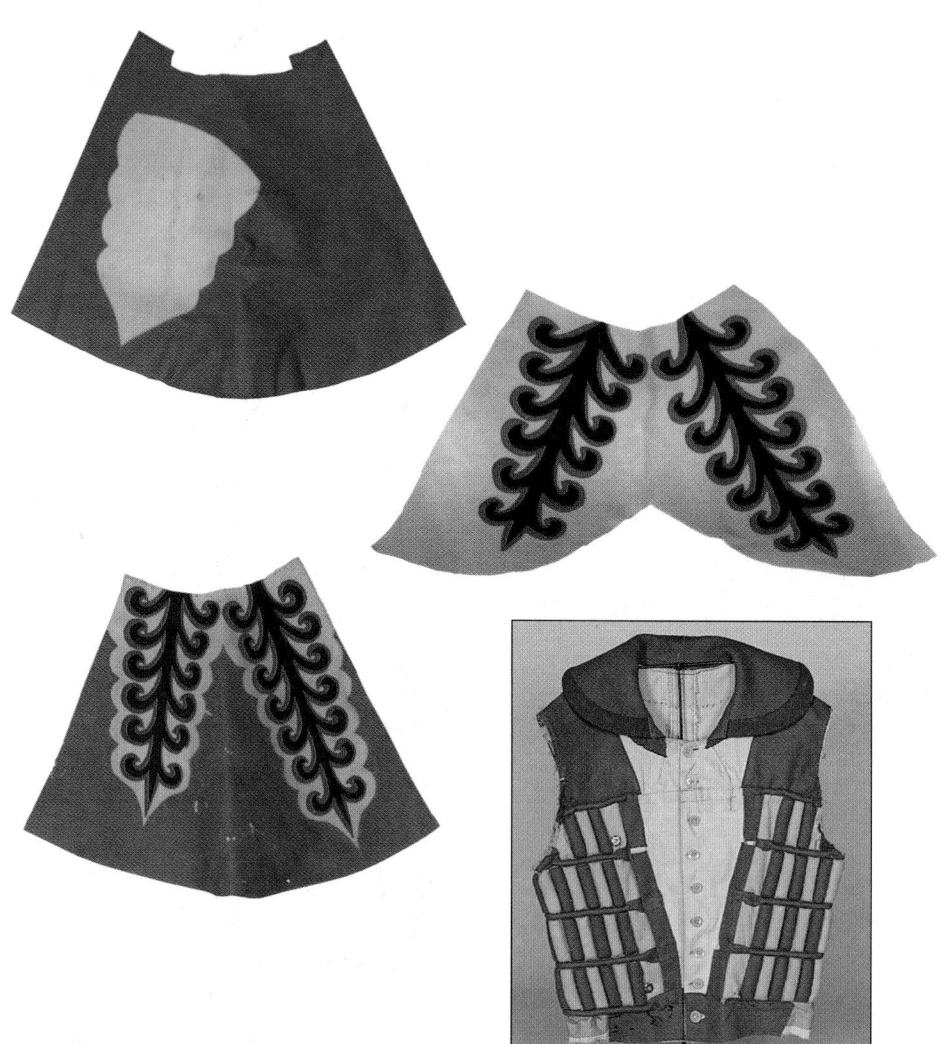

Anatomy of costume construction: wool felt panels, fabric appliqués, and vest for an uncompleted Winkie costume. ***Courtesy Eric Daily; photo: George Anastassatos***

Costume test still of Ray Bolger modeling his Winkie disguise. Inset: a Technicolor test of Haley, Lahr, and Bolger in similar costumes.

Top: A costume test still shows a Winged Monkey posing with "bat wings," rejected as unwieldy. *Courtesy Charles Schram*
At right is the realized concept for the monkey wardrobe.

Animal impersonator Pat Walshe in costume as Nikko, the Wicked Witch's lackey. Unlike the other monkeys, this costume included only very small wings. This resulted from a July 5, 1938, script treatment that explained how the Witch had "clipped" Nikko's wings in order to ensure his servitude. The smaller wings would also prove more practical when the character moved about inside the Witch's castle.

(According to an interview with Judy Garland prior to the film's release, the star described the monkeys as being "so real, it was just like magic, and I was frightened, *honestly*, when I felt their big wings brushing my arms before they carried me off with them!") The monkeys' wings were the subject of much trial and error before it was determined to pattern the wings after the South American condor, the largest bird in existence.

Of course, the costumes for the stars of *The Wizard of Oz* received the greatest publicity for their unusual nature and great discomfort; however, their fabrication wasn't nearly as challenging as effecting wardrobe for the hordes of extras. Studio publicity noted that Judy Garland was the only member of the cast to act with any degree of comfort: "She was to be the only normally dressed person in the entire Land of Oz." *Photoplay Studies* wrote: "Judy wears only one dress throughout, but it took a week of tests to find the one which was most attractive yet rural in appearance. Once found, it was duplicated nine times, and Judy wore out all ten dresses."

The bodice for this Thorpe Dorothy dress is tagged "Judy Garland" but was left uncompleted after Garland's costume was altered to blue gingham. The lacy, bowed blouse is tagged "Bobby [*sic*] Koshay" and was tested only on Garland's double before being quickly rejected. *Photo: Tim McGowan*

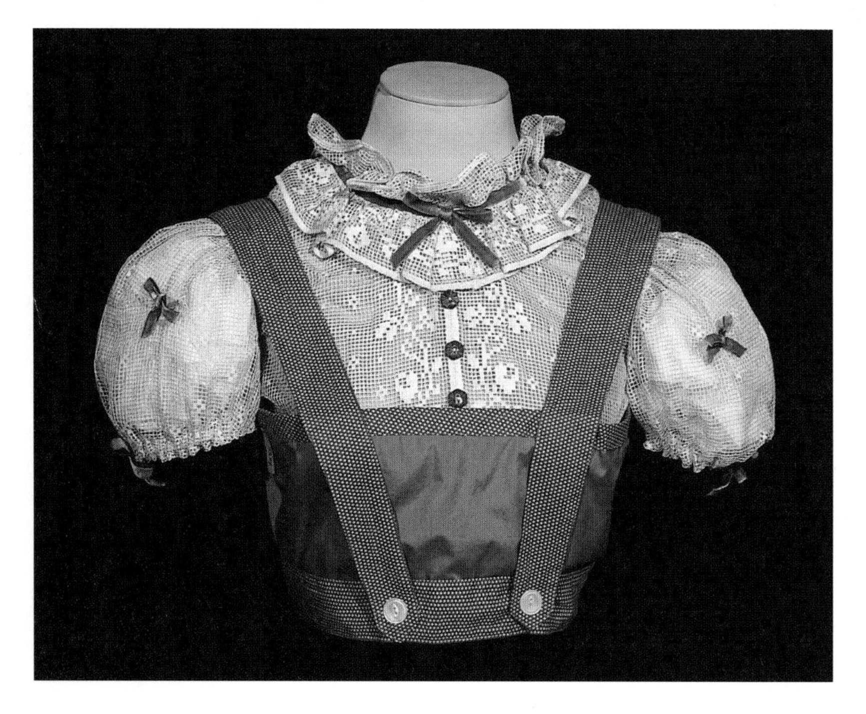

In actuality, it took nearly two months of intermittent tests and film footage to decide upon the dress that best suited Garland. In accordance with the initial concept of Dorothy, Adrian had designed a series of dresses which, while contemporary in appearance, were of the frilly, "party dress" sort. When Technicolor filming began on October 13, 1938, Judy Garland was dressed in a blue cotton pinafore with blue-polkadot border, which also circled the hem border of the dress. Her blouse was constructed of white organdy with puff sleeves, a Peter Pan collar, and a front button panel with six pleats, finished with a matching blue-polkadot bow attached at the neck. The dress befitted a young girl who imagined herself a modern-day storybook princess, but was ultimately implausible for fraternizing amidst the pig stys and hay bales of a Kansas farm.

The final version of Garland's dress was a simple pinafore typical of any pre-teenage girl of 1938. The jumper featured a hidden pocket on the right side of the skirt (for Dorothy's handkerchief) and was worn with a cotton underblouse with a cream gauze bib and puffed sleeves trimmed in

At left: Judy Garland, immobilized. A production still taken during the first two weeks of filming *Oz* reveals Garland in her blonde wig, fancy party dress, and alternate-style ruby slippers. Once Richard Thorpe was dismissed from the picture, Garland's appearance underwent drastic revision. At right: A completed version of the dress Judy Garland would wear during initial filming on *The Wizard of Oz*. Garland's double, Bobbie Koshay, would wear identical pinafores, in addition to one marked "double harness" for the scene in which she portrays Dorothy being captured and carried aloft (on wires) by the Winged Monkeys. *Courtesy The Debbie Reynolds Hollywood Movie Museum; photo: David Hardy*

matching blue ric-rac. The dress also echoed L. Frank Baum's original description, "It was gingham, with checks of white and blue; and although the blue was somewhat faded with many washings, it was still a pretty frock." Standard for Adrian's labor-intensive designs, the pattern was perfectly aligned along the seams of the skirt. For the purposes of Technicolor photography, the jumpers were given a pink overdye to tone the contrast of the blue and white check.

Regardless of the dress Judy wore, her figure was more mature than the Dorothy of the Oz books. To soften her silhouette and make her body appear childlike, Garland's blouses ended in ribbons of bias tape that would tie around her upper waist—and the corset used to flatten her bosom. Child actress and Munchkin Donna Stewart-Hardway remembered, "Judy looks like such a little girl [in

Seeing double: Munchkin maiden Olga Nardone stands between mirror images of Dorothy, December 17, 1938. On the left is Judy Garland, and to the right, Bobbie Koshay, who served as both Judy's double and stand-in. Star doubles and stand-ins needed to be of the same height, weight, and coloring as the actors. Stand-ins took the place of the stars during lighting of the sets and camera focusing. In contrast, doubles actually appeared on-camera for long shots, scenes shot from behind, or for close-ups of body parts. Doubles were occasionally called upon for stunt work as well. *Courtesy Pierre Koshay*

the picture], but she wasn't. She was considerably older than the character was supposed to be. She would pull at the bindings they had on her, just above her breasts. It must've hurt. When you're that young, your breasts are very tender. She kept pulling with her right hand on the right side of her collarbone."

The list of actors requiring costumes also specified "Color—One Costume for Dorothy (Changes in Emerald City)." It is uncertain if this was meant to be a separate change of clothes, as in the book, or an indicator that, as in the finished film, Garland's skirt was to be made subtly fuller.[6] What is certain is that a separate dress for the Kansas scenes was made. And while there has been much

[6] A July 2, 1938, draft of the *Oz* script describes a scene in the Emerald City with Dorothy "being dressed in a charming green dress and having her hair brushed and curled" by attendants while her companions are similarly refurbished. Set to music, the scene became a montage for the song "The Merry Old Land of Oz."

One copy of the jumper designed for Dorothy was apparently worn by Bobbie Koshay for the moment when Koshay (as Dorothy) opens the farmhouse door, and backs out of the frame as Garland (in her blue gingham jumper) steps forward. The dress was made of black and white gingham, tinted with an ochre wash for contrast during the transition to Technicolor. *Courtesy Joseph M. Maddalena, Profiles in History*

speculation as to the extent to which it was worn, it was likely used for a few fleeting seconds—during the transition from black and white to Technicolor. This shot was filmed in color. The interior of the farmhouse was painted in sepia tones, and the lighting was as muted as possible. Garland's double wore a black-and-white-checked jumper dyed with an ochre wash. The outfit was otherwise an exact copy of the blue gingham dress worn by Garland throughout the Technicolor scenes. To create the color change, Garland's double ran to the front door with her back to the camera. As she drew the door open, she stepped back out of the frame as Garland stepped forward and through the door, giving the illusion of one seamless take.

As in Baum's book, the on-screen Dorothy was to inherit the magic shoes of the Wicked Witch of the East. The author describes silver shoes that make a tinkling sound as the heroine walks. To take full advantage of the color photography, the silver shoes became the ruby slippers. (Red being the most vibrant contrast against the bright yellow brick road.) Several versions of the footwear were contrived before settling on the hand-sequinned pumps with flat jeweled bows applied at the toes. Altering the color of the shoes was a significant adjustment in the translation to screenplay, and the change was minimized publicly. If the shoes were even mentioned in press layouts, they were singly referenced

A publicity Kodachrome of Judy Garland in her Dorothy costume, under Victor Fleming's direction. Metro kept Judy on a strict diet, but Baum granddaughter Florence admitted, "Judy would have me . . . go to the commissary at noon and order a double portion of mashed potatoes and gravy, and sneak it to her on the set." For her photo-gallery portraits, photographer Eric Carpenter seated Garland leaning forward with her arms resting in her lap in order to slim the youngster's jawline and flatter her facial contours.

This design for the ruby slippers is reminiscent of the silver shoes in *The Wonderful Wizard of Oz.* Though they would have been appropriate on the protruding feet of the dead witch, they would not have flattered Judy Garland as the child making her way to Oz. *Courtesy The Debbie Reynolds Hollywood Movie Museum; photo: David Hardy*

as "magic slippers," "magic red slippers," or "magic ruby shoes." However, one bit of exploitation generated by M-G-M suggested the following.

> The plot action of *The Wizard* is wrapped closely around possession of a pair of magic red slippers which Dorothy obtains from the Witch of the West [*sic*]—and is her only protection against the other witches. Supposedly the slippers are fashioned of precious stone but a smart designer can get the same luminous effect with cloth. Get a shoe store to make up a pair for window display. Borrow them later for a lobby case during the run of the picture.

In *The Wonderful Wizard of Oz*, the Scarecrow wears the native Munchkin costume, albeit worn discards. His clothing includes a blue jacket and pants, and in addition, "an old, pointed blue hat, that had belonged to some Munchkin, was perched on his head." Herman J. Mankiewicz's March 19, 1938, script of the scene in which Dorothy meets the Scarecrow quotes Baum's description of the Strawman's clothing verbatim.[7] But Adrian took the same artistic license in creating the movie Scarecrow's outfit as he had in designing the Munchkins' wardrobe. Bolger's costume essentially remained unchanged during the preproduction phase. The dancer acknowledged, "What you've seen was what we started with. Adrian somehow just got the right feeling at once. . . . We discussed the fact that I had to move!" As in the book, the

The magical ruby slippers (one of several existing pairs). Each shoe was covered with red satin and lined with cream-colored kid leather, to which was applied 2,300 sequins. Each leather bow comprised 46 rhinestones, 42 bugle beads, and 3 costume jewels. Red or orange felt on the shoes' soles minimized the sound of footsteps. Typical of the early Technicolor process, the shoes' sequins were a deep burgundy or crimson color in order to shimmer a bright red on film. ***Courtesy Tod Machin***

[7] Mankiewicz was the first screenwriter in a veritable roulette of no less than fourteen individuals who had a hand in shaping the *Oz* script. The writer had a reputation for expedient turnaround but his contributions to *Oz* were limited to three weeks in March 1938. By 1941, Mankiewicz had gained lasting recognition for scripting *Citizen Kane*.

Ray Bolger shrugs at smoking in his straw-stuffed outfit while posing for a costume test still. Ironically, a June 9, 1938, draft of the *Oz* script contains a cigarette reference that was quickly excised due to its risqué nature. The Scarecrow informs Dorothy, "I was crazy about a girl once—I'd have married her, only her mother told me she smoked in bed." ***Courtesy Eric Daily***

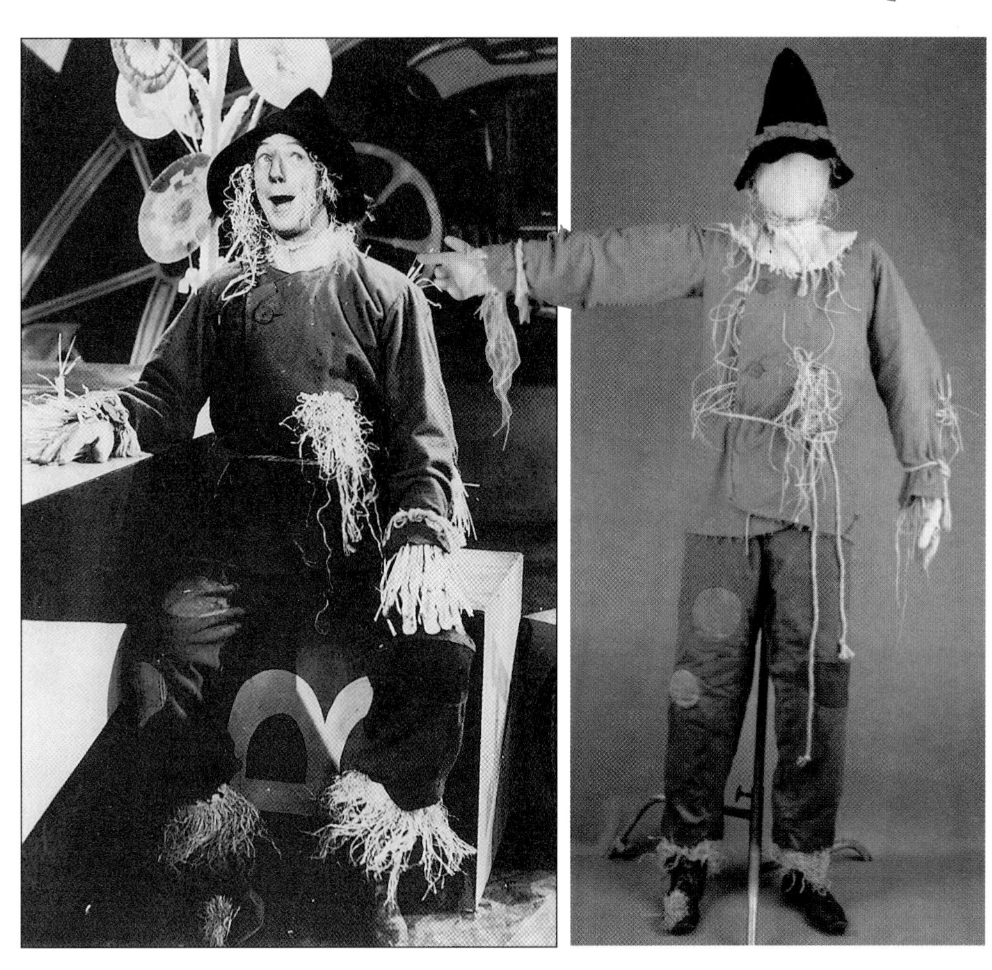

At left: Though making *The Wizard of Oz* was a test of endurance for cast and crew, the experience was fondly recalled by Ray Bolger. Bolger retained his film costume, including the hat, gloves, jacket, trousers, and boots, and appeared as the Scarecrow once again on ABC-TV's *The Ray Bolger Show*, December 24, 1954; the show was repeated April 3, 1955. *Courtesy Photofest*
At right: Ray Bolger's Scarecrow costume from *The Wizard of Oz*, donated by the actor to The Smithsonian Institution. *Courtesy The Smithsonian Institution*

Scarecrow's jacket and pants were ragged, with straw sprouting generously from tears and holes. The patched trousers were now brown; the flannel jacket a dark green; and, atop Bolger's head, a black peaked hat with green trim. Huge white gloves—like those of the Scarecrow in the 1902 stage musical—completed the picture. In 1983, Bolger described the costume fitting: "The top just hung on me; the rope tied to make a blouse effect into which the straw was stuffed and sewn on. The pants were tied with a rope. Considering that I was stuffed with real straw, my costume was the most comfortable of all the characters."

Bolger also recalled the exacting attention to the arrangement of his straw stuffing in order to ensure continuity from shot to shot, though this was little more than an exercise in futility; the straw shifted or dislodged with his very first gesture. Because the script called for the Scarecrow to have a few close brushes with fire, the costume was said to have been flame-proofed with asbestos. This also safeguarded against accidental ignition from the stray ash of the cigarettes Bolger occasionally enjoyed. *M-G-M Studio News* added, "Because Ray

Bolger's costume was straw-stuffed, he was a fire hazard and a man with a fire extinguisher was always nearby in case of accident."

Once it was decided that the Cowardly Lion would not be portrayed by a real animal, Adrian was charged with envisioning the next best thing. The *Rochester* [New York] *Times-Union* erroneously reported what followed.

> Bert Lahr, the comic, played the Cowardly Lion. The studio sent to a taxidermist for his suit, which was delivered a couple days later, furry and resplendent. It soon developed a peculiar odor, which eventually became so potent Lahr could stand it no longer. The taxidermist confessed he made the suit from the skin of a circus lion, recently deceased. He had to produce an odorless lion suit made from a rug.

Opposite: Bert Lahr's Cowardly Lion costume was comprised of at least two authentic lion pelts. The skin zipped up the front, with zippers on either arm; the Cowardly Lion's feet were shoelike slippers. The costume was stifling and uncomfortable and was punctured throughout with small holes, thought to provide some ventilation for the actor while working under the intense lighting required for Technicolor photography. *Courtesy The Comisar Collection, Inc.*

Several copies of the Cowardly Lion costume were produced, made from actual lion skins with the modern convenience of sewn-in zippers down the chest and along each arm. The suits were also punctured throughout the torso with small holes to provide some measure of ventilation. While Bert Lahr appears to wear the same costume throughout the picture, others were available for dress rehearsals or for the stunt double to bound onto the yellow brick road, leap through a window in the Emerald City, or scale the cliffs outside the Witch's castle. Fortunately, Lahr was not expected to crouch down on all fours, but could walk freely on his "hind legs." Still, wearing the heavily padded costume was smothering, and estimates of its weight ranged from fifty pounds to "about seventy pounds," according to Lahr. Make-up man Charles Schram recalled that Lahr wouldn't dress for the part until he absolutely had to.[8] After each shot, the actor unzipped the costume and rolled it down to his feet. During breaks, he took the suit off completely. Without adequate ventilation, it was ringing wet with perspiration, and the skin was aired out in a large drying bin.

For comic relief, the Cowardly Lion's tail was given a life of its own. When the tail was swinging loose from the costume, it was supported by fishing line from the catwalk above the stage. For dancing, running, and posing for publicity stills, the line was attached to a small metal ring on back of the costume. The tail was

[8] That Charles Schram would assist Lahr in dressing was highly unusual. Make-up artist Del Armstrong remarked, "Make-up and hair people would not assist in dressing the actors. . . . There were wardrobe people for that." Still, Schram recalled, "it was always a great delight to me after working an hour or so on a character make-up to walk on the stage and see the actor in the proper wardrobe. It was like putting an oil painting in a fine frame."

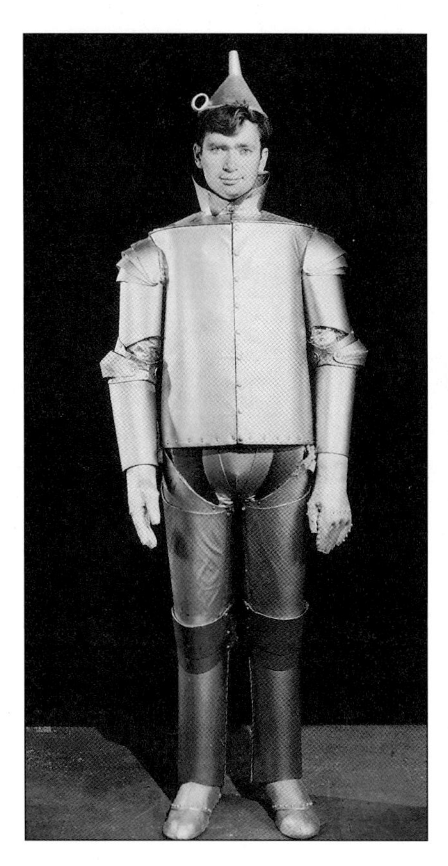

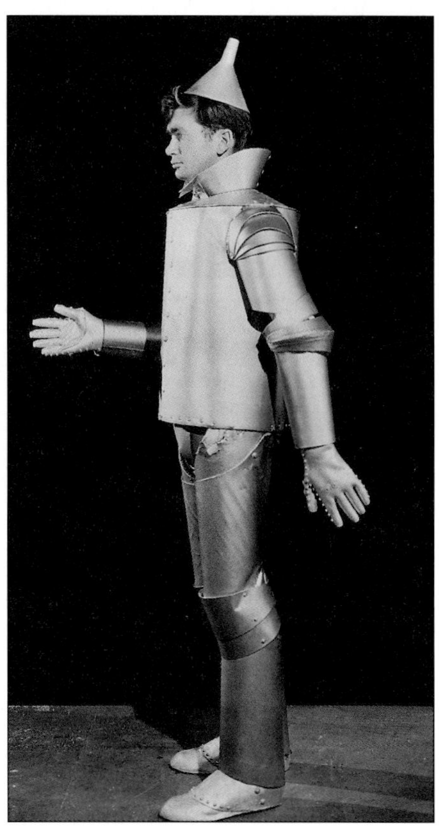

The near-final Tin Man costume, as modeled by Buddy Ebsen, October 17, 1938. ***Courtesy Eric Daily***

Script clerk Wallace Worsley consults with Ebsen's replacement, Jack Haley, who wears the same costume as Ebsen (although temporarily relieved of the trademark funnel cap). This photo was apparently taken early in production of *Oz*, as Haley's make-up would be revised to include extra rivets as well as darkened lips. Women's wardrobe dresser, Sheila O'Brien, is dimly visible in the background on the right. ***Courtesy Sue Worsley***

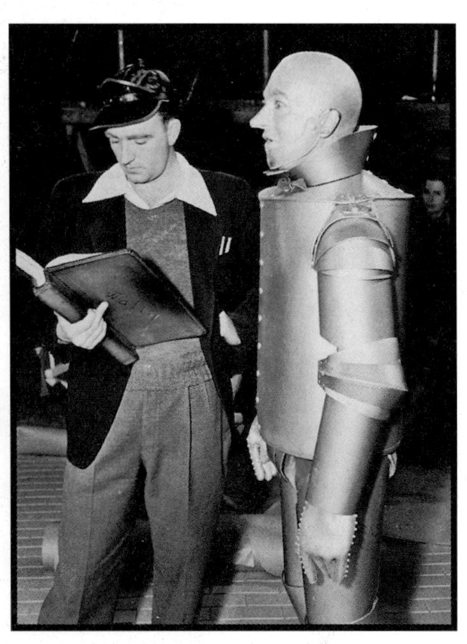

also flexible enough for Lahr to wring it in his paws, or dab at his tears with its tip. But a separate, rigid tail was waved above the rocks for the scene where the Cowardly Lion and his friends are assaulted by the Winkies.

The Tin Woodman's costume was especially challenging. W. W. Denslow drew the character with a drum-shaped torso and tapered limbs. Buddy Ebsen, the original Tin Man, endured the brunt of tests to determine a costume that resembled Denslow's depiction, was functional, and allowed some measure of movement for skipping and dancing. The result was closer in appearance to the costume worn by David Montgomery in the stage show. Attempts at a similar likeness for the movie Tin Man ranged from an authentic, but noisy, aluminum suit to one built of a bamboo-ribbed frame covered in buckram and layered with silvery leather. The latter was finally selected, worn initially by Ebsen and later adapted for Jack Haley. The Tin Man costume was reported to have been "freshly electroplated every two days." In reality, however, a wardrobe woman hand-sponged the taut silver covering every few evenings.

Jack Haley's completed suit of armor was confining and uncomfortable at best. One account quipped, "One day it took

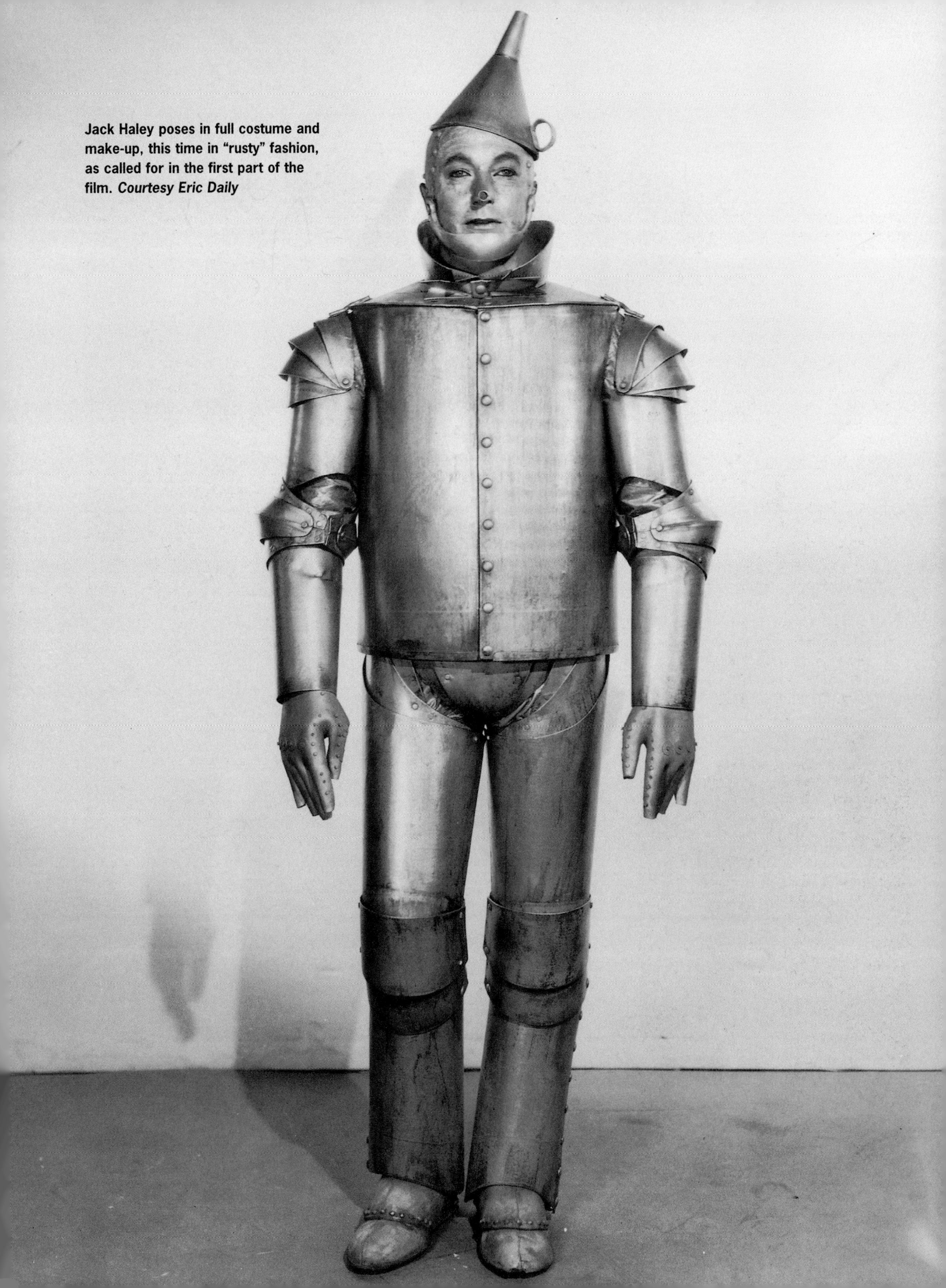

Jack Haley poses in full costume and make-up, this time in "rusty" fashion, as called for in the first part of the film. *Courtesy Eric Daily*

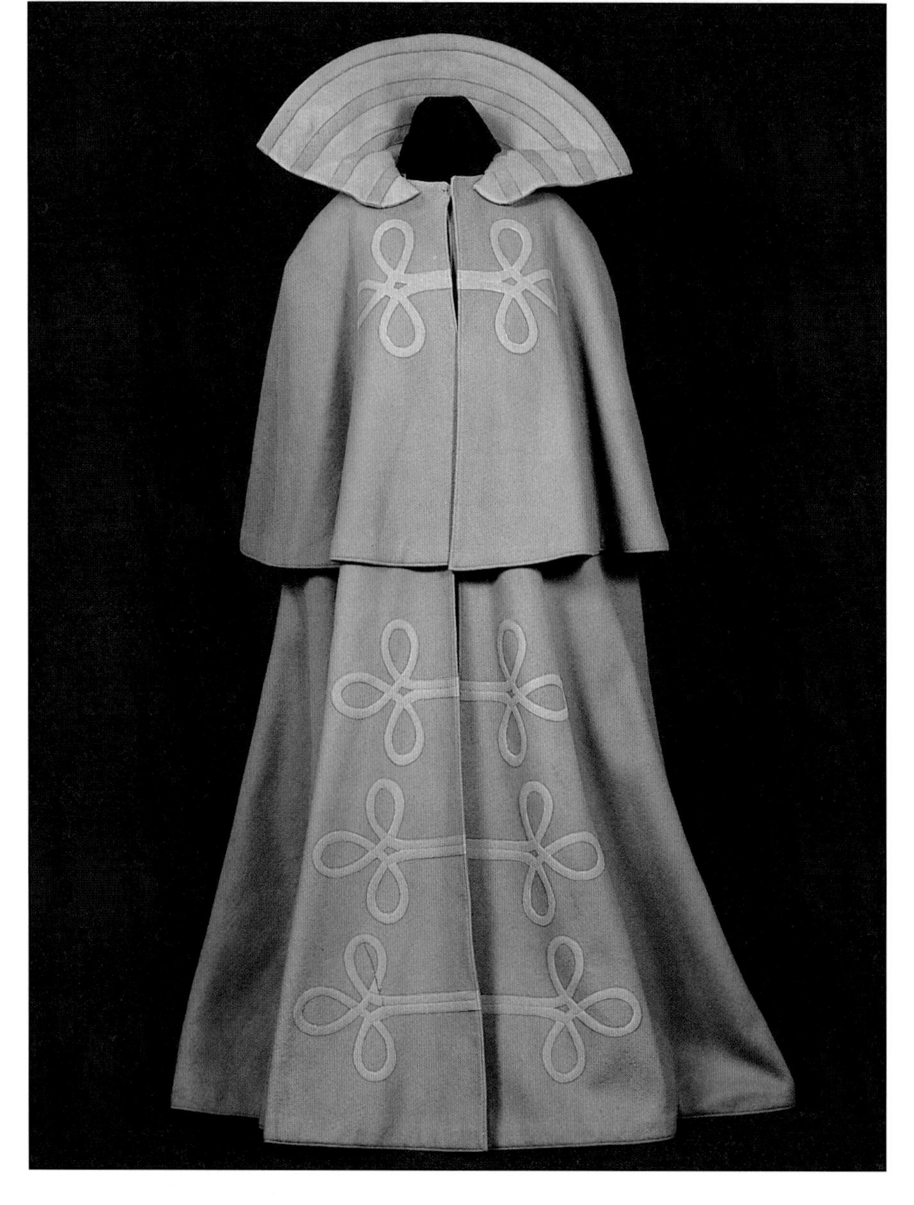

Frank Morgan's cloak, worn by the actor as the Emerald City guard who admits Dorothy into the Wizard's throne room. The cloak is inked with Morgan's name and "No. 1060-3893." ***Courtesy the Hufty family; photo: Todd Bush***

The Winkie spearheads were likely influenced by Adrian, and feature an inverted gryphon design made of cast aluminum painted silver. The spears measure a formidable 8 feet in height; the spearheads alone are 32 inches with a 4-inch iron pin at the base (which inserts into the staff). ***Courtesy Eric Daily; photo: George Anastassatos***

thirty Munchkins to get him out of a chair." The press, reiterating M-G-M publicity, further described the actor's predicament: "Covered from head to foot with a cumbersome, jointed tin costume, even to hands and feet, he had to do an eccentric dance. The outfit, which weighed more than fifty pounds, was perfected so that he had ample use of legs, arms, and body for the dance." Ed Sullivan added in his column: "The studio technicians . . . forgot to rust [the costume]. . . . In order to get the rust effect, they doused it with acid. Unfortunately, the acid soaked

The Cowardly Lion's badge of courage, awarded him by the Wizard of Oz. Once the design was determined, molds for props like the badge and Tin Man's clock heart were created.

The Wicked Witch's hourglass was re-created as a wood and papier-maché prop for the scene in which the Witch shatters it in a rage. The hourglass measures 20 inches in height and 11 ½ inches in width. The glass is handblown; its frame is decorated with six winged gryphons.

through and bit into some of the Haley cuticle. The roars of the Tin Woodman had more resonance than the roars of Lahr as the Cowardly Lion."

The oil used to relieve the Tin Man's corrosive condition was also artificial. As Haley himself recalled, "The oil Ray Bolger squirted at me, to loosen up my joints, was not oil but chocolate syrup. They squirted chocolate in my face, because the oil wouldn't photograph right, but chocolate will."

Dressing Frank Morgan as the Wizard of Oz didn't require time-consuming tribulations to devise some otherworldly attire. Nevertheless, Adrian dreamed up an unusual assortment of jackets and cloaks for the Emerald City disguises donned by the veteran actor—the most fanciful of these being the futuristic-looking doorman's coat with its rings of Saturn shoulders. Like the remaining cast appearing as Kansans, Morgan's Professor Marvel suit was comparatively (and intentionally) simplistic.

Costume accessories, like the inverted gryphon design of the Winkie's spiked spears, were probably influenced by Adrian as well.

(A model spearhead was carved from wood and used to create a sandstone mold from which duplicates were made of cast aluminum.) Other costume pieces included Glinda's wand, the Wicked Witch's broomstick, the Munchkin Mayor's pocketwatch, and the badge of courage and clock heart awarded by the Wizard. Such items were precisely drafted in blueprints before their execution. More complex props like the Witch's hourglass and crystal ball (rimmed with sculpted Winged Monkeys) and the floral design of the Munchkinland coach also required blueprints. However, the task of creating these pieces from concept to realization was delegated to the staff of Cedric Gibbons, overseer of the art department.

Once production was underway, it was the duty of women's dresser, Sheila O'Brien, and Jack Rohan, dresser for men, to ensure that the costumes needed for each day's shooting were brought from the wardrobe department (where they were stored, cleaned,

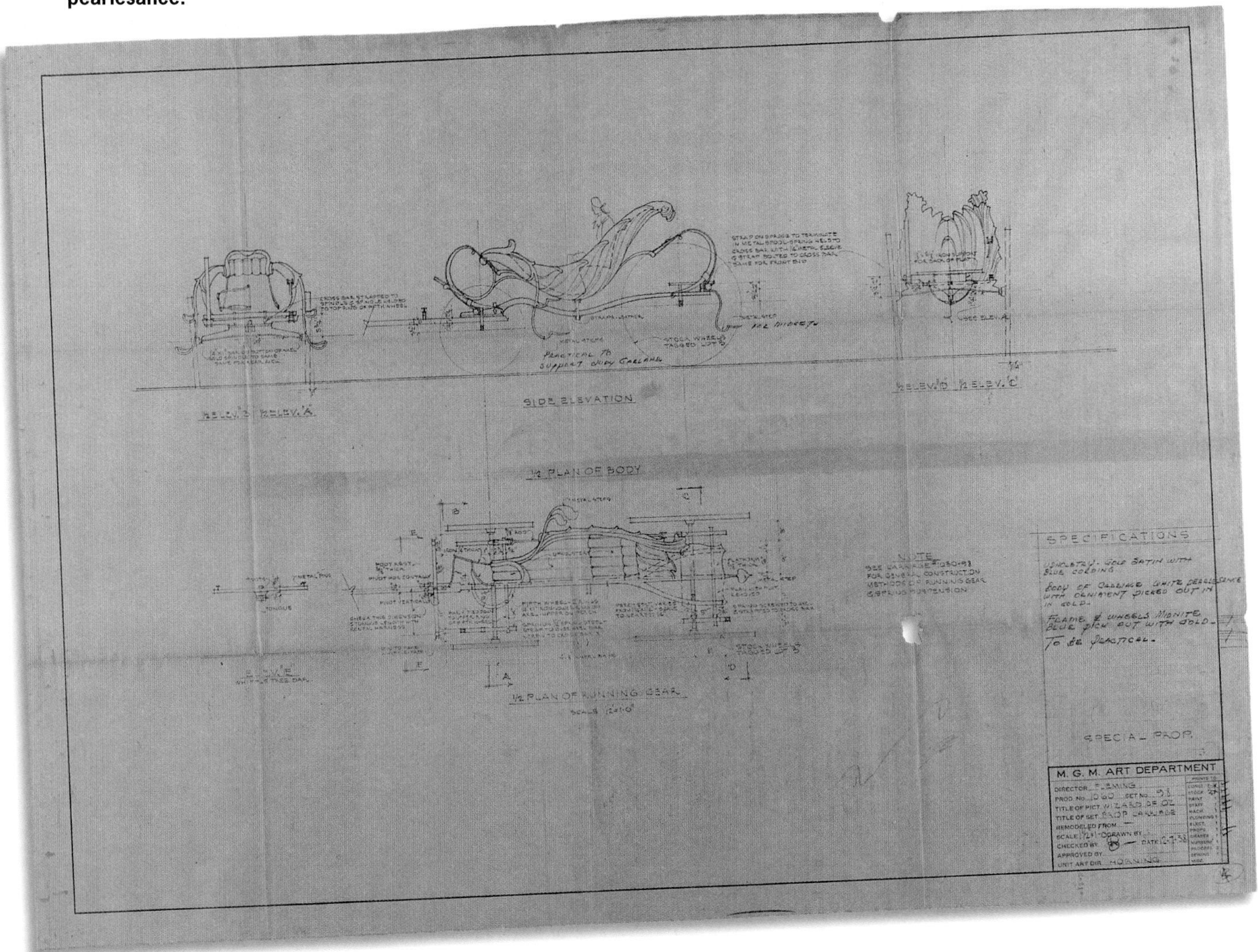

Blueprint draft of the miniature Munchkinland coach, inspired by curving flower petals. This special prop needed to "support Judy Garland" for her tour of the town; a metal step at the rear is indicated "for midget." The upholstery was to be gold satin with blue cording and the body of the carriage was finished in white pearlesance.

and repaired) to the portable star dressing rooms outside the soundstage. Both O'Brien and Rohan would have as many assistants as were needed for the day to aid in attiring the actors, and inspecting that costume details matched the last scene shot. O'Brien and Rohan would then look over the *Oz* set just prior to shooting, noting wardrobe adjustments and changes in their respective copies of the script.

While the elements of convincingly contrived character make-ups and costuming were perfected, the art department was simultaneously engaged. *The Wizard of Oz* needed a series of imaginary environments in which to unfold its story, and M-G-M's supreme resources were prepared to meet the challenge.

The cast and crew of *The Wizard of Oz* bid farewell to director Victor Fleming, who is leaving Oz to assume direction of *Gone With the Wind*, February 17, 1939. From left to right are: Sheila O'Brien, women's dresser; Margaret Hamilton (sans her witch hat); above Hamilton to the left is Jack Rohan, men's dresser; to the right of Hamilton are Bobbie Koshay and Judy Garland (both dressed as Dorothy); Bert Lahr; Victor Fleming; actress Myrna Loy; assistant director Al Shoenberg; cameraman Sam Cohen (over Shoenberg's shoulder); and Frank Morgan.

A watercolor painting illustrates the interior courtyard of the Emerald City, including the cabby's coach, drawn by the Horse of a Different Color.

SET DESIGN

Creating a Technicolor Dreamworld

Set designers usually re-create with research as a strong ally. For *The Wizard of Oz* everything was creation with no research. [Cedric] Gibbons, instead of making settings which resembled something familiar, began planning sets which looked like nothing in existence.

— *The Wizard of Oz*
campaign-book publicity, 1939

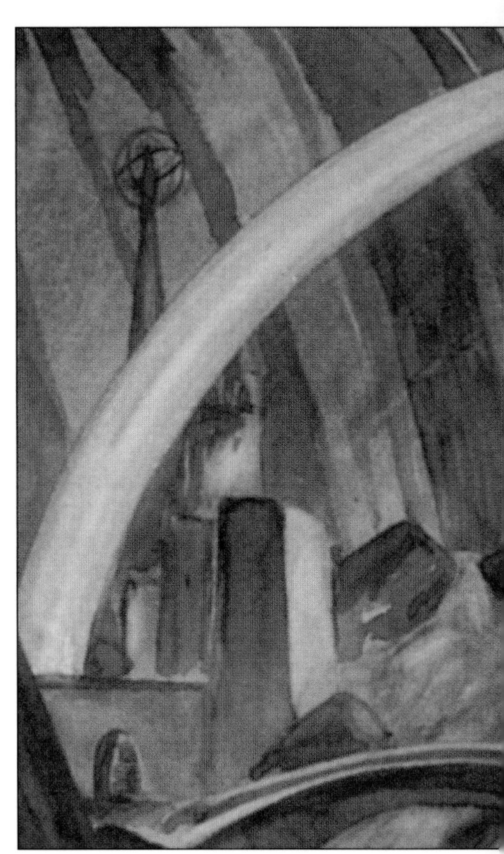

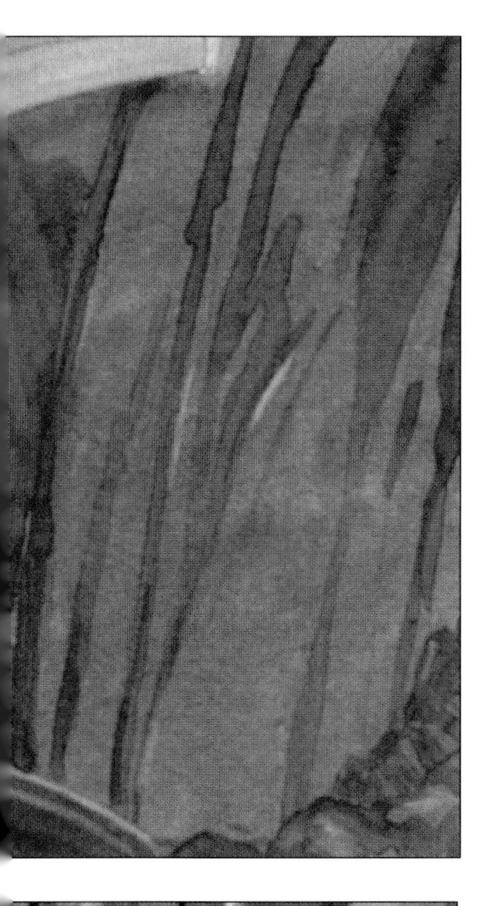

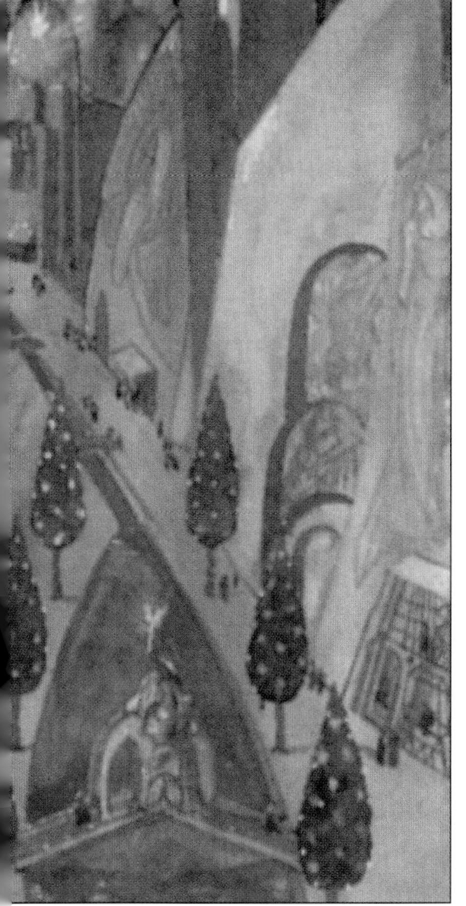

The fundamental components in portraying any motion picture environment of the 1930s required an artful combination of physical setting, realistically painted backdrops, and skillful lighting. However, the creative demands of *The Wizard of Oz* went well beyond the fundamental realm. The script called for a world where settings such as a village populated by little people, emerald skyscrapers, and a sinister fortress were commonplace. The entire picture would also be filmed exclusively on soundstages. George Gibson, director of the scenic art department, recalled, "At that time, making an 'outdoor' movie 'indoors' was something of an innovation and in a sense preceded [films] such as *Brigadoon*, *An American in Paris*, and others." The monumental task of creating a land of Oz that was not only plausible but satisfying to the public's expectations fell to Cedric Gibbons, M-G-M's chief art director.

Gibbons had built his reputation on the merits of visualizing historical epics such as *Ben Hur*, *A Tale of Two Cities*, *Camille*, and *Mutiny on the Bounty*. Recently, he had been more accustomed to designing gleaming black-and-white art deco sets for *Grand Hotel*, *Dinner at Eight*, and *Ninotchka*. But Gibbons's challenge with *Oz* was that of sheer illusion. Moviegoing audiences had reveled in the animated Technicolor delights of *Snow White and the Seven Dwarfs*.[1]

[1] In *The Making of The Wizard of Oz*, Aljean Harmetz quotes art assistant Randall Duell as recalling, "For a while we talked about completely cartooning the background, stylizing it rather than making it realistic, a cartooned cornfield rather than a real one."

Opposite: A sampling of surviving watercolor renderings depict early setting concepts for *The Wizard of Oz*. These include ideas for the Emerald City; Dorothy's farmhouse (being gently transported to Oz by cherubic clouds!); and the Rainbow Bridge—a spell cast by the Wicked Witch. Although highly imaginative, none of these early illustrations resemble anything seen in the finished film.

A rare series of storyboard drawings depicting the chase through the castle of the Wicked Witch of the West. Although the principal characters appear generic in nature, the settings and the action illustrated are nearly identical to what is seen in the final cut of *The Wizard of Oz*. Compare this art with the still and test frames shown here.

The pressure was to sustain a similar air of fantasy through the make-believe surroundings of Oz. At the time, M-G-M noted, "Cedric Gibbons, who has been the studio's art director since 1916 and responsible for many trends in architecture and interior decoration, began work with his staff on an imaginary world."[2] Although he received screen credit for *The Wizard of Oz*, Gibbons served in an advisory capacity to the capable talents of his associate William Horning and lead sketch artist Jack Martin Smith.

From the onset, it was felt that the film should reflect a contemporary quality. An interoffice communication dated February 26, 1938, stressed:

> The whole background should be more modernized than it is in the book to appeal to the modern person's idea of a Fairyland. When L. Frank Baum wrote this story which was before 1900, there were no autos, no radios, no airplanes and I do believe if he had written it today he would have in some manner made it a little more acceptable to the audience on a basis of using some of the modern contrivances that we use today. I think our *Wizard of Oz* background should be a Fairyland of 1938 and not of 1900.

Like the process used by the wardrobe department, determining the preliminary sets and backdrops for *Oz* began with a breakdown of interior and exterior locales as indicated by early drafts of the script. The temporary set list drawn from a script dated May 4, 1938, included:

EXTERIORS
Farm House, Barns, Farmyard, and Road
(Chicken Pen—Haystack—Gate)
Forest of Trees—Trick Apple Trees
Poppy Field—Transformed to Ice Field
Roof of Wizard's Palace and Balloon
Sky over Emerald City, Witch Throwing Scroll
Sky over Oz, Winged Monkeys Attacking Balloon

INTERIORS
Farm House in Munchkinland
Set for Musical Montage in Emerald City

[2] This quote includes Gibbons's work as art director for the Goldwyn studio prior to the 1924 merger with Metro pictures, and his position as art department chief at M-G-M.

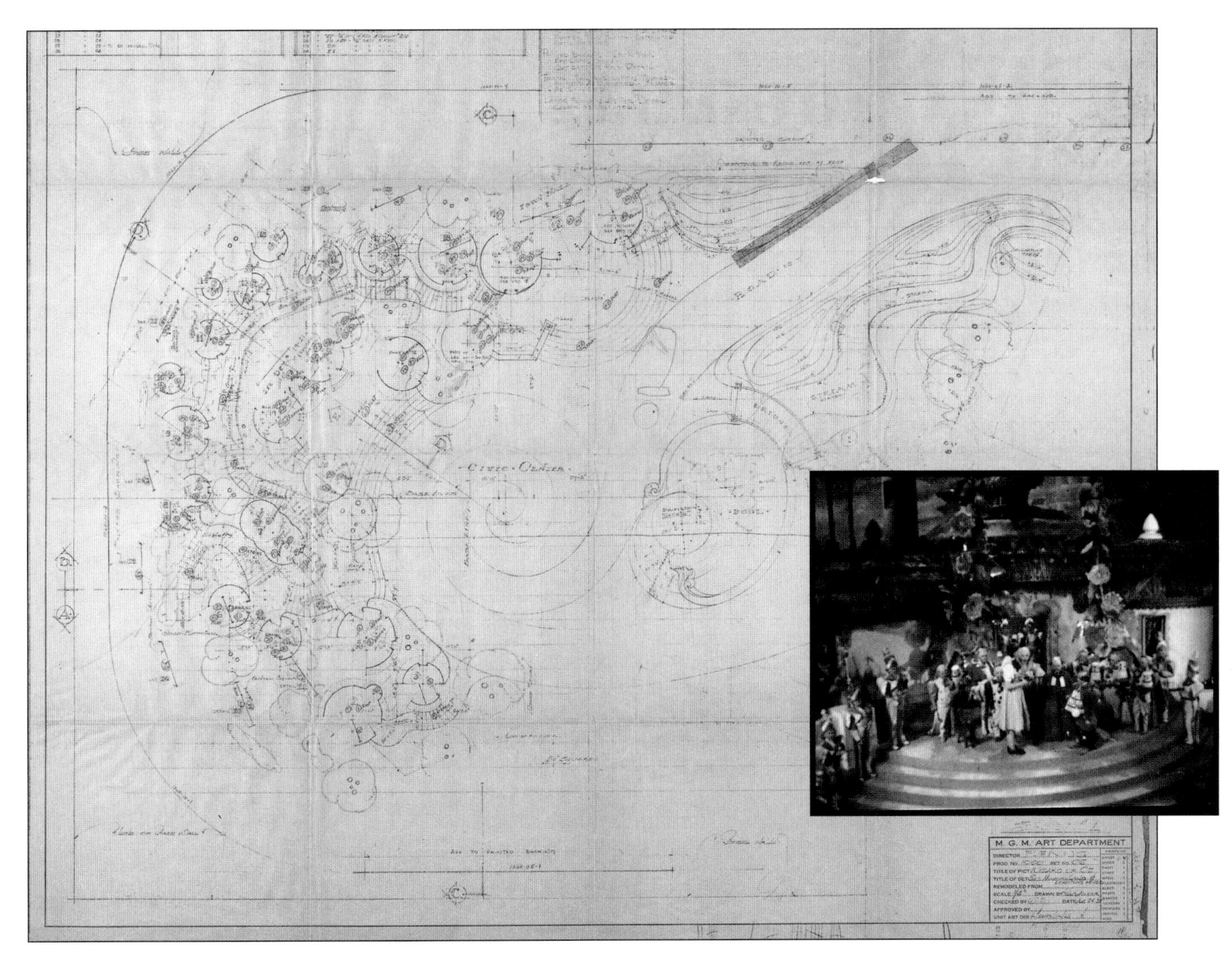

Blueprint of the entire Munchkinland set, an exercise in detail and complexity. Opposite and inset: Two glimpses of the Munchkinland civic center as seen in Technicolor tests (unlike any shots in the completed film). Note the decorative tassle around the thatched roof of the center hut. At right, Judy Garland is counseled by the town dignitaries; Toto is at her feet. *Inset courtesy Charles Schram*

Room with Spiral Staircase—Wizard's Palace
Stone Passage in Witch's Castle
Opening to Pit and Bottom of Stairs in Witch's Castle

The listing would see revision as the plot of the screen treatment was adjusted, but it provided a starting point for the art staff. The text of *The Wonderful Wizard of Oz* offered little in the way of detailed descriptions of Ozian dwellings or landscape (this was perhaps the intent of author L. Frank Baum, who valued daydreaming). "We used imagination as reference. We never used Oz books," said George Gibson, a native Scotsman who was trained in theatrical scenic design before joining M-G-M's art staff in 1934. Indeed, the imagination of the art department's coalition of professionally trained and educated architects and draftsmen rendered innumerable concept sketches. The best of these brainstorming results were approved by Cedric Gibbons and Mervyn LeRoy for further refinement. Gibbons excelled in this area. He was possessed of a remarkable talent for looking at plans brought into his office and spotting the unnecessary elements such as misconceptions of the action the set called for, where corners could be cut, or elements dispensed with. The process of realizing such concepts beyond sketchbooks best employed the department's engineers. Armed with the approved sketches (tinted per Technicolor specifications), these men drafted expansive blueprints and constructed miniature models of the proposed settings. The models aided in staging scenes and determining camera angles.[3]

Committing the land of Oz to paper was not completely without rationale. The creation of Munchkinland was intended to echo the

[3] The camera for *Oz* was operated on a special crane. For low angles, M-G-M camera chief John Arnold designed a special underslung mount that suspended the camera below the crane. This allowed the camera lens to be brought within just a few inches of the stage floor.

The highly fantastic settings of *The Wizard of Oz* provided additional obstacles to filming in Technicolor. Shown is the Munchkinland set, which often proved especially difficult from a lighting perspective. With its large cellophane foliage, light was often reflected into the camera. Consequently, cameramen were kept busy watching for "hot spots"—and adjusted the lights or the set as necessary. *Still courtesy Eric Daily*
Inset: A Technicolor view of the completed Munchkinland set peopled by actors. *Courtesy Charles Schram*

logical imaginings of any youngster who finds themself in a world where they tower over the populace. By extension, flowers would grow larger than life, the domed Munchkin huts would resemble mushroom caps, and the sweeping spiral of the yellow brick road would be conceived of the candy swirl of an enormous lollipop tipped on its side. Such creative abandon was enjoyed by Metro's artists. "Those were good times working in the studio," remembered James Roth, who came to the art department in 1936 as a set designer. "You never woke up in the morning thinking, 'Aw hell, I gotta go to work!' It was a great feeling of contributing something . . . of being interested in your work." Roth was one of a number of young men who drafted blueprints of *Oz* sets, including the poppy field.

Judy Garland and the Munchkins are poised for the scene in which Dorothy is first instructed to "follow the yellow brick road." The fanciful progression of this scene, in which the camera pulls back to a high shot such as this, is akin to a Busby Berkeley number. However in a June 13, 1938, version of the script, Dorothy is led—undramatically— to the border of Munchkinland at which point the yellow brick road merely intersects. Dorothy repeats, "Follow the yellow brick road and I can't go wrong." ***Courtesy Charles Schram***

Once authorized, the art department's blueprints were next delivered to the construction department, where carpenters, sculptors, and painters worked diligently according to the shooting schedule to re-create in three dimensions the inventings of Gibbons's staff.[4] Although existing set blueprints number nearly one hundred, it is believed that just over sixty sets were made for *Oz*. Typical of filmmaking, only that which would be seen on-camera was constructed. Dwellings like the Kansas farmhouse, the Tin Woodman's cottage, and the exterior of the Emerald City were facades. Some of the Munchkin huts were flat background pieces, known as cutouts, made of painted muslin attached to sturdy Masonite frames shaped like the huts' contours. More elaborate presentations of buildings and vistas necessitated double exposure using matte paintings to supplement live film footage. Utilizing wood, plaster, cellophane, and artificial trees, bushes, and flowers, the construction crew would physically erect what they could in-house before piecing the set components together on soundstages. They were also responsible for tearing it all down.

The Wizard of Oz took full advantage of M-G-M's newest soundstages, usually Stages 24, 25, 26, and 27. Considered state-

[4] According to existing blueprints for *The Wizard of Oz*, adjustments in set design were made with the change in directors from Richard Thorpe to Victor Fleming. Altered were the Kansas farm, locations in and around the Witch's castle, and the Scarecrow's cornfield.

A view of Munchkinland from the farthest edge of the set reveals that Dorothy's house is a facade. (Note also the mops required for wiping the yellow brick road between takes.) Compare this with the exacting blueprint of the crashed house (below). Temporary structures such as this were little more than glorified stage scenery. Inset: A similar view with Judy Garland surrounded by Munchkins.

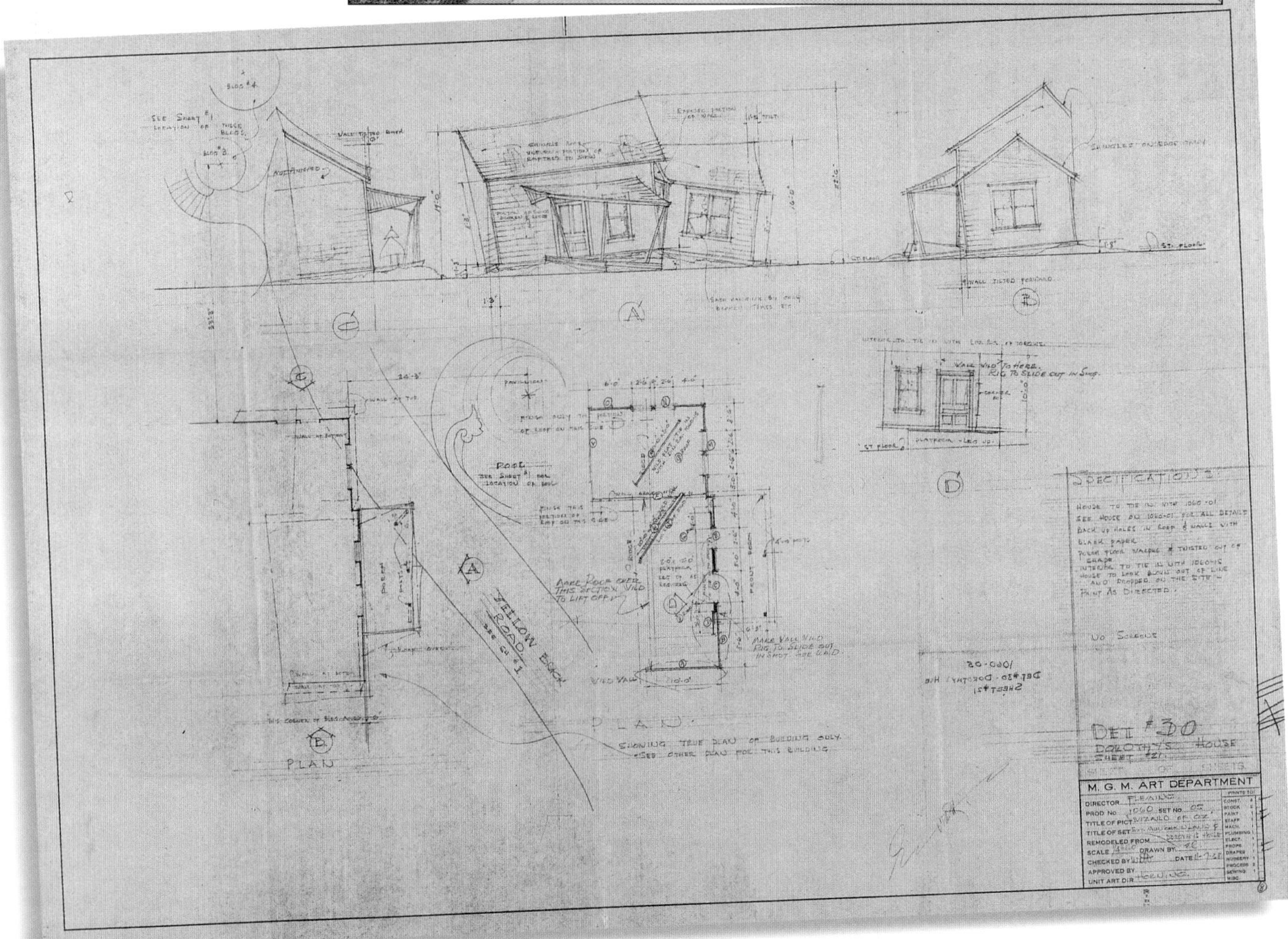

of-the-art, the stages were constructed like huge rectangular factories without any interior roof support. The exterior walls were of thick poured concrete with a layer of sound insulating material held within by a layer of ¼-inch hardware screen. The height of the soundstages was over 40 feet. At the top of each stage were air conditioning ducts where cold air, produced in a separate refrigerator building common to all the stages, blew down over the hot sets. During the recording of dialogue, the air conditioning was turned off for the duration of each take. Despite the call for "Quiet on the set!" some noise was unavoidable. The rustling of the poppies; the clicking of horses' hooves; the scuffling feet of the Munchkins; and general reverberation necessitated dubbing in the appropriate dialogue in postproduction.

At one corner of each soundstage were large double sliding or lifting insulated doors. They were about 20-by-20 feet and each weighed tons. When lowered and sealed, they shut out all outside noises. Through these doors large sections of prefabricated sets were rolled in, as were other materials such as the backings, lights, props, trees, and shrubbery. Near the large doors was a smaller sound-insulated door with a 6-by-6-foot room between, where studio personnel entered.

The sets for *The Wizard of Oz* were built on elevated wooden frameworks, which the construction department kept in stock. These variously sized structures were planked over, like flooring, and nailed together by carpenters on the stages. The frames could then be covered over by jute tarps and topped with grass sod from the studio nursery. For the Kansas farm, the apple orchard, and the Scarecrow's cornfield, the tarps were covered with dirt that was stockpiled on the lot and shipped to the set by trucks. Foliage and other decorative accents were next put in place. The trunks of smaller trees were authentic, and augmented with artificial leaves. When situated, the trees were affixed to the stage floor and secured to the top of the set with wires. Larger trees, like those in the Cowardly Lion's Forest, were made of plaster-molded bark.

One of the first sets constructed, the Scarecrow's cornfield was proclaimed to have covered four acres and consisted of ten thousand

The Scarecrow's cornfield set as it initially appeared under the direction of Richard Thorpe. Elmer Sheeley, Jr., was ten when his father, on staff in the art department, showed him the cornfield after Victor Fleming was at the helm. It was an impressive sight for a ten-year-old, and Sheeley remembered, "The corn was a stalk with a green Celluloid leaf—and there were lots of 'em!"

Judy Garland and Ray Bolger make their way down the yellow brick road on the Scarecrow's cornfield set. The set was refurbished following the change in directors from Richard Thorpe to Victor Fleming, The yellow brick road was now made of Masonite tiles instead of stenciled, painted-on bricks. Likewise, fencing was added to the backing (where previously there had been none). Production stills such as these were taken during dress rehearsals.

real cornstalks stuck into the ground.[5] (George Gibson contended that this claim "stretches things somewhat. The actual field . . . was about 75 by 50 feet, but then publicity people are prone to doing a little exaggerating where statistics are concerned.") For Munchkinland, it was reported that forty painters worked a week after the carpenters were finished. Once assembled, the finished set was described in 1939 as containing "ninety-two tiny houses, giant flowers, a public square, a bridge over a tiny river, a fountain, market places, and streets. The whole set stood ninety feet high and contained every color possible to photography." In contrast, many of the other sets were designed to be more monochromatic in the way that colors appear in nature. The poppy field, for instance, was simply a mass of reds ranging from "light pink" to "deep rose," and accented by varying light intensities on different sections. Likewise, the Emerald City was decorated throughout with green glass spires, and was quoted as being the film's largest interior set.

The walls of substantial structures like the Emerald City and the Witch's castle were made of mortar "skins" contrived by the plaster shop. The skins were created by slathering one to two inches of plaster onto burlap of varying lengths. A series of molds in stock produced a variety of impressions, from masonry to brick. The plaster surface of the skins was particularly conducive to forming an imprint of the desired texture. When dry, carpenters nailed the skins to wooden skeletons of the set. Plaster men would then "point up the joints," smoothing over the seams and nails to make these areas imperceptible. Painters finished the structures by brushing the entire surface with the appropriate colors and shades, completing the effect.

Masonite made of compressed sawdust and plastic was used extensively as flooring, and for the tiled look of the yellow brick

5 Early blueprints for the cornfield indicate that real corn was required, "green as possible." In examining stills taken during Richard Thorpe's direction, the cornstalks do appear authentic—and authentically wilted under the arc lights. When the scenes were reshot by Victor Fleming, resilient Celluloid cornstalks were ordered.

road. For the Emerald City sets, 8-by-4-foot sheets of the ¼-inch-thick material were nailed to the wooden stage floors. When spray painted, lacquered, waxed, and polished, it created the same high-gloss look as the dazzling surfaces that Fred Astaire and Ginger Rogers swirled across in their popular 1930s films. The Masonite gave the illusion of a gleaming marble floor yet provided the friction necessary to sustain spinning, leaping and dancing without slipperiness. The flooring was low maintenance but required frequent mopping between takes. Comparably sized sheets of Celotex fiberboard were used for platforms, stairs, and flooring in the Witch's castle sets.

The unusual nature of the *Oz* sets aroused the curiosity of Metro's star players, and celebrity visits were commonplace.

The apple-orchard set in which Judy Garland and Ray Bolger are pelted with fruit from perturbed trees. ***Courtesy Eric Daily*** **Inset: Garland and Bolger wait for a Technicolor test on the orchard set.**

The Tin Woodman is rescued by Dorothy and the Scarecrow on this portion of the Oz set. The rocky hill was transplanted from the edge of the cornfield set and artfully disguised here with trees. Inset: The actors during a color test on the same set.

According to Ann Rutherford, "If you were a contract player, you could get on the set. You just didn't dare open the door when the red light was on [during a take]!" Having been weaned on the Oz books, Rutherford was anxious to see Munchkinland in particular. "I wanted to see everything brought to life that I had grown up reading . . . so for the rest of my life I could say I had been to the land of Oz!" Accessing the *Oz* set otherwise was by pass only. Being Baum grandchildren, eighteen-year-old Stanton Baum and his younger sister Florence put their passes to good use. "I had one to get in the [front] gate and one to get on the set," Stanton recollected. "The doors closed after a certain time and there was a guard who would check your pass." Stage-door security would also protect the picture's mystique from unauthorized leaks.

In the years prior to his 1938 ascent as head of the scenic art department, George Gibson and his brother, William, worked through the ranks of an apprenticeship program similar to that of the make-up department. Like many others, Gibson didn't receive screen credit for his work on *The Wizard of Oz*, not that he minded. "At M-G-M, everybody felt secure in their work and their job," he recalled of his tenure. "Everybody contributed, everybody collaborated." In overseeing the creation of the backdrops that would complement the sets, Gibson relied on the collaboration of the men he supervised. Painting the huge cloth canvases was, in a way, as challenging as creating the physical sites they meshed with. "In Britain, the biggest thing I ever painted was 36 feet by 24 feet," said the artist. *The Wizard of Oz* required backdrops in excess of 300 feet in length.

Gibson remembered that the scenic art department received notice of the *Oz* project as they were finishing ceilings and tapestries for *Marie Antoinette*. Having done theatrical backdrops, George Gibson was an outstanding illustrator, and sketched ideas of the *Oz* panels for Cedric Gibbons's approval. Like all department heads, Gibbons expected excellence, and would caution Gibson about any margin of error, admonishing, "Be advised, George, you will be remembered by the failures long after they have forgotten the successes." Gibson never allowed himself to forget these words, and strived to surpass the studio's requirements. Too busy to be concerned much with the communal lunches at the art department's commissary table, Gibson was occasionally torn when Gibbons would remark, "I don't see you at the table any time." George Gibson was also chided for his work attire, which contrasted starkly with that of his supervisor. Cedric Gibbons was a handsome Irishman who dressed immaculately. The white smock Gibson wore over his shirt and tie was practical but did not connote the professional example set by Gibbons. Instead, the smock prompted one *Oz* grip to joke, "Are you the ice cream man?" and Gibbons to urge, "George, goddamn it, why don't you get yourself a jacket!"

November 11, 1938. The Wicked Witch of the West is filmed atop the Tin Woodman's hut. In its review of *The Wizard of Oz*, *Esquire* magazine declared, "Margaret Hamilton as the green witch is something Disney could never equal in *Snow White*."

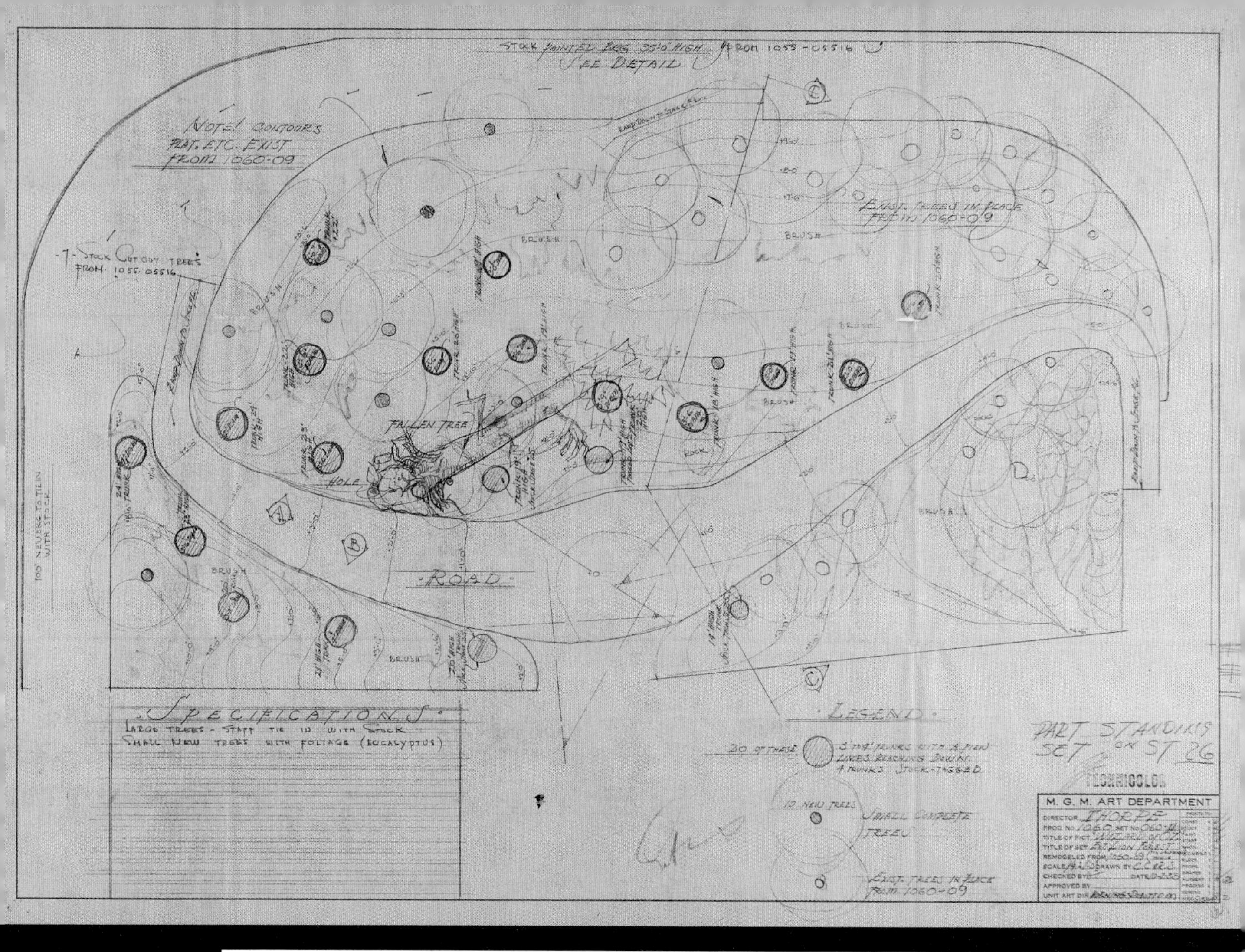
STOCK PAINTED BKG 35'-0" HIGH FROM 1055-05516
SEE DETAIL
NOTE! CONTOURS PLAT. ETC. EXIST FROM 1060-09
-7- STOCK CUT OUT TREES FROM 1055-05516
EXIST. TREES IN PLACE FROM 1060-09
FALLEN TREE
HOLE
ROAD
BRUSH
SPECIFICATIONS
LARGE TREES - STAFF TIE IN WITH STOCK
SMALL NEW TREES WITH FOLIAGE (EUCALYPTUS)
LEGEND
20 OF THESE
10 NEW TREES
SMALL COMPLETE TREES
EXIST. TREES IN PLACE FROM 1060-09
PART STANDING SET ON ST 26
TECHNICOLOR
M. G. M. ART DEPARTMENT
DIRECTOR THORPE
PROD. NO. 1060 SET NO. 060-11
TITLE OF PICT. WIZARD OF OZ
TITLE OF SET EXT. LION FOREST
REMODELED FROM
SCALE
DRAWN BY
CHECKED BY
DATE
APPROVED BY
UNIT ART DIR.

Lion Forest

A blueprint of the Cowardly Lion's Forest (featuring a large fallen tree), a still of the completed set, and two Technicolor outtakes. (Note Bert Lahr's double perched on the tree trunk.) A separate blueprint details the painted backing that augmented the artificial trees of the forest.

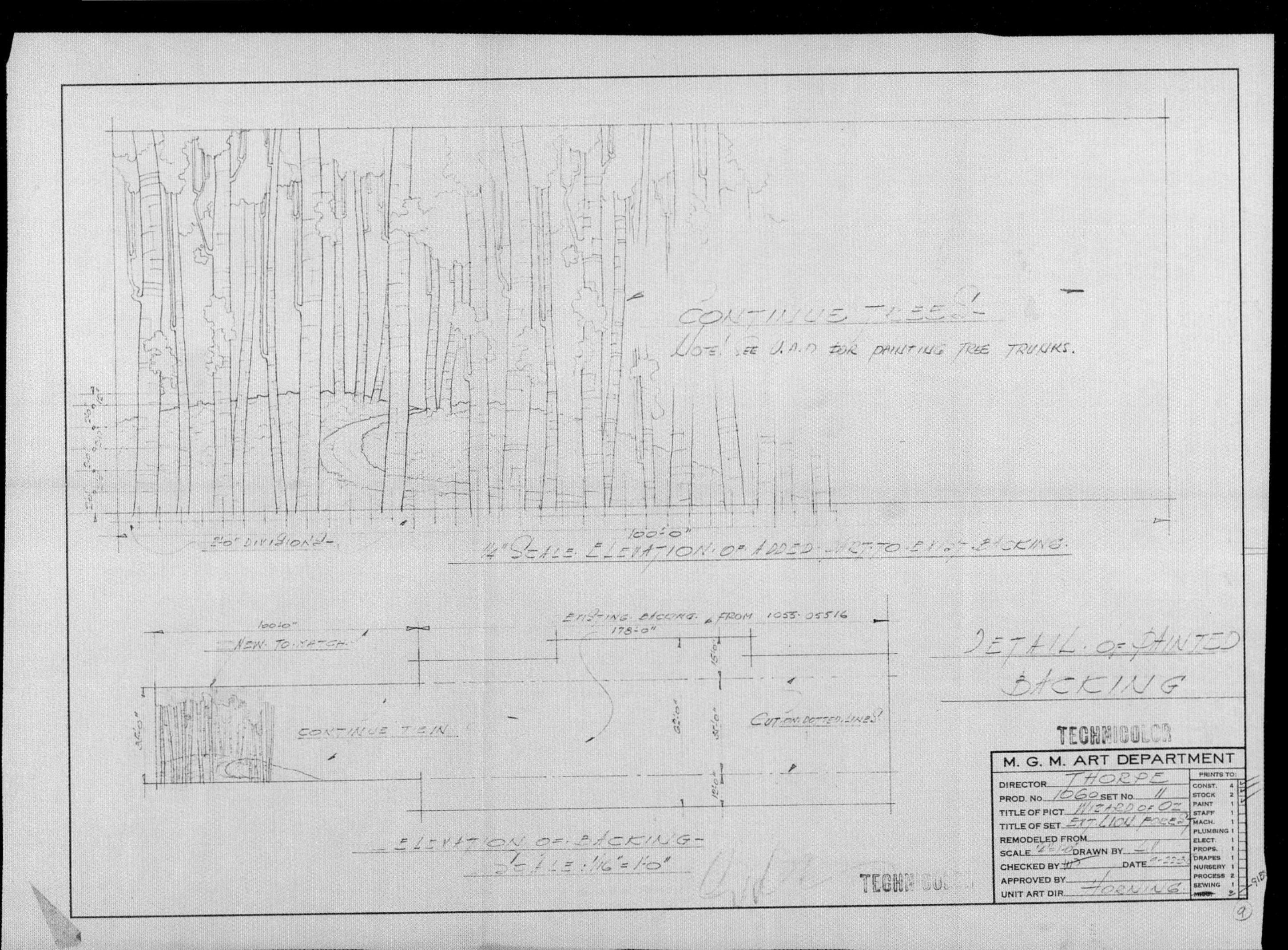

The glorious poppy field during Technicolor lighting tests. Of all the *Wizard of Oz* sets, the poppy field was most frequently singled out as memorable and breathtaking by those who recall visiting the set.

A set still of the poppy field, taken from the perspective of the actors, reveals a seemingly infinite vista of artificial blossoms.

FLEMING
PROD. 1060
SET NO.
13
Poppy
Field

A set constructed for *The Wizard of Oz* for a "montage song," according to the original blueprint, but unseen in the finished film. This scene apparently took place as the characters emerge from the poppy field en route to the Emerald City (see inset). Sheets of cardboard protect the yellow brick road from scuffing.

By early fall 1938, the scenic art crew had set up the cornfield backdrop at one end of Stage 26 while Judy Garland and the other actors began rehearsals at the opposite end of the soundstage, accompanied by pianist Eddie Becker. Gibson remembered, "Judy, Jack Haley and Bert Lahr used to come over and look at what we were doing. I had about ten artists working on [the backings] at the time, and [the actors] were curious and interested. Of course, being of the theatre, they were familiar with scenic artists and what they did." A scaffolding arrangement set up in front of the large panels enabled Gibson's painters simultaneously to work within the grid outlines that would guide them. Gibson could direct these operations and attend to other matters from a desk that could be rolled about the studio.

Prior to *The Wizard of Oz*, scaffolding for scenic backings was stationary, limiting the efficiency with which the backdrops were painted. The majority of the *Oz* backings were done this way, with an eye toward recycling them throughout the course of filming. (The fantastic nature of the scenery meant that none of the backings could be reused in other pictures, and they were eventually painted over for cost efficiency.) "The same backing, about 300 feet long by 40 feet high . . . doubled on the cornfield, apple orchard, and Tin Woodman's–hut sets. . . . Of course there was another arrangement made in front of it each time so that it wouldn't be recognizable," said George Gibson. However, before the picture completed filming, the backdrops were painted in the new scenic art building using immense vertical easels engineered by Norwegian designer John

The gates of the Emerald City and an inset frame of the actors during a test. *Still courtesy Eric Daily*

A blueprint of the Emerald City Wash and Brush Up Parlor, and two views of the set taken on January 5, 1939. (Note that the order of the salon stations changed from the draft to construction.)

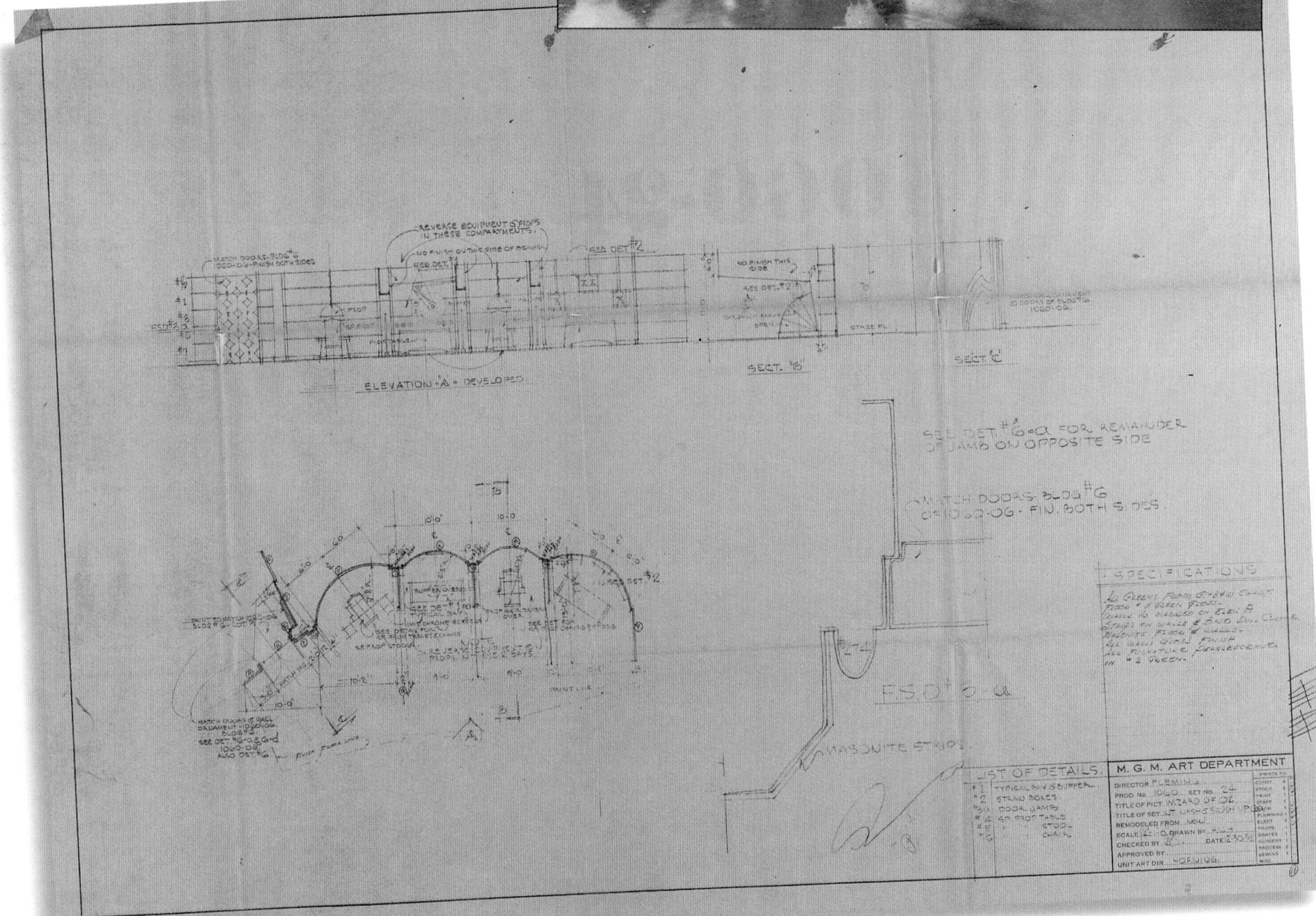

Bossert. Gibson aided Bossert in the building's design by providing specifications such as the weight of the cloth backings and the size of the frames needed. One publicist aptly dubbed the finished scenic art department a "two-story building ten stories high." Housed in the 110-foot-tall building, five frames were electrically operated via motors installed in the rafters. Three frames measured 100 feet long by 40 feet high; the next was 60 by 40 feet; and the smallest frame was 40 feet square. By pressing a button, the huge easels could rise up or be lowered to the desired height. Without ladders, the artists stayed on one level and raised the easels to the ceiling to paint the bottom backing, or lowered them to paint the top. The threatening clouds of the Kansas sky were done on these frames, painted in shades of burnt umber for the film's prologue and closing.[6] The umber color was painted using the same number of values—light to dark—as was used in black-and-white photography, the darkest value necessitating the addition of black.

"In painting the backings for the Kansas farm, the main element, of course, was the sky," recalled Gibson of the intentional foreshadowing for the cyclone, "and Leo F. Atkinson was the artist in this area." Atkinson was known as the undisputed cloud authority, and he intensely studied cloud formations: cirrus, stratus, cumulus. Given his reputation, Atkinson personally painted all the skies for *Oz*, including those in Kansas. To create the sky effect, the artist used a paint spatter gun instead of an air gun. This appliance kept the spatter separated and allowed for more control of the paint. The clouds could then appear dense, not misty or foggy.

Readying the backdrops and the paint used to cover them was an art in itself. The absorbency of the muslin backings had to be sealed off with cornstarch size, a preparation medium. Once the cloth was wetted with the size and allowed to dry, the paint could be applied without running or bleeding. The paint used was a type of watercolor made of ground, dry pigment mixed with a glue binding to create a sort of poster paint. (The powdered color was

The same set populated by the principal characters and Emerald City attendants. Assistant dance director Dona Massin (seen as a manicurist, far left) had worked with producer Mervyn LeRoy at Warner Bros. prior to coming to M-G-M. As LeRoy enjoyed success with the Warner Bros. pictures in which Massin appeared, he asked her to make a cameo in *Oz*. "And I told him I didn't *want* to be in the picture," she recalled. "He said, 'You'll bring me luck.'" *Courtesy Charles Schram*

6 Even though the Kansas scenes were filmed in black and white, the footage was printed in sepia. Not only were the backdrops in brown tones, the matte paintings used for these sequences were in sepia as well.

Opposite: Stills of Emerald City, the film's largest interior set. Much green glass was reportedly used to create the ornamental structures. Decades later, set designer James Roth remained impressed, "My chief recollection is of the Emerald City . . . which was terrific! It was just an outstanding set."

The blueprint for the interior of the palace corridor contains exacting specifications for executing the walls, floors, woodwork, and windows—a portion of which was "breakaway" so that Bert Lahr's double could vault through the glass in panic. The arched hallway was created with a painted backing and also as a separate matte painting.

requisitioned by the pound from paint companies.) Gelatin glue in dry chips of about ⅛-inch thick and no more than two inches square were put into a double boiler. The pigment was added to the mix until the color ran a certain thread consistency, formed a bead, and dropped down into a paint bucket. This was the only way to tell if the amount of glue was sufficient or needed tempering. The general recipe for backing paint was a teacup of glue to a gallon of water. The paint itself was 60-to-70 percent dry color to 40 percent water, mixed in 5-gallon crocks. In later years, huge quantities of paint were mixed in the 100-gallon drums on Lot 3, which had a paint shop to accommodate its own huge backing around the water tank used for miniatures at sea.

It was on *The Wizard of Oz* that Duncan Spencer got his first break. Since starting with M-G-M in January 1937, he had worked his way up from pot boy, a position cleaning up paint buckets technically known as "assistant to journeyman." Twenty-seven

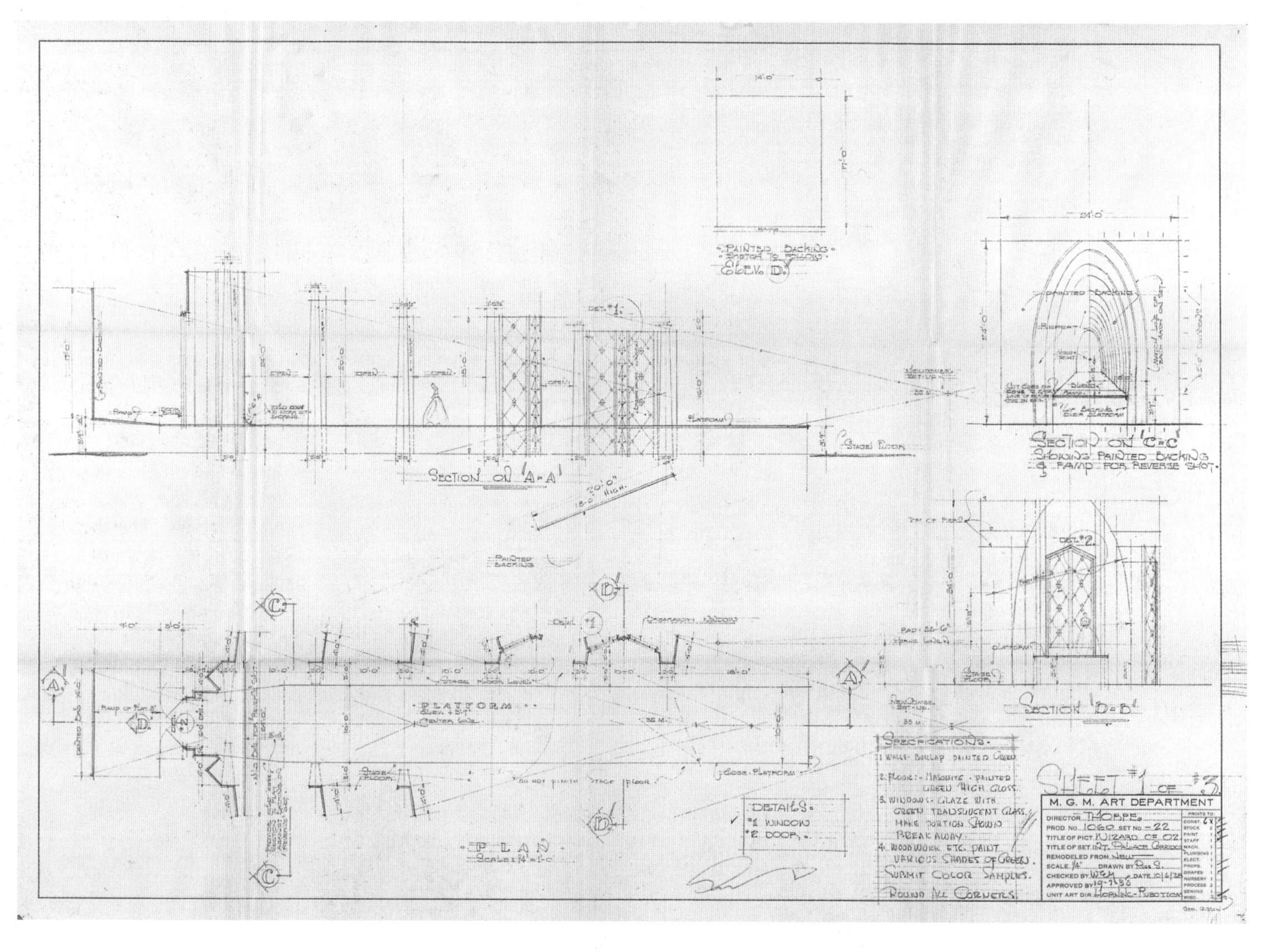

59
60
61
62
FLEMING
1060
City

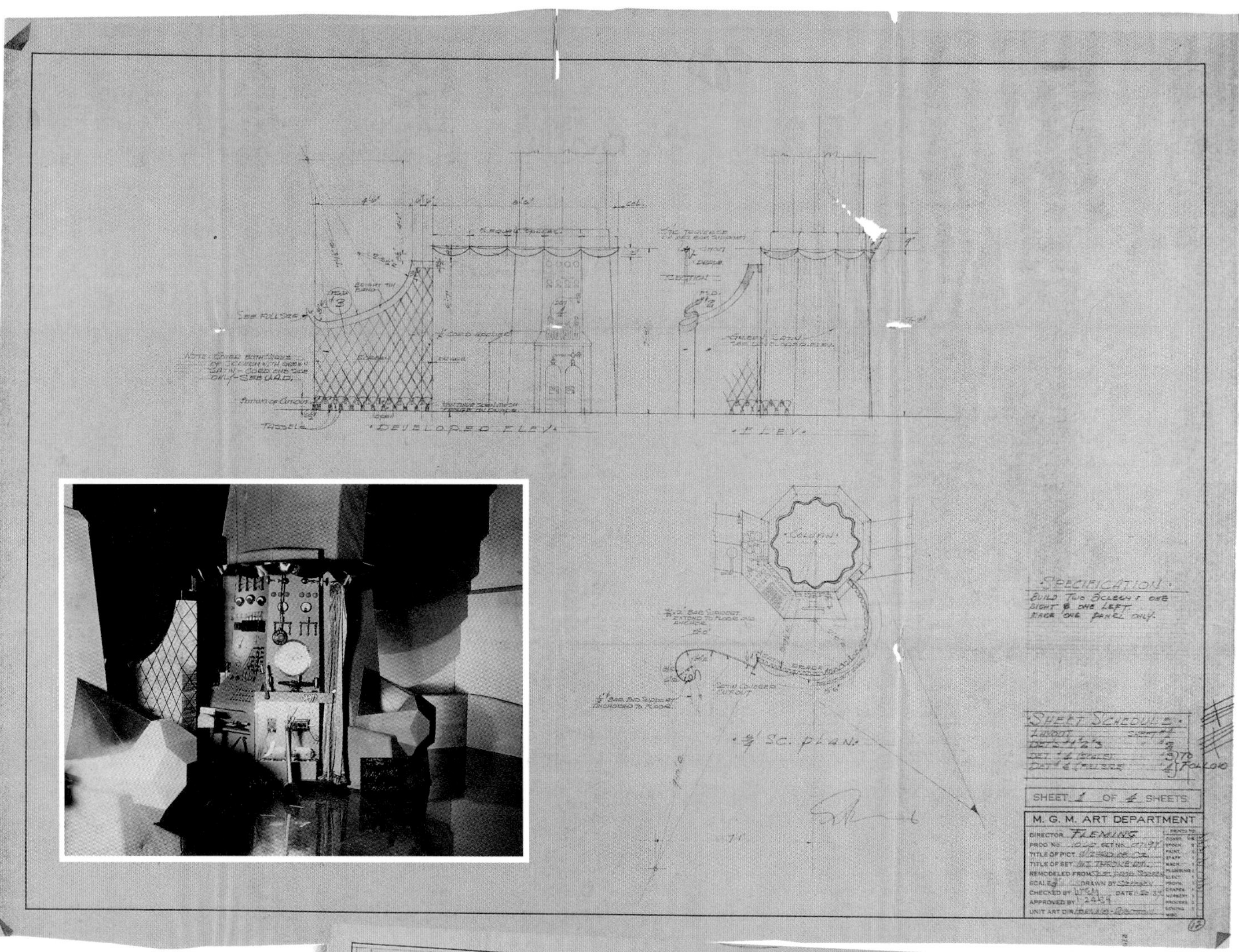

The set for the scene in which the humbug Wizard is exposed as "that man behind the curtain," in blueprint and (inset) as a finished set.

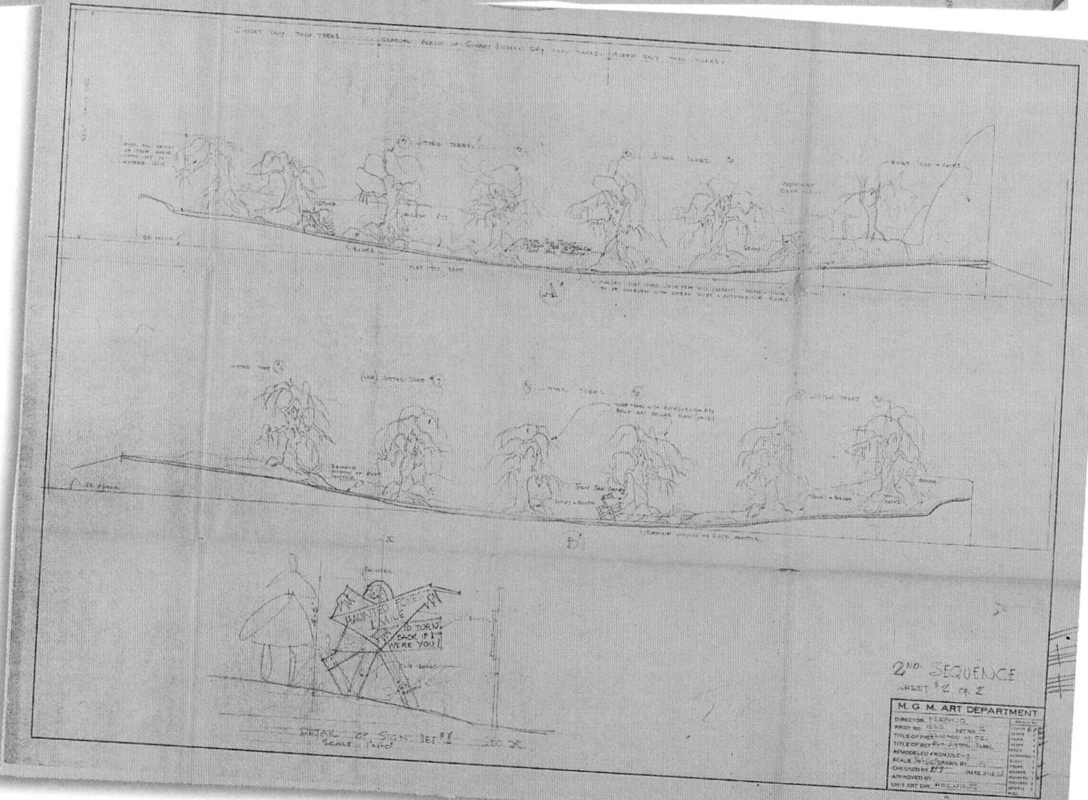

A November 18, 1938, blueprint details the positioning of the Haunted Forest's Jitter Trees, as well as the "warning" signpost.

Set stills provide different views of the Jitterbug Forest and the Haunted Forest. During a break in shooting (inset top), Garland and company are shown on the same set, as are their doubles (inset above).

Above and opposite: Two views of the completed Witch's tower room, both under Richard Thorpe and (later) Victor Fleming's direction. Although the set itself remained unchanged, the placement of various decorative props was altered with the switch in directors. Artificial cobwebs (like those seen hanging from the ceiling) were reportedly made by whirling machines spinning gum rubber. *Courtesy Eric Daily*

Insets depict Judy Garland and Margaret Hamilton on the set.

years old at the time, he made seventy-five cents an hour painstakingly painting the Oz landscapes for maximum effectiveness. "I remember most of the time we jumped between Stages 25 and 26. The attitude of most of us men in scenery was 'we got to do our best,'" said Spencer. "Other studios were not as specific about detail, in my opinion. They were *all* inferior to the scenic department of M-G-M."

His care for detail led to Spencer's assignment to independently paint one of the smaller background panels used in *Oz*: that of the precipitous mountains and cliffs seen outside the Witch's tower-room window. In actuality, the backing was just 18 by 20 feet. Before he began, Spencer was advised against making the scenery too green. "I was a little on the color-blind side," he confessed. As it was painted to correlate with Technicolor stipulations, this smaller-sized panel,

and others like it, were ideal as background for the on-film testing of costumes and make-ups.[7]

The lighting for *The Wizard of Oz* received a great deal of attention as one of the film's "believe it or not" expenses. Of her visits to the *Oz* set, actress Marsha Hunt contended, "It was *very* bright. It was lighted so that you missed no detail. Metro believed in *lighting things* so you could see what you were watching." The *Baltimore Sun* estimated that "as many as 350 huge lights were used on a single set, generally enough electricity to light 550 five-room homes with two 60-watt globes in each room." The intense heat generated by the lamps was equally notorious, and quickly won over

Overleaf: The October 6, 1938, blueprint for the Witch's tower room exemplifies the great care for detail that went into such set construction, most of which is unnoticed on film. Note the zodiac on the floor around the crystal ball, and the miniature sketch of the old crone herself.

[7] Prior to the advent of Technicolor, the backdrops for all motion pictures were either painted in black, white, and shades of gray, or in shades of a single monochromatic hue.

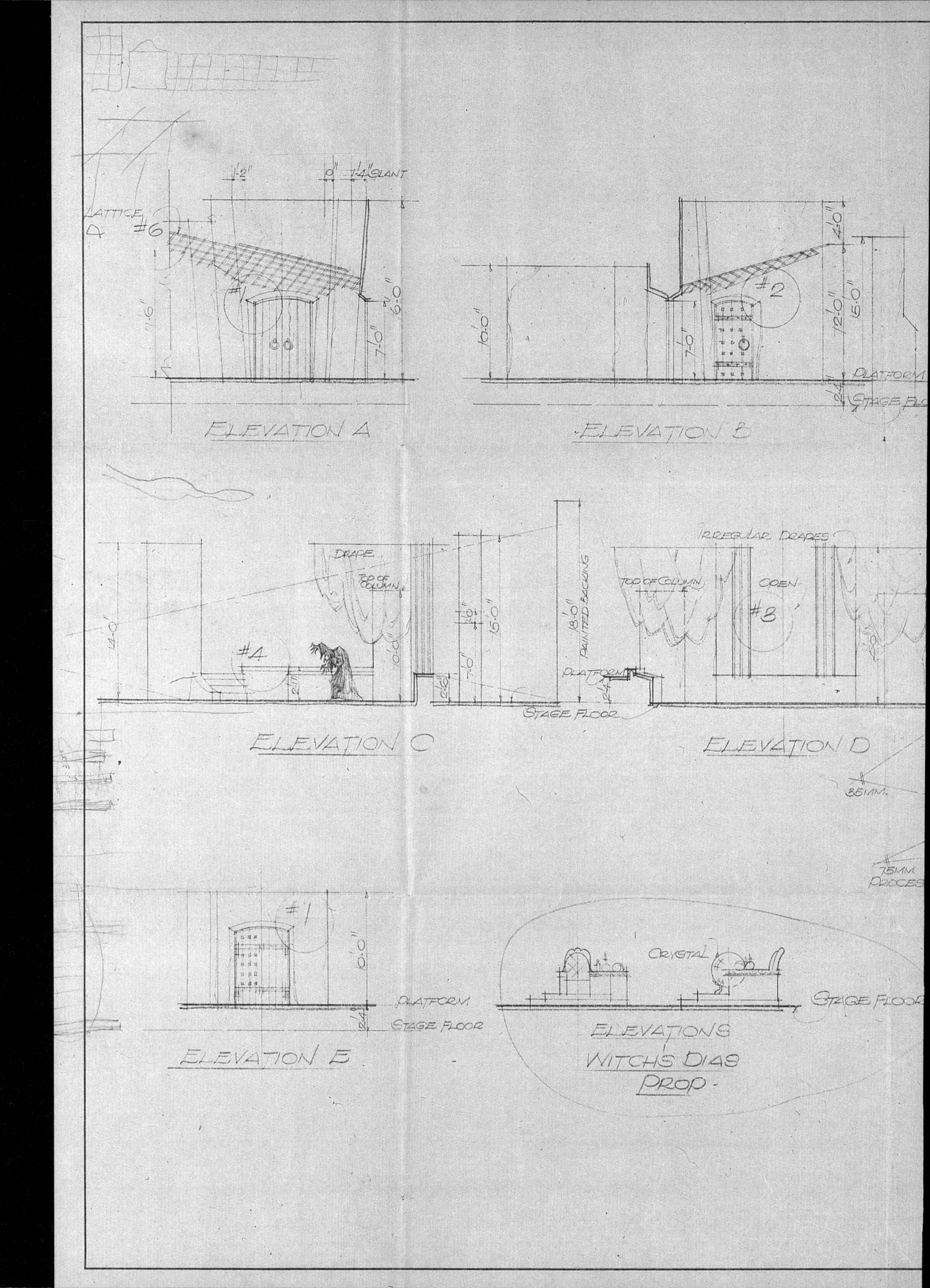
LATTICE
#6
#1
ELEVATION A
#2
PLATFORM
STAGE FLO
ELEVATION B
DRAPE
TOP OF COLUMN
#4
18'-0" PAINTED BACKING
PLATFORM
STAGE FLOOR
IRREGULAR DRAPES
TOP OF COLUMN
OPEN
#8
ELEVATION C
ELEVATION D
35MM.
75MM.
PROCES
#1
PLATFORM
STAGE FLOOR
ELEVATION E
CRYSTAL
STAGE FLOOR
ELEVATIONS
WITCHS DIAS
PROP

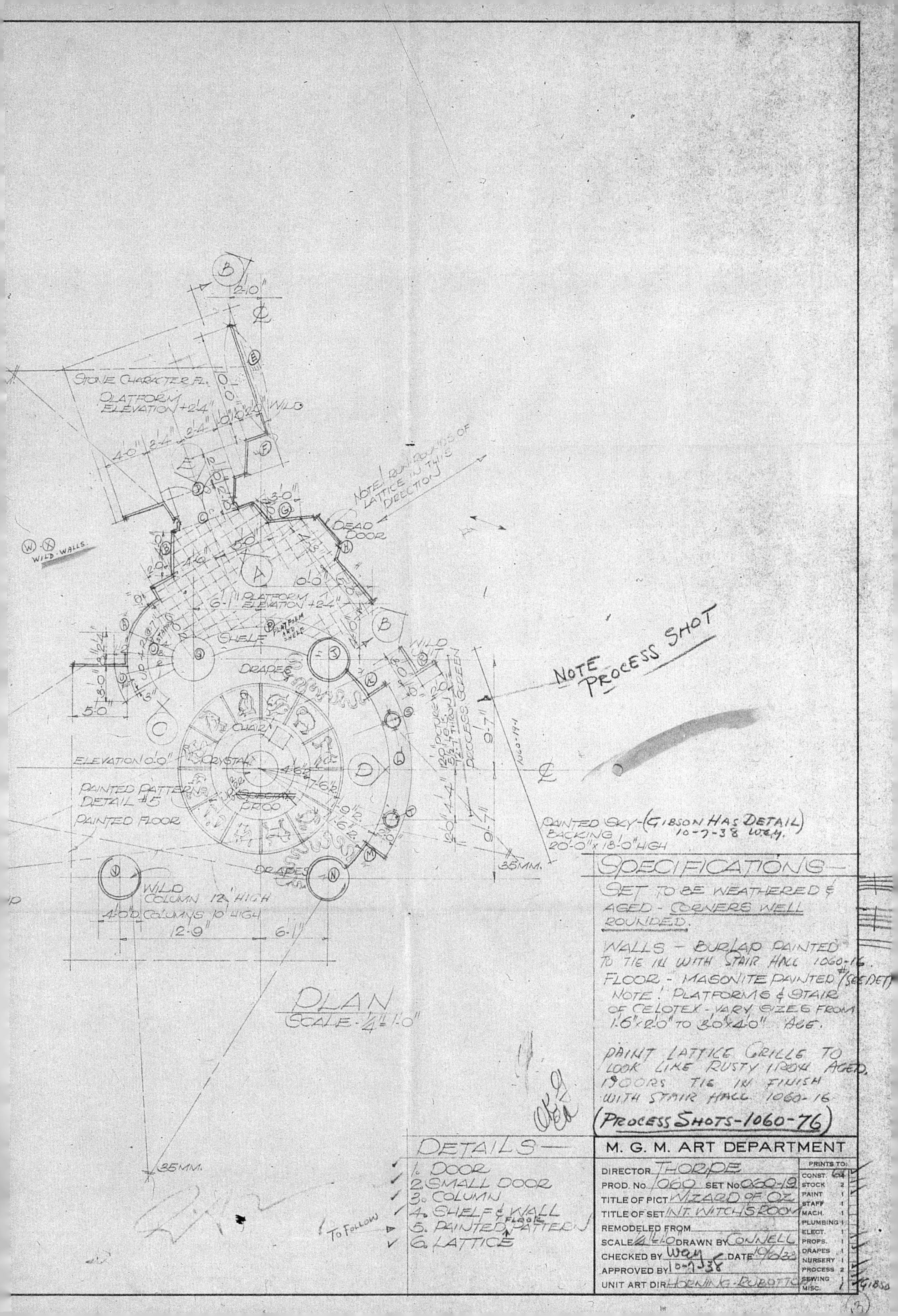

STONE CHARACTER FL.
PLATFORM ELEVATION +2'4"
WILD
NOTE! RUN ROUNDS OF LATTICE IN THIS DIRECTION
DEAD DOOR
W.-X. WILD-WALLS.
PLATFORM ELEVATION +2'4"
SHELF
DRAPES
WILD UNIT
CHAIR
CRYSTAL
ELEVATION 0'0"
PAINTED PATTERNS DETAIL #5
PAINTED FLOOR
SPECIAL PROP
PROCESS SCREEN
NOTE PROCESS SHOT
PAINTED SKY-(GIBSON HAS DETAIL) 10-7-38 W.C.M.
BACKING! 20'-0" x 18'-0" HIGH
35MM.
DRAPES
WILD COLUMN 12' HIGH
4'-0" D. COLUMNS 10' HIGH
PLAN
SCALE-1/4"=1'-0"
SPECIFICATIONS—
SET TO BE WEATHERED & AGED - CORNERS WELL ROUNDED.
WALLS - BURLAP PAINTED TO TIE IN WITH STAIR HALL 1060-16.
FLOOR - MASONITE PAINTED (SEE DET)
NOTE! PLATFORMS & STAIR OF CELOTEX - VARY SIZES FROM 1'6"x2'0" TO 3'0"x4'0" AGE.
PAINT LATTICE GRILLE TO LOOK LIKE RUSTY IRON AGED.
DOORS TIE IN FINISH WITH STAIR HALL 1060-16
(PROCESS SHOTS-1060-76)
DETAILS—
1. DOOR
2. SMALL DOOR
3. COLUMN
4. SHELF & WALL
5. PAINTED FLOOR PATTERN
6. LATTICE
TO FOLLOW
M. G. M. ART DEPARTMENT
DIRECTOR THORPE
PROD. No. 1060 SET No. 1060-19
TITLE OF PICT. WIZARD OF OZ
TITLE OF SET INT. WITCH'S ROOM
REMODELED FROM
SCALE 1/4"=1'0" DRAWN BY CONNELL
CHECKED BY DATE 10/6/38
APPROVED BY 10-7-38
UNIT ART DIR. HORNING-RUBOTTOM
PRINTS TO:
CONST.
STOCK
PAINT
STAFF
MACH.
PLUMBING
ELECT.
PROPS.
DRAPES
NURSERY
PROCESS
SEWING
MISC.

the air conditioning. After each take the stage doors would be opened to allow giant 6-foot wind machines to circulate in the outside air. Electricians worked out the lighting setup for each scene, and banks of numbered arc lights were installed on the catwalk platforms above the soundstages, secured with heavy chain. The amount of electrical current needed for Technicolor filming far exceeded the studio's typical capacity. Southern California Edison had built a small substation on a corner of M-G-M's acreage, which generated the extra power needed.

The structure of the lighting platforms was critical to the placement of the backdrops. The finished painted panels were attached to sandwich battens, lengths of wood 4 inches wide by

A set still of the tower and battlements of the Witch's castle includes the water bucket crucial to the film's climax. A July 5, 1938, script sees Nikko, the Witch's monkey slave, pressing the bucket into Dorothy's hand at the critical moment. *Courtesy Eric Daily*

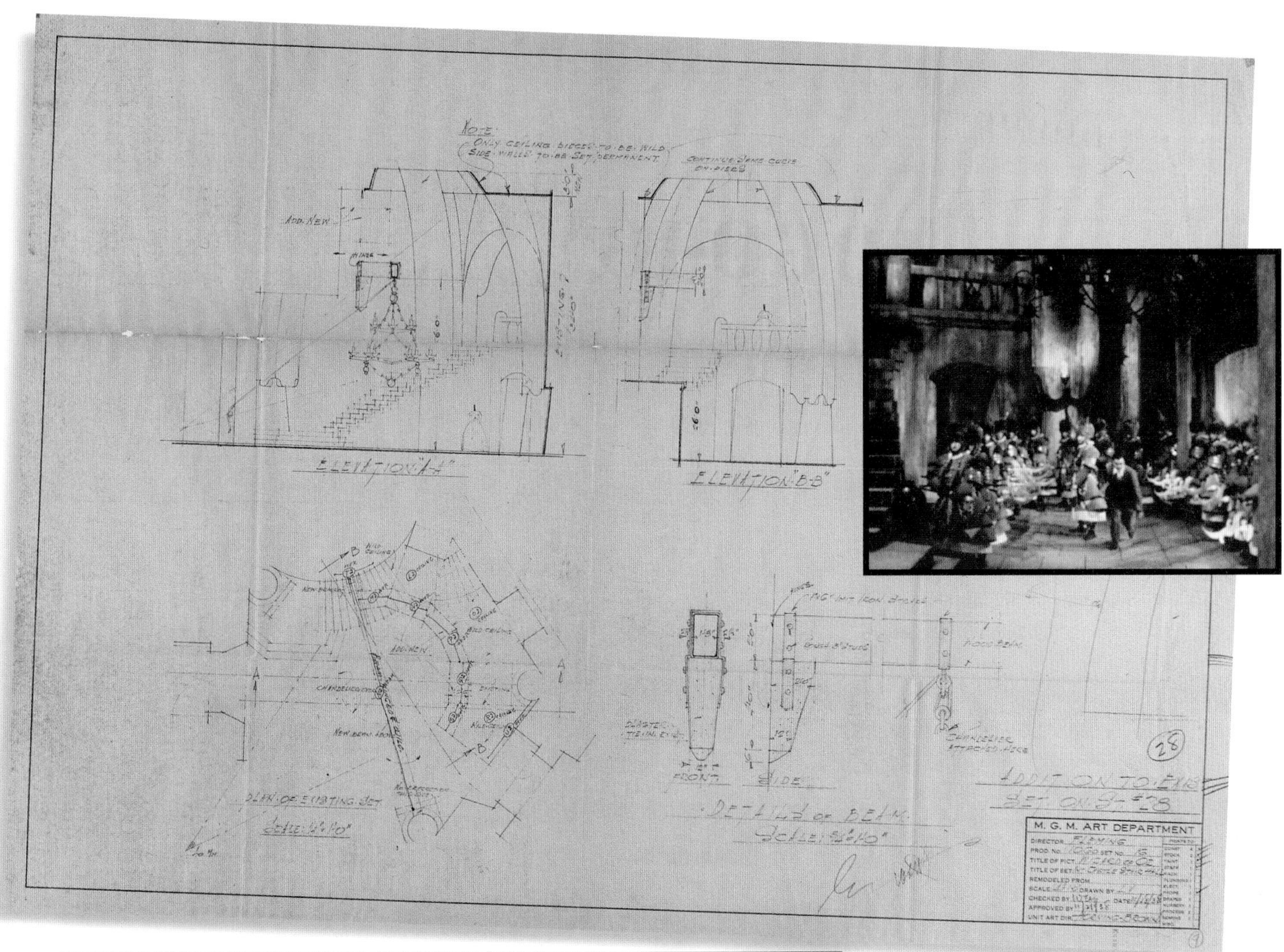

The entrance hallway of the Witch's castle: in blueprint rendered November 28, 1938; as a completed construction; and during a Technicolor test. ***Still courtesy Eric Daily***

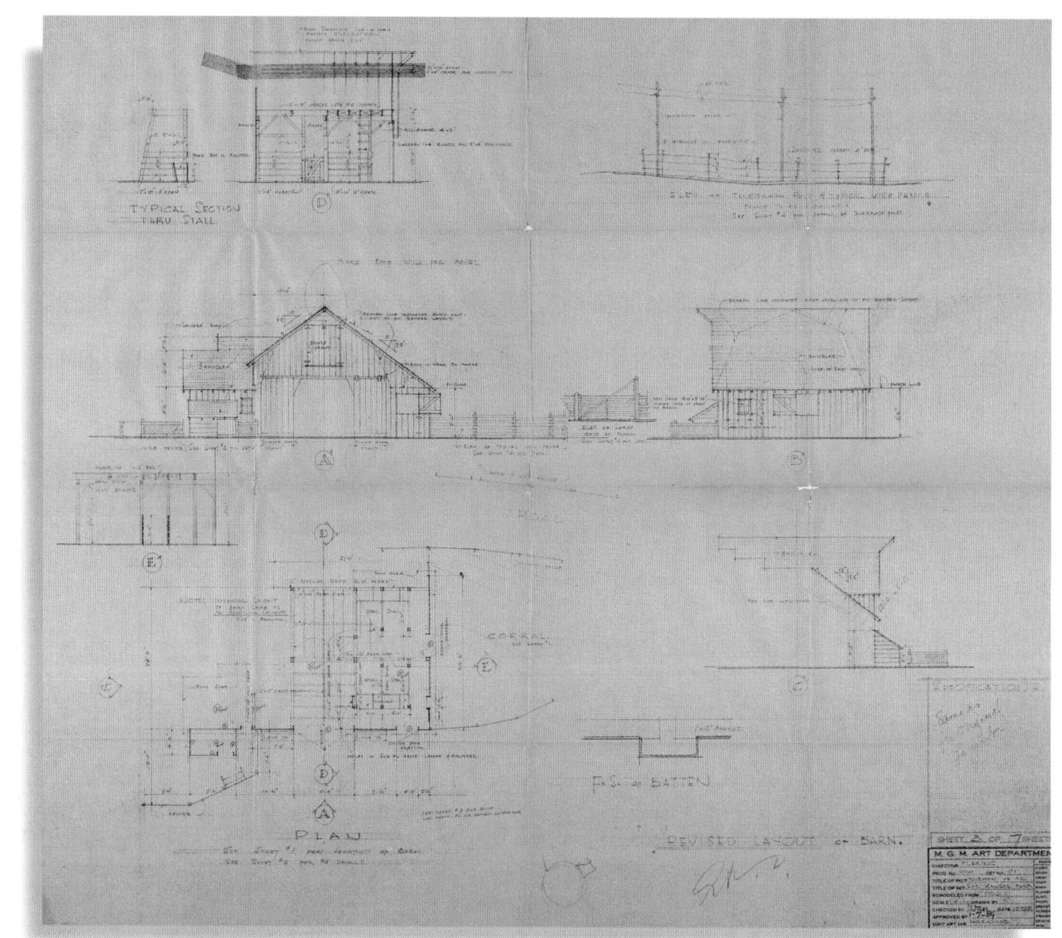

January 1939 blueprint for the barn on the Gale Farm set.

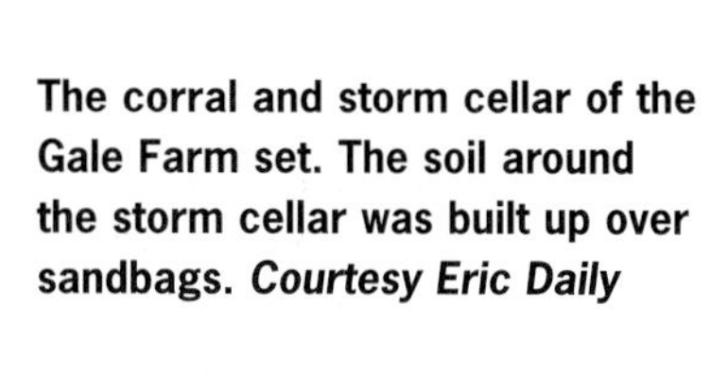

The corral and storm cellar of the Gale Farm set. The soil around the storm cellar was built up over sandbags. *Courtesy Eric Daily*

The back of the Gale farmhouse, where Aunt Em and Uncle Henry are first seen counting chicks. The Kansas farm set evokes the images of Farm Security Administration photographers who captured the dignity and despair of the Depression. *Courtesy Eric Daily*

Another view of the Gale farm. The hay bale and reaper shown served as the site for Judy Garland's famous "Over the Rainbow" number. *Courtesy Eric Daily*

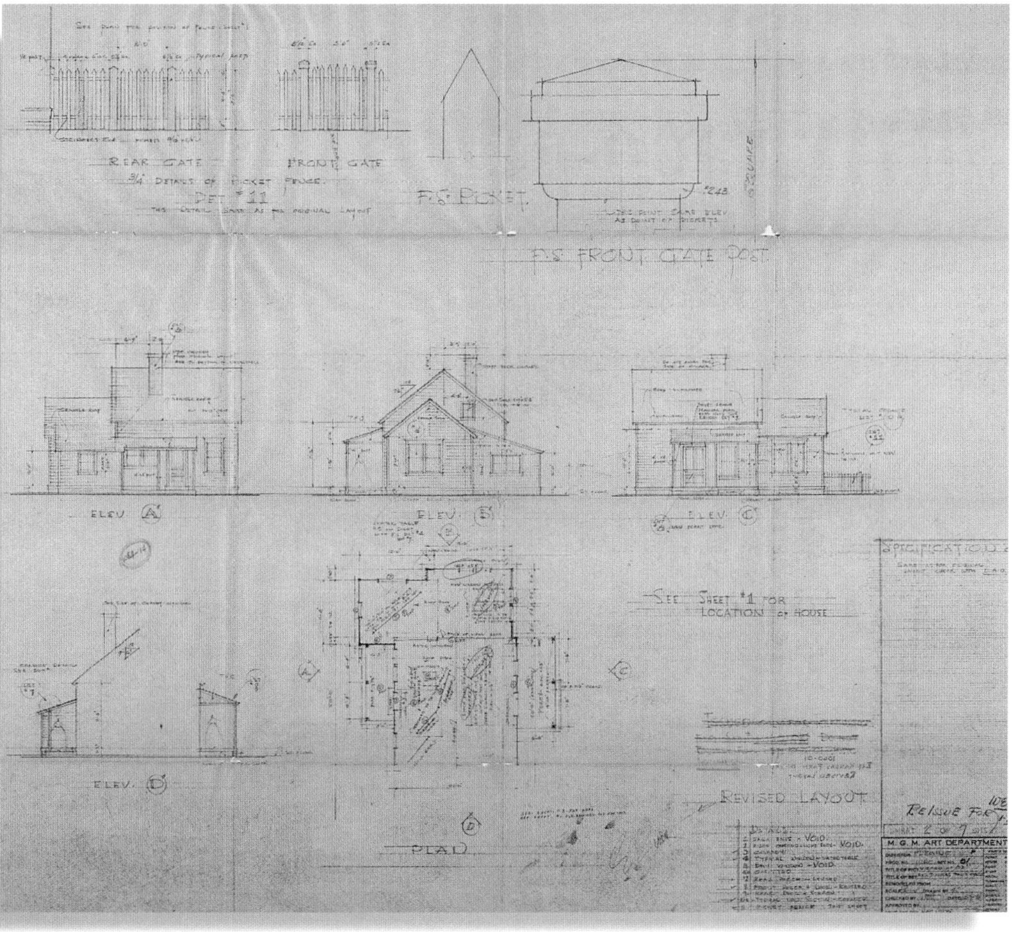

Blueprint of Dorothy's Kansas home. After a more ornate rendition is rejected, the final draft is dated December 7, 1938. (This concept needed to be firmed up quickly to match the battered version of the house on the Munchkinland set, construction of which was imminent.)

¾-inch thick. The battens formed a framelike structure that provided stability to the backings. The backing cloth was tacked to one batten and another batten was aligned over the top and nailed in place. The panels were rolled up bottom to top, and carried to the set by grips, walking one every ten feet. There, the backings were hung from the lighting platforms, pulled taut, and anchored to the stage floor with clamps. As a measure of quality assurance, George Gibson would stop by a newly erected set on the first couple mornings of filming to see if the cameraman had any needs or required adjustments.

When combined with the physical set structures, Gibson's scenic backdrops were especially impressive achievements. "Birds, pigeons flew into [Gibson's] backings!" said James Roth. "They thought they were outside!" Charles Schram recalled, "As I entered the soundstage with the poppy field set for the first time, I saw the 300-foot-long poppy field backing that George Gibson had made along the far two sides of the stage. The full length of the wall to my left was an upper and lower row of klieg lights placed as close together

The side and rear elevation blueprint for Professor Marvel's wagon abode. Interestingly, there are detailed indications for the wagon's colorful decoration—even though it would appear only in the sepia-tone Kansas scenes. (Margaret Hamilton recalled the wagon as especially attractive.) In June 4-8, 1938, script drafts written by Florence Ryerson and Edgar Allan Woolf, the Professor (then named Winkle) returns Dorothy to the front gate of her farm in his caravan.

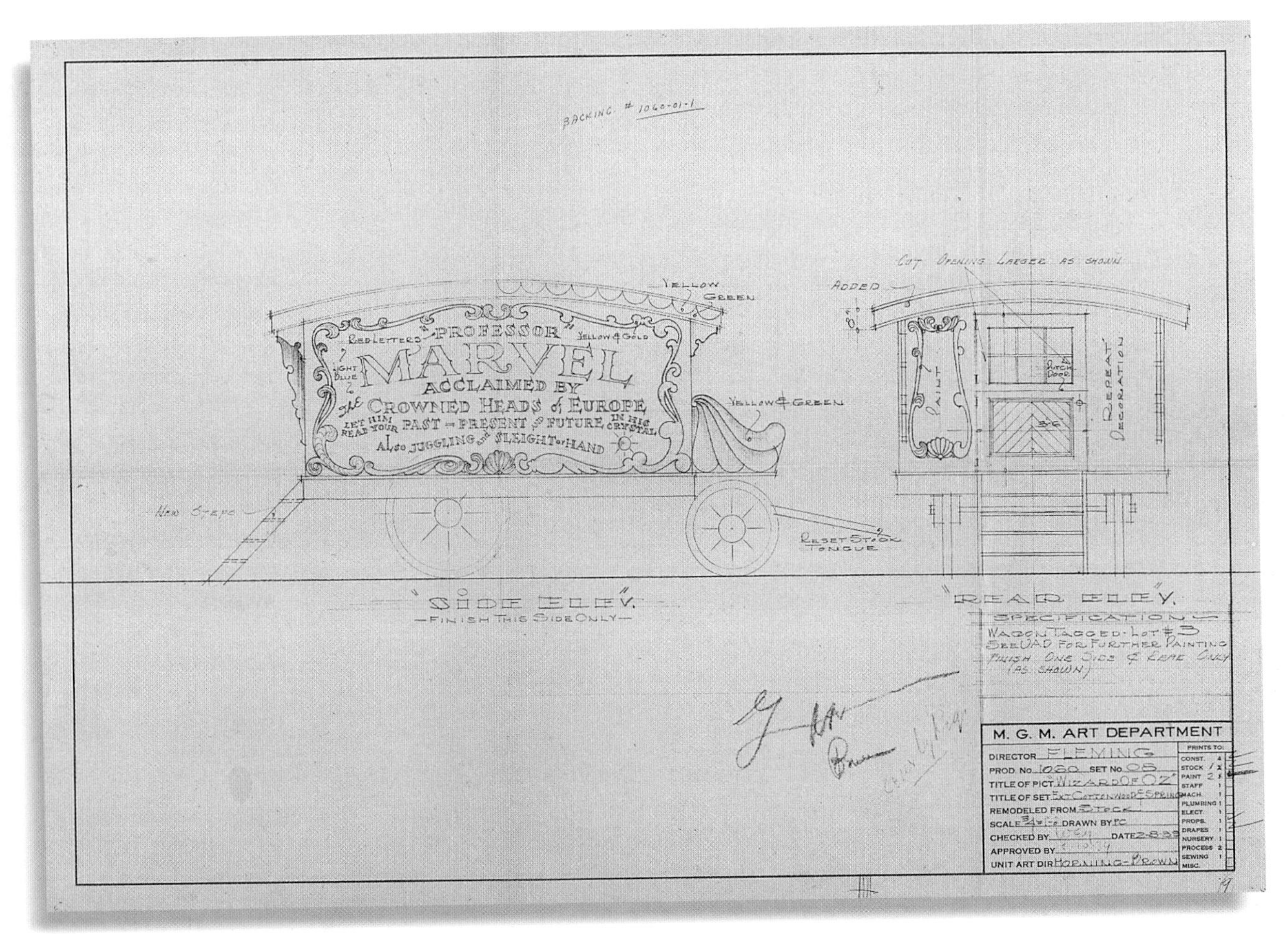

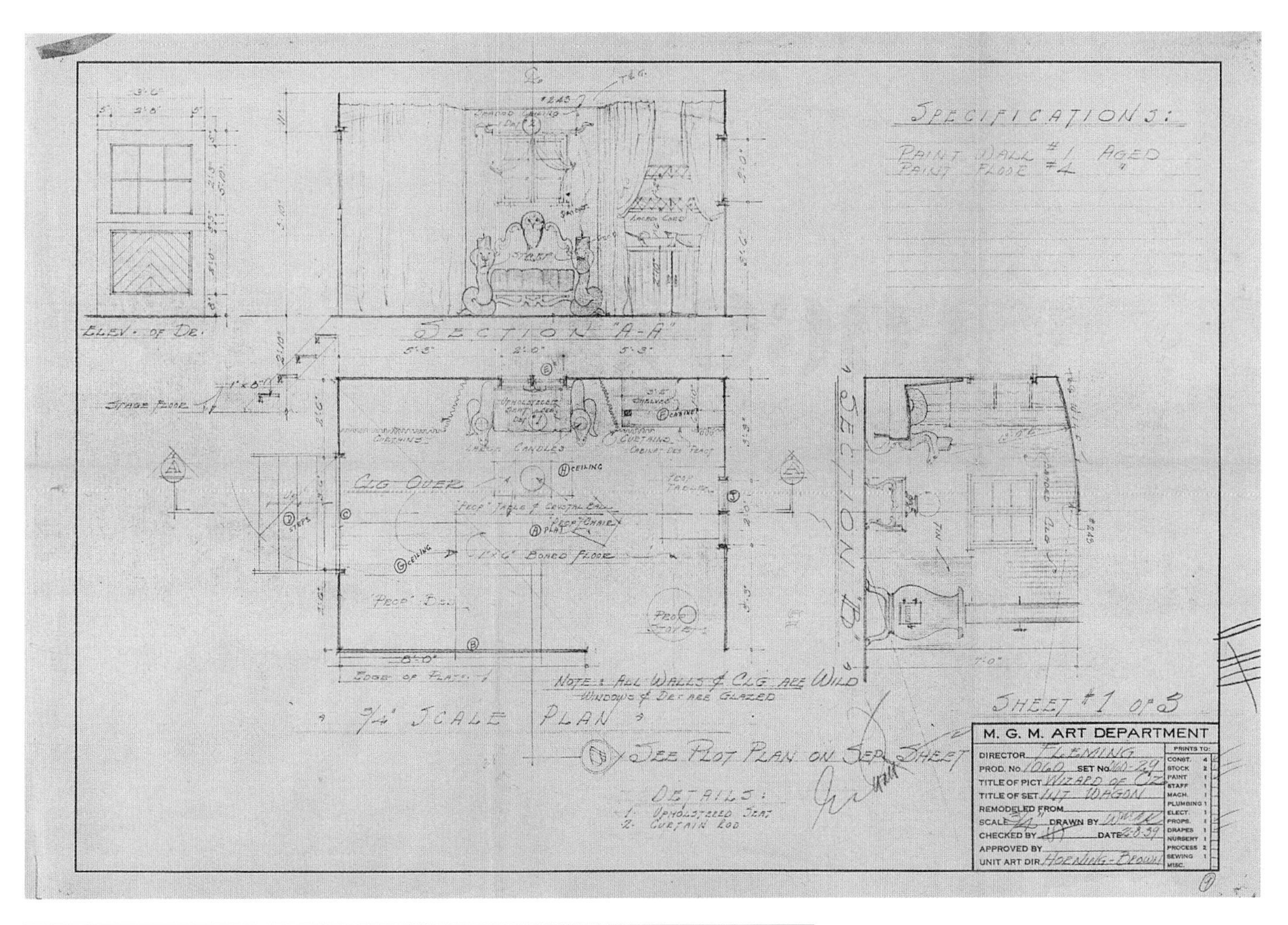

One drafted concept of the interior of Professor Marvel's wagon is marked "Set 29" and dated February 8, 1939. (The notation "wild" refers to a portion of any structure that could readily be removed to allow for a specific camera shot.) By February 11, the set was completed, decorated with mystical ornaments largely unseen on screen.

as possible. The floor of the stage was covered with artificial poppies, and the winding yellow brick road curved and blended perfectly with the painted backing located at the rear of the stage."

The art department was not only charged with envisioning the fantastic countryside and structures of Oz; visualizing how the script's magical feats would play out in those environments was

A view inside the scenic art building, circa 1954, shows one of the huge backing frames. On the extreme right is John Coakley; F. Wayne Hill stands foreground center reviewing a sketch. Both men contributed to the backings for the Kansas scenes in *Oz* after Leo F. Atkinson had filled in the sky. *Courtesy George Gibson*

Several grips designate gobos for use in filming *The Wizard of Oz.* Gobos were frameworks used to control lighting by softening, shading, or eliminating the amount of light used in a scene. When filming in Technicolor, it was as important to limit lighting in certain spots as it was to determine the direction of the lighting. (Constant, flat lighting usually lacked depth.) Gobos were covered on one side with black cloth to cast shadow; white muslin on the other side reflected light. The frameworks were generally 4 feet wide and in excess of 8 feet tall, with a telescoping piece in back that could be sandwiched on pulleys and raised by ropes to greater heights.

also the responsibility of Cedric Gibbons's crew. The artists on staff painted concepts of the Kansas cyclone and illusions for the Wizard's throne room and the Witch's castle. However, fulfilling these visions was beyond the scope of sketch artists and architects; and collaboration was required with another division within the art department crucial to *The Wizard of Oz*: special effects.

One of the most famous settings in film history. Long shots of the Emerald City's exterior were—in actuality—matte paintings. The towering spires were given special illumination by miniature lights that glimmered through holes punched in the illustration board.

SPECIAL EFFECTS

Illusions of Grandeur

AMAZING SIGHTS TO SEE!

The Tornado

Actual photographs of the inside of the tornado that whirls Dorothy to a land more excitingly real than life itself!

Horse of a Different Color

Ever see a blue horse? Ever see a green horse? You will—when you see this magic "horse of a different color"!

Startling Balloon Ascent

Up in the stratosphere! What lies beyond the stars? See the glistening Emerald City . . . The wonderful Palace of Glass!

The Flying Monkeys

Most amazing camera effects since *San Francisco*!

Trees That Talk and Throw Apples

— 1939 newspaper advertisement for *The Wizard of Oz*

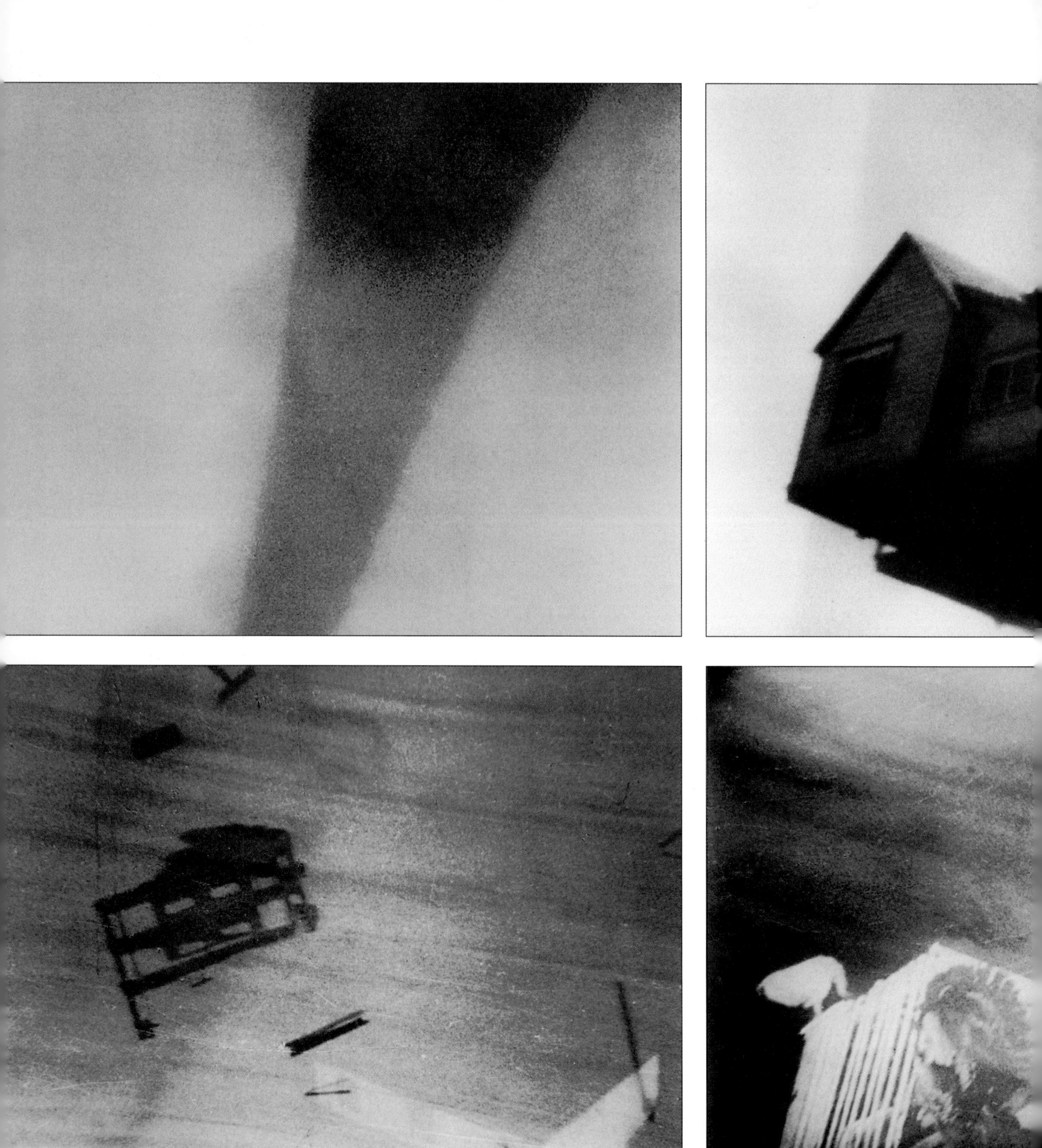

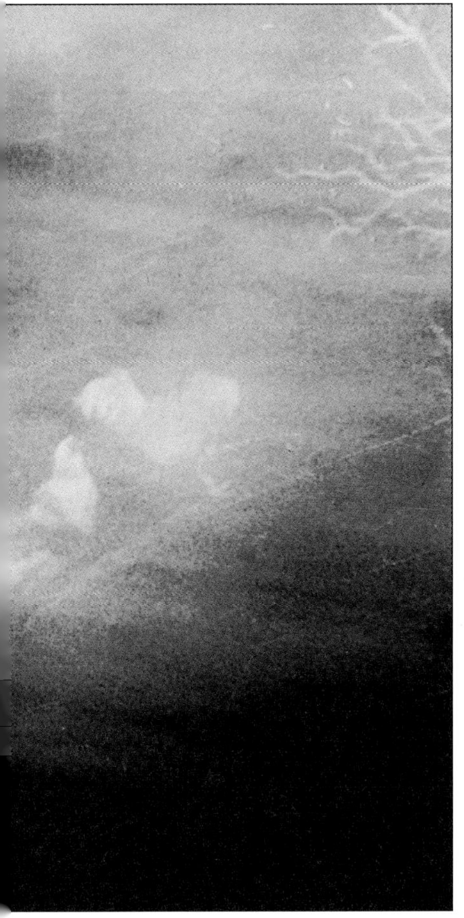

Of the many elements that have upheld *The Wizard of Oz* as a triumph ahead of its time, the film's special effects are still considered technical feats of wizardry. L. Frank Baum imbued *The Wonderful Wizard of Oz* with all the wonderment of traditional European storytelling but in a straightforward, uncontrived manner. The book contains countless instances of magical events that do not detract from the humanity of the characters or their fantastic adventures. That Dorothy's friends are implausible yet articulate and feeling is merely happenstance. In Oz, magic is a science; its methodology is as natural as breathing and as concrete as the laws that govern it. For example, in order to summon the Winged Monkeys, the owner of the Golden Cap must reenact the spell written in the cap's lining.[1] The cap is a talisman with a rationale underlying its power. Translating such fairy tale devices to live-action film was historically precarious.

Earlier in the century, Baum had experimented with similar trickery himself in a traveling Oz show that combined live actors with slides and motion pictures. A 1910 Selig film production of *The Wizard of Oz* features a Kansas windstorm, magical transformations, and a melting witch (made possible via double-exposure

[1] In a brief bit cut from the final version of the M-G-M film, the Wicked Witch orders her monkey commandant to retrieve the Golden Cap so that she may compel the Winged Monkeys to capture Dorothy, who has been subdued in the poppy field. On-screen, Glinda intercepts the poppy spell with a snowshower, causing the Witch to angrily throw the cap across the room.

Opposite: A series of frames from test footage of the cyclone effects. Of the assorted debris seen through Dorothy's bedroom window, the chicken coop appears first on screen. Appropriately enough for a farm girl, Dorothy is awakened from her unconscious state by a crowing rooster.

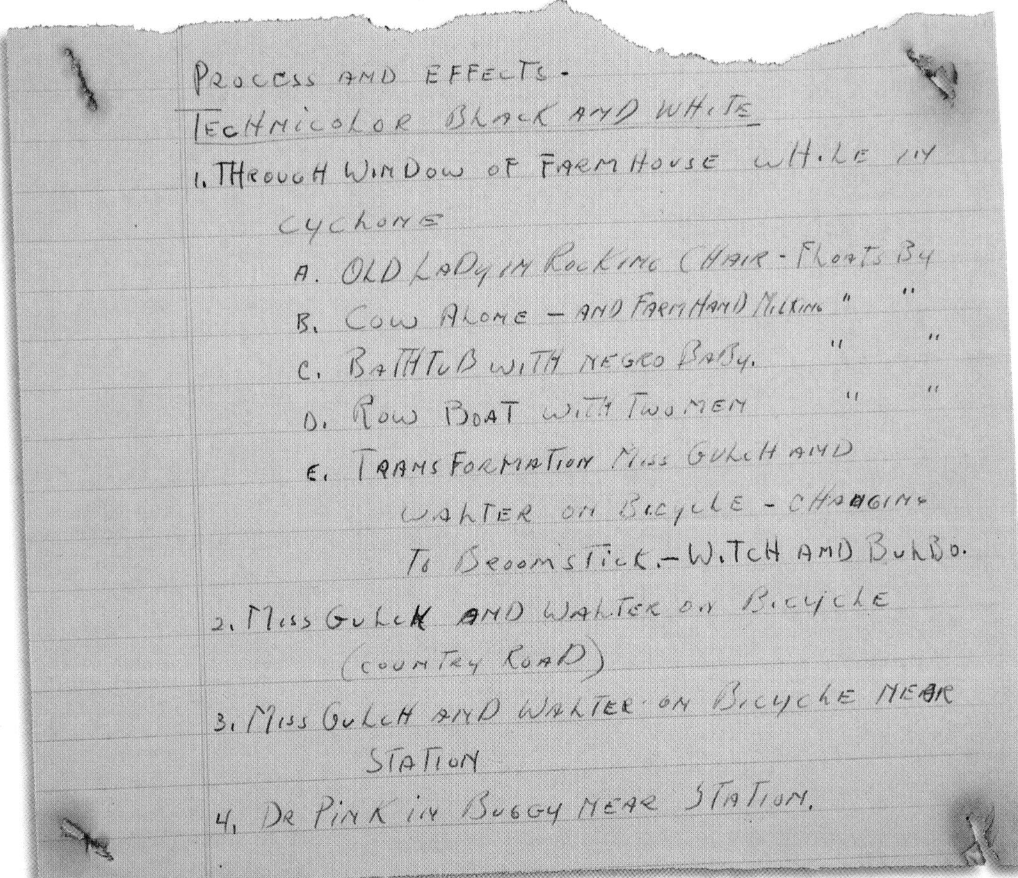

PROCESS AND EFFECTS -
TECHNICOLOR BLACK AND WHITE

1. THROUGH WINDOW OF FARMHOUSE WHILE IN CYCLONE
   A. OLD LADY IN ROCKING CHAIR - FLOATS BY
   B. COW ALONE - AND FARMHAND MILKING " "
   C. BATHTUB WITH NEGRO BABY. " "
   D. ROW BOAT WITH TWO MEN " "
   E. TRANSFORMATION MISS GULCH AND WALTER ON BICYCLE - CHANGING TO BROOMSTICK. - WITCH AND BUMBO.
2. MISS GULCH AND WALTER ON BICYCLE (COUNTRY ROAD)
3. MISS GULCH AND WALTER ON BICYCLE NEAR STATION
4. DR PINK IN BUGGY NEAR STATION.

Racism in Oz? A May 1938 list of special effects for "Technicolor Black and White" (meaning sepia-tone) filming includes "Bathtub with Negro baby" as one of the entities that floats past Dorothy's window during the twister. The reference—intended for comic effect—was dropped, but a similar slur occurs in a June 29, 1938, script draft. In the Emerald City beauty parlor, Dorothy's ruby slippers are polished by the Wizard character as a Bootblack in blackface. The Bootblack's dialogue (complete with racial inflection) is, "Yo sho is goin' make a hit with the Wizard, Missy—on' you won't never get it." ***Courtesy The Lilly Library, Indiana University, Bloomington, Indiana***

dissolve). Baum's own Oz Film Manufacturing Company founded in Hollywood a few years later, though short-lived, did showcase some state-of-the-art effects. In *The Patchwork Girl of Oz* (1914), the studio's first offering, the quilted mannequin of the title is invisibly assembled piece by piece and brought to life via stop-motion photography. *His Majesty, the Scarecrow of Oz* includes a magic wall of water, the freezing of a princess's ice-cold heart, and the Strawman being abducted by an oversized crow.

Prior to the M-G-M production, modern screen adaptations of the Oz stories were tentative, minor, or founded in rumor. Until *Snow White*, Hollywood had had few successful bouts with fantasy. Apart from Metro's own *Babes in Toyland* in 1934, such contemporary films were limited to Walt Disney's *Silly Symphony* shorts, Flash Gordon serials, and the nightmare inducements of Universal's horror pictures. Updating *The Wizard of Oz* replete with its cyclone, flying monkeys, fighting trees, and assorted witchery was largely dependent on credible special effects.

At M-G-M, anything that burned, moved, exploded, flew, or was made of rubber was the responsibility of the art department division known as the property shop, or simply the prop shop. The prop shop was located next to the studio's lumber mill, which housed all the equipment necessary to construct nearly anything a picture required. Like all department heads, A. Arnold "Buddy" Gillespie wore a suit and tie and spent most of his time in his office, lunching with other executives in the commissary, reviewing dailies, or attending production meetings to plan the effects for all the pictures to be shot on the Metro lot. Gillespie often supervised process scenes involving live action film shot in front of a rear-projection background on a completely black stage. He relied upon Jack Gaylord to lead a team of men known for their knack in overcoming the kind of difficulties *Oz* would present. Gaylord wore overalls and got his hands dirty alongside his staff in making hallucinations perfectly tangible.

Re-creating the Kansas cyclone that transports Dorothy to the land of Oz was the greatest challenge. In previous endeavors, M-G-M had quite competently replicated natural disasters like the earthquake and consuming blaze of *San Francisco*, the locust swarm

Jack Haley, Judy Garland, and Ray Bolger react following the scene in which the Wicked Witch tosses a ball of fire from the rooftop of the Tin Man's cottage. The fireball-throwing illusion was accomplished by simple double exposure. The moving ball of fire printed over the live-action footage was made by using a gas torch fastened to a car traveling a track laid out for the desired path. With the track assembly painted black, the torch was photographed at night against a black backing. Fire photographed especially brilliant in Technicolor, and was used as frequently as possible throughout *The Wizard of Oz*.

in *The Good Earth*, and the jungle perils of the occasional *Tarzan* picture. For a film chiefly set in a mystical realm, the cyclone was the critical plot catalyst originating in the real world. Its authenticity required total acceptance to be believable on screen.

A list of "Wizard of Oz Effects" dated June 22, 1938, segmented the action into specific shots; for example:

1. Kansas Farm
    - A. Cyclone Approaching Kansas Farm
    - B. Cyclone Hitting Farm
    - C. Cyclone Lifting Farm House into Air
    - D. Key of Cyclone Approaching—for Cellar Door Cut
    - E. Farm House Whirling Around in Cyclone

Additionally, the outline called for a shot of the cyclone leaving the farmhouse in midair and passing on, and one of the house falling until it blocked out the camera.

Standing 35 feet yet considered a miniature, the cyclone was filmed on Stage 14, an old tin-roof stage reserved for such models. Stage 14 wasn't soundproof. Only footage that would later be dubbed could be shot due to the noise of grinding motors and other machinery. The exterior of the Kansas farm—built twice due to a change in design—was constructed on a platform at ¾ scale. After painstaking experimentation, the exterior effects of the tornado were achieved using a large canvas stocking affixed to a gantry crane traveling the length of the stage. The tornado-shaped canvas cone was rotated by a D.C. motor on a speed control. The motor assembly was arranged to tip sideways. The base of the tornado cone was fastened to a car traveling along a predetermined track and containing an arrangement for Fuller's earth to act as dust. The car was moved by operators below the set.

The principals are refreshed from the sedative poison of the poppies with a snowfall. White gypsum, a mineral used in making plaster of Paris, simulated the snow but was hazardous to inhale. The gypsum particles were up to a half-inch in diameter (Charles Schram recalled, "I picked a lot of 'em out of wigs") and left a dust in the air that was irritating to breathe. Though the substance was banned shortly afterward, the actors were advised against inhaling too deeply.

Cloud-shaped shadows were projected on a white backing, which served as the sky. This was accomplished using large frames (about 8 by 4 feet) covered with heavy cellophane. George Gibson painted clouds onto the cellophane, which was lit from behind with open arcs in a huge light box. This projected the shadows onto the white backing but as Gibson recalled, "I had sore eyes for weeks." The cloud shadows were augmented by cotton clouds affixed to glass panels set up in the foreground. The cotton clouds were also created by Gibson using an airbrush and black paint. The glass panels were manually shifted to simulate turbulence.

Judy Garland herself was reported to have singled out the film's Kansas twister when interviewed by *Movie Mirror*. "Perhaps the audience won't be able to see me for dust. . . . There are such clouds of it in some scenes!" mused the actress. "The cyclone, for instance—just wait until you see that scene where my little house is tumbled over and over in the air until it comes to rest right in the Land of Oz!"

Gillespie's cyclone was a remarkable achievement, but not everyone was universally impressed. In his review of *The Wizard of Oz* in the *New York Times*, critic Frank S. Nugent was virtually alone in his dissension.

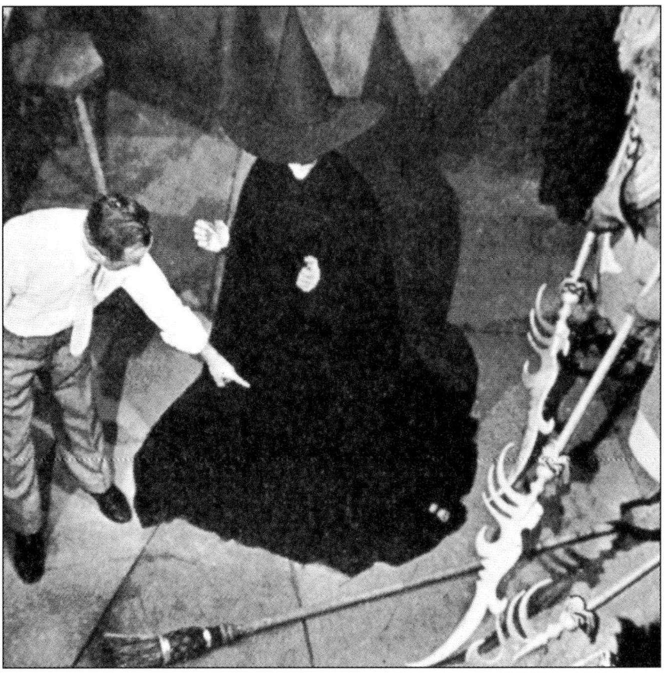

Margaret Hamilton is readied for the climactic witch-melting scene. The intended trick was to have the Witch lowered beneath the floor using a trap-door-like elevator, while dry ice and compressed air beneath her dress created a steam effect. Many years after appearing in the film, Hamilton recalled the first dress rehearsal of this famous scene—and how the compressed air caused her hat to blow completely off and her dress and cape to billow up over her head! To alleviate this, the actress remembered, six to eight big nails were used to tack down the dress (and contain the air stream).

> Mr. Baum wrote of a cyclone that picked up Dorothy's house, with her and Toto in it, swept it to the top of its cone, carried it along and dropped it safely on the Wicked Witch in the Land of Oz. Mr. Disney could have done that in a twinkling. Remember *Mickey's Band Concert*?[2] Mr. LeRoy and his technical crew have done it too; but it doesn't much look like a cyclone, and the house, once aloft, looks like a miniature, and one never really believes Dorothy is being borne away by a twister.

Creating a realistic twister was ineffectual without the genuine roar of its ferocious winds. This was no simple task either, as the following M-G-M press release explained.

> Delicate mathematical calculations were conducted by the man Albert Einstein pronounces one of America's five greatest mathematicians, to work out a formula for the sound of a cyclone in terms of decimals and electrical requencies. The object was to reproduce the noise of such a story for *The Wizard of Oz*. . . . As sending sound apparatus in search of unpredictable cyclones was impossible, O. O. Ceccarini, mathematician, was put to work. From scientific

[2] *Mickey's Band Concert* was the first Mickey Mouse cartoon to be produced in Technicolor. The 1935 short included an animated tornado that sweeps through the park where Mickey is conducting an orchestra. In its wake, the storm uproots shrubbery, a farmhouse, Donald Duck, and the musicians. Nonplused, Mickey continues directing the band through the finale of the *William Tell Overture*.

Technicolor tests for "The Merry Old Land of Oz" number. Horse wrangler Freddy Gilman steadies the "Horse of a Different Color" in the top frame. Two white horses were alternately hand-colored with vegetable dye to humanely pigment their hides. (Make-up man Charles Schram recalled that "the horses did not come white again for a long time.") Note the blue-hued horse, cut from the film. Unsuspecting encounters with the steeds were unnerving at best. M-G-M starlet (and Jack Dawn's fiancée) Marla Shelton was startled driving through the back lot when she passed a pink horse "statue" that moved! The horses caused exotic Metro newcomer Hedy Lamarr to do a double-take and think to herself, "If this is America, I'd better go back to Austria!"

> weather figures he obtained the pressure, velocity, air density and electrical characteristics of cyclones. From these facts he calculated volume and pitch of the sounds that would naturally accompany these phenomena. These calculations completed, he worked out practical methods of creating the sounds; 4,698,271 separate figures and algebraic symbols had gone into 200 pages of calculations before the task was completed.

One of the most publicized illusions was that of Dorothy looking out of her bedroom window while caught up in the twister—hyped because no one had ever seen the inside of a cyclone and lived to tell about it. To relieve the traumatic events of the storm striking the farm, a humorous variety of familiar entities was to blow past the window. These included the "old lady in rocking chair," "cow alone" and "row boat with two men" that appear in the completed film. However, a circa May 1938 list of the effects includes "Bathtub with Negro baby floats by." Though obviously intended for comic effect, the baby and the bathwater were thrown out by the June 22 version of the list, replaced with "crate of chickens."[3]

The parade of floating people and animals was created by double-exposing film of the stationary characters with separately made footage of the inside of a large spinning drum constructed of curved Masonite. Painted to resemble the inside of a funnel cloud, this Masonite backing was filmed with dust, leaves, dead branches and other debris blown over it by wind machines. Over this film was printed footage of "larger pieces of debris in the form of trees, barns, fences, carriages, etc.," all of which were shot against a black backing. As this initial double exposure "lacked speed in rotation," a tubular cloth backing measuring 16 feet in diameter and 12 feet long was rotated from a gantry and shot from inside. This was then printed over the other combinations. Initially budgeted at a cost of $2,100 for construction, operation, and electricity, this seemingly simple process shot instead ended up totaling over $3,200—a heady amount in 1938 dollars. But given the recognition the studio received for spectacular effects in *San Francisco* and other films, the cost of achieving optimal results was rarely scrutinized.

[3] In a film marked by few topical references, perpetuating such a stereotype would both mar and date *Oz* by today's standards. For years afterward, television showings of the Mickey Rooney-Judy Garland musical *Babes in Arms* (1939) deleted a scene in which the two stars appear in blackface.

A huge model of the Wizard's disembodied head was sculpted with far more detail than the description called for in the *Oz* script: "Through [a cloud of smoke] two bright green eyes, each about two feet wide, gaze out. . . . The shadowy outline of a mouth appears." *Courtesy Charles Schram* Below, the star doubles tremble before the Wizard mockup for a Technicolor test. Bottom: Blueprint detail for the Wizard's inner sanctum, dated January 3, 1939. There is indication for a pit beneath the stage floor, needed to contain the light, steam, and smoke effects. The principals' reaction shots were filmed separately; colored sheets of gelatin over the lights enhanced the "fire" effect.

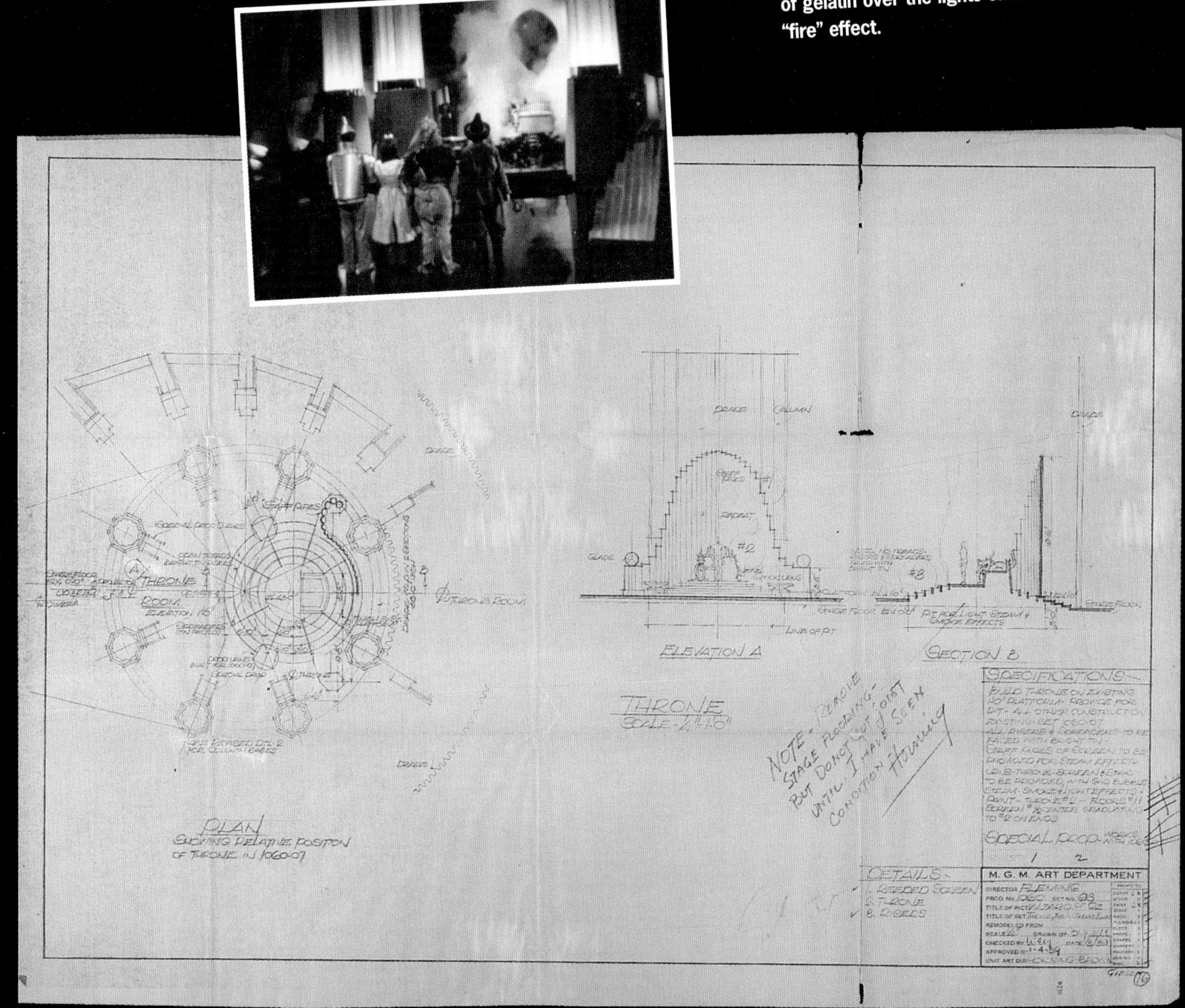

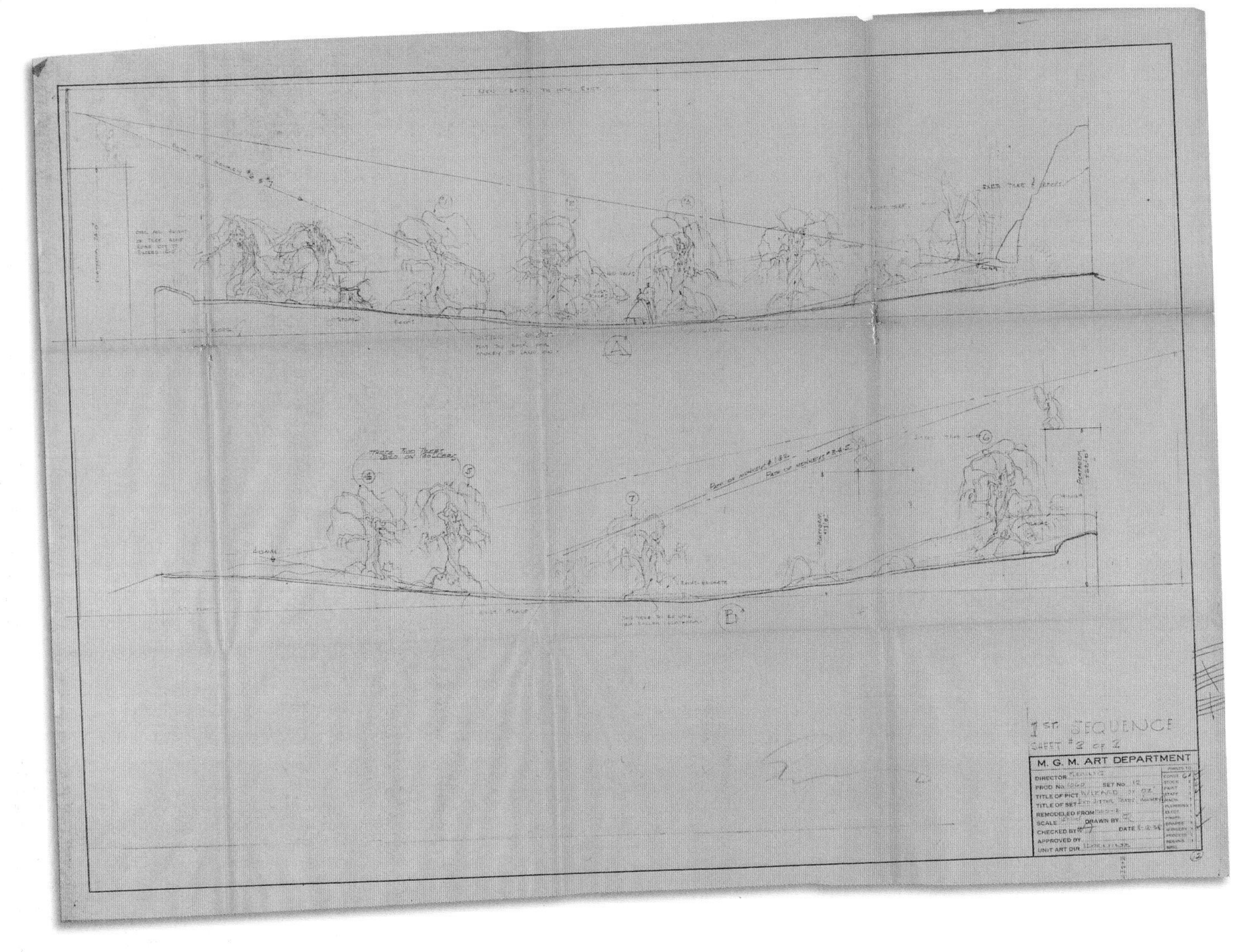

Opposite: Several Winged Monkey actors prepare to "fly" with the help of wires, pullies, and leather harnesses. Above: A blueprint elevation of the Jitter Trees indicates the path of flight for the monkeys that abduct Dorothy and Toto. The artificial rock platforms, to which the monkeys would ascend, are also shown.

Once completed, the film of the tornado interior was combined with live-action footage of Judy Garland and Toto via rear projection onto a screen outside Dorothy's bedroom window. A separate set for Dorothy's bedroom was erected and the camera was fixed—like a ship's compass—to a gimbal mount that allowed it to twist and turn, rather than only pan up, down and sideways.[4] This gave the impression of the house swaying and floating on air current. A wallpapered muslin backing was set in place for those shots of the bedroom in which the camera (looking in from the window) captured Dorothy and Toto's reactions. The set for Dorothy's bedroom was also adapted so that the room could be tilted at will to create a violent rocking.

Double-exposure effects in black and white were commonplace at

[4] The most ingenious use of a gimbal mount was Fred Astaire's famous dance up the wall and across the ceiling in *Royal Wedding* (1951).

the time *The Wizard of Oz* was being filmed. However, such processing was not as easily accomplished in Technicolor without making a mess of the colors. This prompted alternate ingenuity for at least one of the film's effects as reported in the August 1939 issue of *Minicam* magazine:

> In black-and-white photography, . . . the image of home and relatives which the heroine sees in the crystal ball would have been double-exposed into the globe. Technicolor made this method too complicated, so the "visions" were filmed first. Prints were projected onto a mirror which reflected the picture into the ball. With the images moving inside the globe, the entire scene was photographed in a single regular exposure.

Undaunted, the special effects wizards of *Oz* did make use of Technicolor double exposures for several of the film's other images—albeit with a good deal of experimentation. Glinda's traveling bubble, for instance, went through at least one failure before achieving the desired outcome. At first, a glass bubble about 8 inches in diameter was suspended on wires from an overhead track plotted for the travel required in the scenes. The bubble was then lighted with reflected color from a cloth-covered tunnel outside of camera range. Lighting the moving bubble in this manner, however, contaminated the solid black background necessary to surround the image for double printing. To correct this the bubble was mounted stationary against a black background, this time lighted from behind. Filmed by a camera on a moving dolly, the stationary bubble appeared to be traveling along the plotted course.

One method of attaining the luminous glow of Glinda's bubble was a process electrician Raymond Griffith distinctly remembered. Among the anecdotes he relished sharing with family was how the sphere was lit with four huge spinning arc lights, one at each corner of the room. The lights were directed to the precise center of the room, and the intersecting beams enhanced the radiance of the "bubble." His niece Linda Reyes recalled:

> I know my uncle was very proud of the fact that special effects had done such a great job with the lighting of the globe that the Good Witch floats into the Munchkin City. I remember him showing me with his hands how the

> spinning effect was achieved with lights. He said it took two weeks to get it right. . . . I can still see the look of wonderment and pride in his face as he told the story to me and used his hands to show us how the big lights were spun about, making the motion that we see today in the Munchkin City scenes.

Oz* artifact: rubber remnant of a model monkey. The prop's legs and wings have disintegrated, but the pipe-cleaner tail remains intact. Sculptor Marcel Delgado made the models; he had previously done similar work for *The Lost World* and *King Kong*. *Courtesy Linda and Rudy Reyes; photo: Tim McGowan

Other reports of the bubble effect were creative—if inaccurate—perhaps generated by test accounts. *Citizen Magazine* wrote, "Most difficult laboratory job was making a bubble float into scene, burst, and reveal Billie Burke. You can't double expose on color. [It was] done with matrices to block off parts of film." The August 17, 1939, edition of the *Cleveland Press* stated, "Double exposure could not be used on the iridescent floating bubble because the colors blurred with the background. The experts put a white spot on each frame of film, making thousands of white spots in all, and then tinted each by hand." Even for some associated with the film, Glinda's lofty sphere will forever be a mystery. Munchkin maiden Margaret Pellegrini has remained incredulous, "To this day I don't know how they got Glinda down in that big bubble!"

Another double-exposure shot that required some trial and error was the scene in which sparks fly from the ruby slippers as the Wicked Witch attempts to remove them from Dorothy's feet. Initially the sparks were made by masking off all but the portion of the scene in which they were to appear and filming high tension electrical juice shot at speed. The end result, it was determined, "lacked violence." Alternatively, the effect was achieved by shooting in stop-motion streaks of light made on the surface of glass painted black on the camera side and illuminated from behind.

The spinning rings double-printed with the close-up of Dorothy during her transition from Emerald City to Kansas ("There's no place like home . . . There's no place like home . . .") also saw more than one test. One aborted attempt began by shooting straight down from a rotating camera mounted at the top of Stage 30. A 20-foot circle stood 6 feet above the floor and contained ports through which colored smoke was forced. This proved unsatisfactory since the volume of smoke could not be controlled well enough to keep it from completely covering the camera lens. Instead, a second test was made using a striped plaster cone mounted upon a turntable and rotated about 200 rpm. As the cone rotated, it was filmed directly overhead by a stationary camera positioned six feet above the point of the cone. This was done using four different-colored striped cones shot separately. The different-colored shots were then printed in succession to give the illusion of color-changing rings.[5]

The success of many of Buddy Gillespie's special effects was owed in large part to Max Fabian. Fabian was the cameraman for virtually everything Gillespie shot on *Oz*. Fellow artisan George Gibson commented, "Fabian was the closest to being an artist of any cameraman I knew. He understood light and objects. He painted with light." It was Fabian's skilled camera lens that enhanced the picture's make-believe and miniatures, making them laudable.

Many of the large structures and awe-inspiring landscapes in *The Wizard of Oz* would have been too costly, impractical, or virtually impossible to build—even as miniatures. To create such images, a process that combined live-action film footage with matte paintings was employed. Named after their creator, Warren Newcombe, these combinations were referred to in the industry as Newcombe shots. Basically, the portion of the scene that would not be built was drawn on a 22-by-28-inch black board using crayon pastels and pencil, with a black area preserved where footage of the live characters would be shown. The painting would then be filmed, while the corresponding live-action footage was filmed separately. The two pieces of footage were then combined so that the live action would fit into the blackened-out area of the painting, thereby creating the final image.

Although filming Newcombe shots in Technicolor did not present as many problems as some of the other Technicolor double exposures used in *The Wizard of Oz*, there were some added delays. Each night the cameras were taken back to the Technicolor plant in order to have color filters changed, lenses polished, and mechanisms adjusted and tested. According to the Newcombe shots log for *Oz* dated February 24, 1939, this caused each morning's setup to be thrown out of line during the process of getting the camera back in place. As a result, two or three hand-developed tests usually needed to be made each morning before the shot was made to line up. Each hand test required approximately twenty minutes for negative development and fifteen minutes drying time.

In an interoffice memo dated March 27, 1939, Warren Newcombe provided a list of Technicolor Newcombe shots yet to be completed

[5] In the rough cut of the film, this scene included a montage of Oz images as Dorothy wishes herself back to Kansas. Double-exposed over the ring effect were shots of the witches, the Munchkins, the Cowardly Lion, the Wizard, and scenes from Kansas—all preceding the farmhouse crashing back to earth. Given that this sequence ran over a minute, the color shifting of the rings was obvious prior to editing, unlike the brief few seconds seen in the finished film.

259

for *The Wizard of Oz*. The listing represented only a partial roster of the numerous scenes utilizing matte paintings and included the following.

1. Exterior of the Witch's castle as the Scarecrow, Tin Man, and [Cowardly] Lion creep up
2. Exterior of the poppy field as the principals head toward Emerald City
3. Emerald City corridor as the principals enter the Wizard's throne room
4. Emerald City corridor as the [Cowardly] Lion runs from the Wizard's throne room
5. Exterior of Emerald City gates as the principals approach to ring the bell
6. Exterior of Emerald City inside the gates
7. Exterior of Emerald City with the Wizard's balloon present
8. Exterior of Emerald City after the Wizard's balloon has left
9. Exterior of the Witch's castle on the hillside (an all-over painting with no live-action combination)

Not all of the on-screen magic for *Oz* necessitated a clever camera lens. The studio contended that actual magicians were consulted to learn theatrical feats involving appearances, disappearances, fire, and sleight-of-hand illusions. An improved version of the stage-floor trapdoor was pressed into service when the Wicked Witch was required to melt and make her fiery entrances and exits. The accident that resulted from one such vanishing act has become the sort of legendary Hollywood anecdote that only grows more distorted with time. The incident occurred December 23, 1938, on the Munchkinland set. Make-up artist Jack Young recalled:

> I had just made up Margaret Hamilton as the Wicked Witch. The scene . . . was where she was threatening the Good Witch and Judy Garland. At the end of her tirade, the Wicked Witch disappears in a puff of smoke and a flash of flame. Special effects had rigged up an elevator type contraption that would quickly lower her below the floor. [Around the circular floor-level rim of the elevator was a metal tubing punctuated by countless holes to allow for gas and smoke jets.] Something went

Opposite: The sepia-tone matte painting of the road leading to Dorothy's Kansas farm. *Courtesy The Comisar Collection, Inc.* The blank, black area of the board indicated where live action footage was needed, similar to the image beneath it. Below: The combined images provided a complete picture of the scene that begins the film, similar to this still.

256
FLEMING - EXT. MU
STAND - 2
HOLE 43

"The Munchkins will see you safely to the border of Munchkinland." A matte painting depicting the path of the yellow brick road beyond Munchkinland, and a frame of the illustration paired with live action.

The principals march "off to see the Wizard," but only on a portion of the yellow brick road, as shown in the set still, top; the winding path and distant trees seen in the film are a matte painting, bottom.

> wrong. She screamed she was on fire, her voice muffled from beneath the floor. Without a moment's thought, I leaped into the pit and smothered the flames. I was proud of that make-up job and I would be damned if I would let anything happen to it. Fortunately no one was injured, including the make-up.

Munchkin Coroner Meinhardt Raabe confirmed Young's assessment of the incident. His memory was that a fireman with a soaking-wet blanket was off-camera waiting for just such possible emergency. Raabe reported that, for this scene, the fireman was down in the elevator with Margaret Hamilton and extinguished the flames with the blanket before anyone knew what had happened. "And all that happened to [Hamilton]," said Raabe, "was that her facial heavy cream make-up melted and her eyebrows were singed, because she was back on the set the next day. So she was not physically injured." Another Munchkin performer maintained it was he who saved the day by quickly filling his hat with water from the nearby Munchkinland pond and dousing the flames! Charles Schram was also on the set that day and remembered that a prop man sustained third-degree burns on his hands from beating out the fire.

Of course, injury did occur and Margaret Hamilton suffered severe burns to her face and right hand, which laid her up for six weeks. Regardless of how the incident was perceived, no one can quibble with the indelible impression the event left in the mind of a child—Margaret Hamilton's three-year-old son, Hamilton Meserve. Almost sixty years later, Meserve still recalled "being led into her bedroom, and there she was, mummylike—in her four poster bed—swathed in bandages." Margaret Hamilton's training as a kindergarten teacher led to her select sensitivity in discussing not only the Witch but any potentially disturbing circumstances with her son. She broke the ice by beginning their talk with, "Well, I had a bad burn . . ." The actress could have just as easily dispensed with the precautions; little Ham thought his mother's new appearance was more fascinating than frightening.

The Witch's disappearance, though technically a stunt, was—fortunately—Margaret Hamilton's most physically taxing *Oz* experience. Miniatures were used for the scene showing the Wicked

Witch of the West soaring out of her castle on broomstick, encircling the castle tower, and exiting the scene. The castle was merely a miniature painted profile set against a painted sky. The Witch was a 1 ½-inch modeled figure carried on an overhead track and pulled by a motor. Wearing a silk gauze cape meant to blow in the wind, the figure was operated at a speed fast enough to smooth out the action and flutter the cape without the need for a wind machine.

Other "flying" scenes featured the Winged Monkeys, which were also done in miniature for long shots. Early attempts at filming miniature flying monkeys in profile utilized two-dimensional cutouts in three different sizes. The cutouts were later replaced by three-dimensional modeled figures, yet they still proved to lack sufficient animation. Finally the monkey models were cast in rubber in four sizes. These were then assembled in front of a small painted backdrop, suspended by two stationary wires at the head and feet and two movable wires on the tip of each wing. This approach allowed for a choice of angles ranging from side view (as they would be seen outside the Witch's tower window) to head-on (as they would appear swooping into the Haunted Forest). As most Oz fans know, the monkeys' descent into the Haunted Forest was to follow "The Jitterbug," a deleted song and dance that involved rhythmic syncopation with the forest's "jitter trees."

The star doubles, in makeshift costumes, arrive at the Emerald City gates, top. The area above the set will be compensated with an elaborate matte painting, bottom, number 289. ***Courtesy University of Southern California***

Another anthropomorphic effect—that of the talking apple trees—was divulged by Frederick C. Othman writing for the *Rochester* [New York] *Democrat and Chronicle* on August 14, 1939.

> One scene you'll see is that of Dorothy plucking an apple from a tree. This makes the tree angry. It snatches the apple away from her and slaps her on the wrist. How do you think Metro wangled that? Well sir, the experts built a flexible rubber tree, put a man inside of it, and zipped the bark up the back. He did the apple snatching.

George Gibson further defined the creation of both the jitter trees and the talking apple trees.

> [The trees] were made by the property shop under supervision of Jack Gaylord, who was a master of gimmickry, and were built to contain a smallish man. . . . [They were made] of light-weight wood and covered with latex skins which were fabricated from molds of tree bark taken from actual trees. They had fixed branches, all except the two where the prop men put their arms like sleeves, with lots of flexibility so they could throw the [rubber] apples.

Not to be underestimated, the film's Oscar-winning musical score was critical in adding an air of charm, whimsy, and dread to on-screen action involving the talking trees and other effects. In grounding the fantasy of Oz, the background scoring was an important atmospheric component. In the article "Film Music and Its Makers," published in the May 27, 1939, issue of *Hollywood Spectator* magazine, Bruno David Ussher summarized composer Herbert Stothart's challenge.

> Stothart tells me that *The Wizard of Oz* will be one of the few pictures for which a 100 percent musical background score is under preparation. This will include some musical, some highly phantastic and grotesque, as well as some humorous episodes. The difficulty is to relate music with special sound effects, such as the swishing of straw as the Scarecrow walks, the clank of the Tin Woodman, the voices of the trees and other nature elements. . . .
>
> All this requires extremely minute work, on the part of musicians and sound engineers. Already some 15,000 feet of such soundtrack, enough for a two and a half hour picture, has been made. Of this enormous mass of sound effects plus music, the most illusionary will be chosen to accompany the screen action.

Stothart philosophically reflected, "In the *Wizard*, music and sound must be highly imaginative, unreal as well as superrealistic. Here, sounds must stir the phantasy and the meaning and power as well as physical attributes of inanimate things. . . . In the *Wizard of Oz* the super-human, super-natural is humanized and speaks in terms of music or musical sounds."

As well as adding musical tracks and special effects, there was a sufficient amount of postproduction work for *The Wizard of Oz* that involved sound synchronization, rerecording, and dubbing. The reasons for this were varied, and included unwanted set noises, technical sound difficulties, machinery noises, and "cue" tracks that needed to be replaced by alternate sounds or dialogue (such as the distorted voices of the talking apple trees and the echo effect of the Wizard's throne room). By early March 1939, some forty unusable and "questionable" scenes in need of possible sound adjustment were identified by Gavin Burns, the film's chief sound technician.

The churning of wind machines was a frequent cause of soundtrack flaws. Used throughout the Kansas tornado scenes, the machine noises necessitated the dubbing of Frank Morgan's lines as he takes Professor Marvel's horse to cover, as well as Bert Lahr exclaiming, "It's a twister! It's a twister!" Most of Judy Garland's lines required attention too, including the deleted "Toto, we're off the ground." Beyond the tornado effect, the more subtle use of wind machines to make the Wicked Witch's dress and cape blow and to effect breezes in scenes like the Haunted Forest created similar sound problems. Yet another special effects machine, that of the open projector used to direct images into the Witch's crystal ball, called for some of Margaret Hamilton's lines to be synchronized.

The castle of the Wicked Witch, a matte painting used exclusively as an establishing shot without live-action footage. ***Courtesy University of Southern California***

merald City
HOLE #27
STAND-3
Stand 2

Opposite: The domed spires above the town square in Emerald City are a matte painting. Above: The live-action portion of the scene pictures extras poised for the deleted "Triumphal Return" number. The combined art and live action are shown in a scene cut from *The Wizard of Oz. Courtesy University of Southern California*

FLEMING EXT.
WITCHS CASTLE
STAND 3
HOLE #42
257

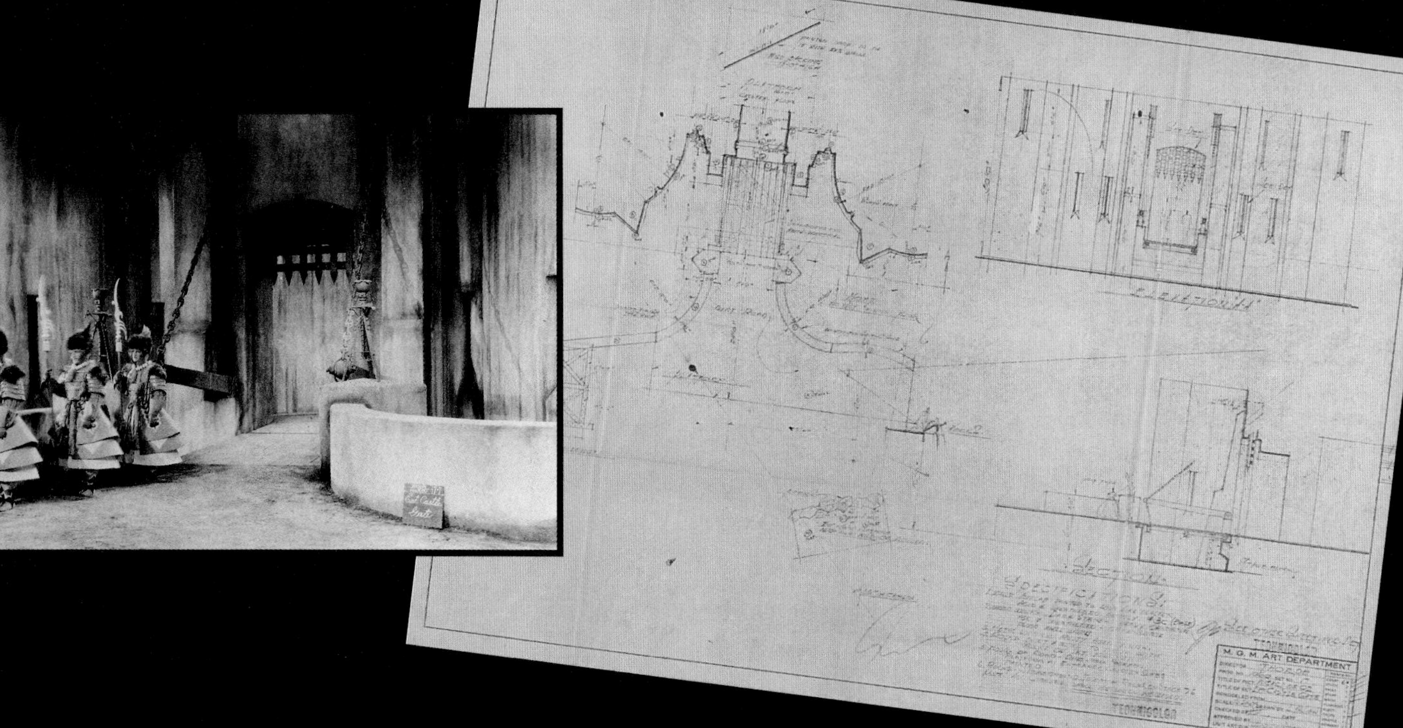
M. G. M. ART DEPARTMENT
TECHNICOLOR

Unwanted footstep noises also resulted in a great deal of postproduction sound editing. Examples included the scene in which the Cowardly Lion chases Toto, the Winkie guards chasing the principal characters throughout the Witch's castle, the hooves of the Horse of a Different Color, and the scuffle with the flying monkeys. In at least two instances—in the Wizard's throne room and during the Witch's melting scene—the use of steam effects interfered with sound quality. And both crowd noise and the use of a balloon hoist caused a number of Judy Garland's and Frank Morgan's lines to be redone for the Wizard's departure scene.

It would not be until June 1939 that the majority of all postproduction work on Oz was completed for the sake of "rough-cut" previews. Audience response to those previews meant further work for editor Blanche Sewell and assistant Ernie Grooney, as several scenes were shortened or eliminated altogether. Retakes and pick-up shots took place as late as June 10. (Technicolor assistant Clifford Shirpser was scheduled to be married at 10 p.m. that evening. The scramble to finish *Oz* pushed the wedding back to 2 a.m. the next day!) By the time the final cut of the film was ready—and several hundred copies were made for distribution to theatres throughout the country—it would be August. M-G-M's *The Wizard of Oz* had its official West Coast premiere at Grauman's Chinese Theatre on August 15, 1939, and its East Coast premiere two days later at New York's Capitol Theatre. Now ready for the public at large, the film would be heralded by a publicity campaign such as no other film in history had seen.

Opposite: A deleted overhead shot of the drawbridge to the Witch's castle would have shown, through matte painting, the surrounding rocks and moat. The blueprint for the drawbridge indicates that it should be "practical" or built fully functional. The set itself was on dry land, with the stage floor serving as the moat.

Gaiety! Glory! Glamour!
GARLAND
MORGAN
BOLGER
LAHR
HALEY
THE WIZARD OF OZ
It's METRO-GOLDWYN-MAYER'S TECHNICOLOR TRIUMPH!
BILLIE BURKE
MARGARET HAMILTON
CHARLEY GRAPEWIN
AND THE MUNCHKINS
A VICTOR FLEMING production
MERVYN LE ROY
THE WIZARD OF OZ

Exploitation essential: the original "Coming Attraction" glass theatre slide. *Photo: Tim McGowan*

Five

A WHIZ OF A PROMOTION

at Home and Abroad

Business is great! Exploitation campaigns are tremendous! The whole nation is Oz conscious. . . . When the final box-office reports are tabulated it will be the consensus of opinion among theatre men that [*The Wizard of Oz*] was the biggest and liveliest promotion natural of 1939. Believe us, we never saw so many contests! . . . Single page and double [page] spreads were twice as plentiful as ever before! . . . Oz characters dominated smash lobbies and paraded the streets in magnetic human form! . . . Roto and Sunday art placements were the rule rather than the exception! All engagements seemed intent on making their patrons feel: “We’re off to see the Wizard, the wonderful Wizard of Oz”!

— *M-G-M Bi-Weekly Co-operative Campaign Service*, circa September 1939

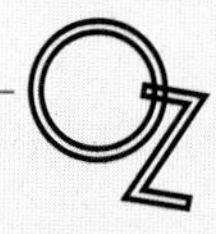

Publicity wiz Howard Dietz conjures up Ozzy poster art for the film's initial release in 1939.

At a total cost of $ 2,777,000, Metro-Goldwyn-Mayer went to great expense in mounting its screen adaptation of *The Wizard of Oz*. The picture was Metro's most expensive to date. Indeed, producer Mervyn LeRoy recalled in later years that the studio almost fired him over the unheard-of costs that *Oz* racked up during the course of its production. Having poured such financial investment into "LeRoy's Folly," M-G-M was banking on the popular success of the film. By spending an additional $250,000, Metro went to equally great lengths in orchestrating a promotional campaign to get the general public of 1939 "Ozified!"

At the time *The Wizard of Oz* was filmed, M-G-M produced an average of fifty pictures a year—not counting about thirty "B" pictures. Promoting these films, including *Oz*, was a task shared between M-G-M's own publicity department and the offices of the studio's parent company, Loew's Incorporated. The West Coast publicity department operated from the M-G-M studio in Culver City, while the Loew's sixteen-story home offices were located above the State Theatre at Broadway and Forty-fifth Street in New York. Together, some 150 people worked on both coasts in various divisions to publicize M-G-M films by arranging features in national magazines; placing photos and stories in newspapers; encouraging promotional tie-ins; and handling fan mail for the stars.

Promotional pin-back buttons herald *Oz* in 1939. *Photo: Tim McGowan*

In 1939, and for years prior, Loew's Incorporated was the most profitable movie company in the world. With Metro-Goldwyn-Mayer as its picturemaking unit, it in essence was responsible for the best movies being made in Hollywood. And Loew's gross film rentals were consistently higher than that of any other studio. Since the death of its founder, Marcus Loew, in 1927, Loew's Incorporated had been headed by Nicholas M. Schenck. Having emigrated from Russia at the age of nine, the thick-accented president of Loew's had faithfully worked for the company since 1906. M-G-M boss Louis B. Mayer referred to Schenck as "The General" and reportedly was accustomed to calling him on the telephone two or three times a day.

Distance was not the only thing that separated the East and West Coast publicity operations. Rotogravures, newspaper art, and other prerelease publicity were handled in California by Howard Strickling

TELL THE WORLD YOU'VE GOT IT!
IT WILL BACK UP YOUR EXTRA EFFORTS!
USE THE ACCESSORIES!
$250,000 ADVANCE ADVERTISING!
EXTRA POSTERS PAY!
A WHALE OF A HERALD! USE IT!

HOLD OPEN EXTRA TIME!
INCREASE YOUR AD BUDGET!
ADVERTISE IT!
SHOWMANSHIP OPPORTUNITY!
PUBLICIZE IT!
PLANT THE NEWSPAPER SERIALS!
EXPLOIT IT!
AN EXPLOITATION NATURAL!
Gaiety! Glory! Glamour!
Judy GARLAND
Frank MORGAN
Ray BOLGER
Bert LAHR
Jack HALEY
THE WIZARD OF OZ
It's METRO-GOLDWYN-MAYER'S TECHNICOLOR TRIUMPH!
POSTERS
READ WHAT HAS BEEN DONE FOR YOU!
PRE-SOLD TO MILLIONS!
MARVELOUS TECHNICOLOR TRAILER!
EVERYBODY HAS READ ABOUT IT!
CASH IN ON EXPLOITATION TIE-UPS!

COMPLETE
CAMPAIGN BOOK
FOR Metro-Goldwyn-Mayer's WONDER SHOW OF SHOWS!
MAGNIFICENT IN ITS BRILLIANT TECHNICOLOR SPLENDOR!
BIGGEST SENSATION Since "SNOW WHITE"!
THE WIZARD OF OZ
with
JUDY GARLAND
FRANK MORGAN
RAY BOLGER
BERT LAHR
JACK HALEY
BILLIE BURKE MARGARET HAMILTON
CHARLEY GRAPEWIN and THE MUNCHKINS
HOW TO EXPLOIT OZ!
HOW TO ADVERTISE OZ!
HOW TO PUBLICIZE OZ!
FOR RECORD BUSINESS!

$250,000 to advertise "THE WIZARD of OZ"
91,912,853
(ACTUAL PUBLICATION CIRCULATION)
MOVIE-GOERS WILL READ M-G-M's GREATEST-EVER ADVERTISING CAMPAIGN TO BRING THEM TO YOUR THEATRE!
THE BIGGEST AND MOST COLORFUL ADVERTISING CAMPAIGN EVER PUT BEHIND A MOTION PICTURE!
THIS BROADSIDE OF FACTS
This giant broadside is vital to your own complete promotion campaign! It contains all the ads in full colors, all the publications and their "On Sale" dates, a list of all the newspapers, all circulations ...and other impressive data! It has already been sent to every M-G-M exhibitor! Read it—study it—and tie up your own promotion with the greatest campaign ever put behind a motion picture!
NATIONAL MAGAZINES
JUVENILE MAGAZINES
FAN MAGAZINES
COMIC SUPPLEMENT ADS
NATION-WIDE TEASER ADS
RECORD PUBLICITY RESULTS
THE PROMOTION COMPANY!—THE FRIENDLY COMPANY!

LOBBY
A WHIZ OF A TRAILER! IN TECHNICOLOR!
SPECIAL EXIT MUSIC TRAILER!
M-G-M's TECHNICOLOR SHOW OF SHOWS!
The WIZARD of OZ
BIGGEST SCREEN SENSATION SINCE "SNOW WHITE"
NEW! SHOWMANSHIP HERALD!
TITLE CARD
GARLAND MORGAN BOLGER LAHR HALEY

A BOOK FAMOUS IN FICTION...
A PLAY CELEBRATED ON THE
AMERICAN STAGE...A PICTURE
THAT IS TRULY A TRIUMPH...
for
Exploitation
The Wizard of Oz
JUDY GARLAND • FRANK MORGAN
RAY BOLGER • BERT LAHR
JACK HALEY
W. R. FERGUSON, Manager of Exploitation

EXHIBITORS' SERVICE SHEET

PRESS BOOK
ADVERTISING SECTION

MGM's THE WIZARD OF OZ IN GORGEOUS TECHNI-COLOR

The elaborate campaign book for *The Wizard of Oz* was distributed only to theatre owners and contained endless opportunities to promote the picture through poster art, advertisements, and gimmicks.

A two-page spread in M-G-M's *Studio News* magazine suggested several *Oz* ad formats.

Opposite: One of four installments in a pen-and-ink art serial illustrated by renowned newspaper artist Michelson. Supplied by M-G-M free of charge to any newspaper wishing to run the serial in its magazine or motion picture section, the comiclike feature provided unique publicity for *The Wizard of Oz.*

at M-G-M. Meanwhile, coverage in national magazines and on East Coast radio networks was attended to by the New York offices of Loew's. Moreover, New York was continuing the business originally started by Marcus Loew in maintaining its own movie theatre chain. In 1939, the company had a reported 125 theatres in the U.S. and Canada. The 26 houses in and around the New York City area were supervised by Charles Moskowitz; Joe Vogel had charge of the remaining Loew's theatres throughout other parts of the country. These two men were assisted by the guidance of Oscar Doob, whose advertising department would cost Loew's some $3 million a year. However, individual theatre managers were expected to generate their own publicity and "exploitation" of films. This included maintaining working relations with newspapers and other local outlets.

Theatre managers, Loew's and independents, were also assisted to an extent by the New York publicity office headed by Howard Dietz. Spending about $2.5 million each year at the time, Dietz's department would, among other things, instruct exhibitors all over the country in the technique of securing newspaper advertising

IMPRESSIONS OF *Metro - Goldwyn - Mayer's* TECHNICOLOR MASTERPIECE

THE WIZARD OF OZ

ILLUSTRATED BY THE CELEBRATED ARTIST, MICHELSON

(1) An awful rumpus arises one day when little Dorothy (Judy Garland), a Kansas country girl, finds that Miss Gulch, a mean neighbor, wants to destroy her dog Toto. She and Toto run away but in the woods they meet Professor Marvel (Frank Morgan), a fortune teller, who says that Aunt Em is grieving for her, so Dorothy races home. (2) That night a cyclone hits. Everything goes sailing through space and a Witch, who looks like Miss Gulch, flies past. Then a bubble bursts, revealing Glinda (Billie Burke), a *Good* Witch. She leads the way to the Munchkins, kindly dwarfs, who give Dorothy the magic slippers of the dead Wicked Witch. But the Witch's sister demands the slippers and when they won't come off, vows vengeance. (3) Now Dorothy starts out for the Wizard of Oz, who alone, can send her back to Kansas. Soon, she meets a dancing Scarecrow (Ray Bolger) who wants the Wizard to give him Brains. (4) A little later, they encounter a Tin Woodman (Jack Haley). *He* wants a heart so he joins them too. Once, the Wicked Witch sends a fire to destroy the Scarecrow but Dorothy rescues him. (5) Suddenly, a Lion (Bert Lahr) jumps out and leaps at Toto but when Dorothy slaps him he begins to sob! He's a Cowardly Lion and *he'd* like the Wizard to give him Courage. Blithely, the friends set out again, all unaware that the Wicked Witch has laid a terrible trap for them. *Don't miss the next adventurous episode.*

Unique in the Annals of Exploitation

A GREAT STUNT FOR SMALL TOWNS AND BIG CITIES!

NOW touring territories playing this attraction is a truly unique creation which strikes the imaginative fancy of children and focuses the interest of adults. This conception, inspired by the picture, glorifies the most important entertainment aspects of "The Wizard of Oz"—the celebrated characters and their wonderful adventures in a land of delightful make-believe.

The picture below shows it in its entirety. The ballyhoo is unique in the sense that it allows youngsters to actually participate and play the roles of the characters. A special motor van also serves the purposes of an exhibition float. Transported within the van are the original two black ponies in the production along with the phaeton that carried Dorothy and her pals. When it arrives at a theatre, the ponies and phaeton are used to carry youngsters lucky enough to be chosen to impersonate the Wizard, Scarecrow, Tin Woodman, Cowardly Lion and Dorothy. Costumes of these picture characters are worn by the kids selected and then they are off on a gay party starting from the theatre, visiting patients convalescing in hospitals, shut-ins, etc. It has great local tie-up and merchandising angles!

To date "The Wizard of Oz Tour" has covered the following territories: New York City, where Mickey Rooney and Judy Garland, appearing in person at the Capitol Theatre, started it off; New Haven; Boston; Albany; Buffalo; Cleveland; Cincinnati; Indianapolis; Chicago; St. Louis; Omaha; Des Moines; Kansas City.

This is only the beginning! Hundreds of other theatres will benefit from the popular Wizard of Oz Tour now covering the country!

space. Dietz's own talents were many, including those as a lyricist responsible for many of M-G-M's songs. Several years earlier, in 1917, it was also Howard Dietz who had designed the Goldwyn Pictures studio trademark of a roaring lion in full-body profile encircled by a banner reading "Ars Gratia Artis" ("Art for Art's Sake"). When Loew's Incorporated completed its merger of Loew's theatre chain, Metro's distribution network, Goldwyn Pictures, and Louis B. Mayer Productions in 1924, Dietz replaced the logo's lion image with that of a regal lion's head—creating the famous Leo the Lion M-G-M trademark.

Typical for most films, publicity-campaign books prepared by the studios were sent at no cost to theatre managers in advance of film play dates. The books were virtual manuals that provided scores of gimmicks designed to hype ticket sales. Pictured were posters, banners, cardboard standees, and other display materials that could be purchased or rented from the film exchanges. For *The Wizard of Oz*, M-G-M issued a campaign book that was characteristic of only the most prestigious films of the day. As lavish as the film itself, the *Oz* campaign book featured a folder with full-color covers depicting a variety of posters available for theatre marquee and lobby display. The colorfully lithographed posters for the film ranged in size from an 8-by-14-inch window card to a billboardlike twenty-four sheet.

Several of the original release posters for *The Wizard of Oz* were graced by the work of either of two renowned artists of the time. The window-card poster, the twenty-four-sheet poster, and a 40-by-60-inch poster all featured renderings of the principal characters by Armando Seguso. An Italian-born musician, painter, and illustrator, Seguso's work had been featured on the covers of such magazines as *Cosmopolitan*, *Good Housekeeping*, *Woman's Home Companion*, *Pictorial Review*, and *McCall's*. His commercial artwork for M-G-M included striking images done in a variety of media, including crayon, pastel, and watercolor. Seguso's poster art would herald another highly anticipated 1939 film, *Gone With the Wind*. Meanwhile, Picassoesque images created by famed caricaturist Al Hirschfeld were incorporated into *Oz* one-sheet, three-sheet, six-sheet, and jumbo window-card posters. His work was also used in magazine advertisements, sheet music covers, and merchandising tie-ins for the film. Another artist with an impressionist style signed his *Oz* publicity paintings "A. Birnbaum."

Other illustrators designed art used in magazine and newspaper features. A charcoal sketch of Judy Garland reading *The Wizard of*

Opposite: A page from the September 1939 *M-G-M Bi-Weekly Co-operative Campaign Service* newsletter announced the "Wizard of Oz Tour," comprised of a decorated Chevrolet motor van. "Transported within the van are the original two black ponies in the production along with the phaeton [the Munchkinland coach] that carried Dorothy and her pals." Mickey Rooney and Judy Garland kicked off the tour, which started at New York's Capitol Theatre, mid-August 1939. (The two are visible in the top left photo.) At each stop of the multicity tour, local children were selected to don miniature replicas of the *Oz* costumes for "a gay party starting from the theatre, visiting patients convalescing in hospitals, shut-ins, etc." The banner worn by the ponies reads, "Original equipment from the M-G-M picture *Wizard of Oz*."

Oz while her otherworld companions waft from its pages was created by Moor Rushey. Wiley Padan drew an *Oz* news mat along the lines of *Ripley's Believe It or Not* titled "It's True." (The feature also noted that Mervyn LeRoy planned to relocate Munchkinland to the New York World's Fair!) And the celebrated newspaper sketch artist Michelson rendered a four-chapter pen-and-ink art serialization, "Impressions of Metro-Goldwyn-Mayer's Technicolor Masterpiece *The Wizard of Oz*."

Contained in the campaign book for *The Wizard of Oz* were three separate sections. One of these, the "Exploitation" section, was completely devoted to merchandising, contests, national print features, and a host of other "ballyhoos" intended to incite interest in the film. A sampling of the offerings included:

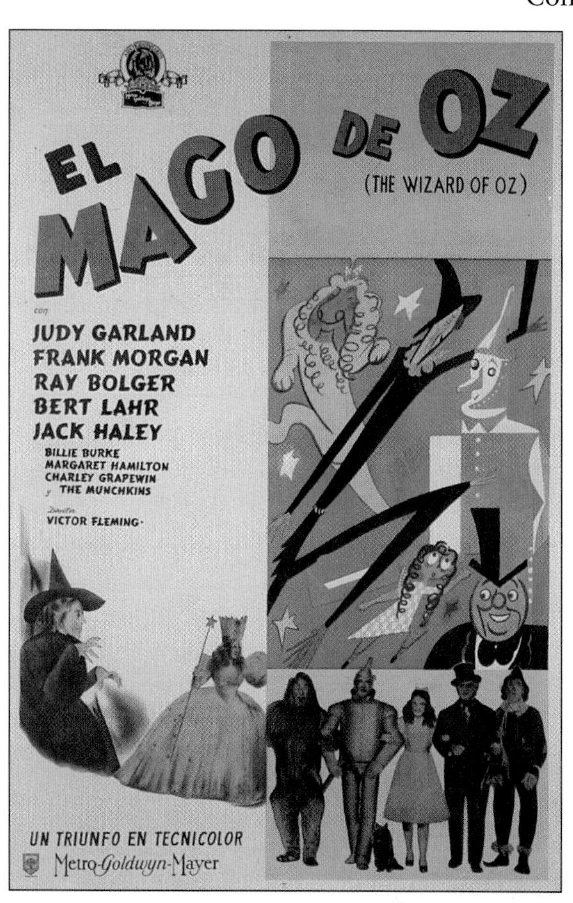

Adjusted for language translation, the original Argentinean one-sheet poster of 1939 was nearly identical to that used to promote *Oz* in America. *Photo: Tim McGowan*

> Exploit the picture's famous book characters! Follow the example set by *Snow White* showmen who made the Seven Dwarfs the most familiar "people" in America! . . .
>
> "Back to School with *The Wizard of Oz*" newspaper promotions and coloring contests. . . .
>
> Run a newspaper, theatre, or radio contest in which you ask movie fans what they would do if they were the Wizard of Oz. . . .
>
> Several of the characters in the picture will make arresting street figures when impersonated by men dressed as The Cowardly Lion, The Scarecrow, The Wizard, The Tin Woodman, etc. Hunt around a costumer's shop for such apparel or create the costumes yourself. . . .
>
> Organize a *Wizard of Oz* Club.

The other two sections of the *Oz* campaign book were geared toward local newspaper advertising and publicity. The "Press Book Advertising Section" comprised a series of print advertisements ranging from a few columnar inches to full-page layouts. Similarly, the "Exhibitor's Service Sheet" contained numerous pages of prepared reviews and stories of interest, such as the creation of the film's special effects, the casting of the Munchkin actors, the musical scoring, and Judy Garland's apparent trials and tribulations while filming around the pigpen of the Kansas farm set ("No More Pigs for Judy Garland").

Touted by M-G-M as its "greatest-ever advertising campaign," the *Wizard of Oz* promotion was pervasive and highly successful. Never before had there been such an outpouring of print advertising for a motion picture that matched *Oz*: in national magazines, juvenile magazines, fan magazines, daily newspapers, and even Sunday comic sections. The number of store-window tie-ups was equally phenomenal. All the chain stores represented the film in some respect; book displays were tremendous; sheet music poured in from

Le Magicien d'Oz **was seen in France shortly after its American release in 1939—complete with a dubbed soundtrack and on-screen titles and credits in French.** ***Photo: Tim McGowan***

Det lyckliga landet Oz
(The merry old land of Oz)
Musik: Harold Arlen
Svensk text: Kar De Mumma — Jokern
Engelsk text: E. Y. Harburg
Ur METRO-Goldwyn-MAYERs
sagolika sagofilm i färg
TROLLKARLEN
från OZ
Melodier ur filmen:
Ovan regnbågen
Om jag hade . . .
Ding, dong, häxan är död
Vi är på väg till trollkarln
Det lyckliga landet Oz
REUTER REUTER
25

every part of the country; children's stores grabbed everything in sight; Judy Garland fashions were offered in retail outlets; and bakeries and grocery and drug stores publicized local screenings of the picture. There was even a "Wizard of Oz Tour" in the form of a unique promotional motor van that traveled to New York, New Haven, Boston, Albany, Buffalo, Cleveland, Cincinnati, Indianapolis, Chicago, St. Louis, Omaha, Des Moines and a host of other cities. With all the media hype, it was likely that few Americans in 1939 hadn't seen or heard of Metro-Goldwyn-Mayer's *The Wizard of Oz*.

Opposite: The *Oz* songs proved as popular in Sweden as they were in the States. *Photo: Tim McGowan*

Hollywood gave *Oz* a gala reception at its Grauman's Chinese Theatre premiere on August 15, 1939; but the East Coast send-off at Loew's Capitol Theatre two days later far exceeded all expectations. To boost the film's opening, Metro sent Mickey Rooney and Judy Garland to New York for a personal-appearance engagement. The experience was overwhelming even for the young veteran performers. Mickey Rooney's voice was still tinged with enthusiasm when he recently recalled the event, "The Capitol Theatre—that's where we kicked [*Oz*] off at! Where do you think we were staying? The Waldorf Astoria! And we'd never seen anything like that in California before! We arrived at Grand Central Station—you know how many people greeted us? Twenty-five thousand!"

The one-sheet poster for the original release of *El Mago de Oz* in Spain, 1945. *Photo: Tim McGowan*

Shortly after the United States had been introduced to the eagerly-awaited *Oz* film, audiences in foreign countries were treated to it as well . . . albeit with the aid of a dubbed soundtrack.[1] Millions of Americans had enjoyed reading *The Wonderful Wizard of Oz* for decades prior to the M-G-M screen adaptation. But the L. Frank Baum book was largely unknown outside the States. As such, most foreign countries were introduced to the story for the first time by Judy Garland and company. "What is *The Wizard of Oz*, M-G-M's new mystery film, which is expected to prove one of the screen's biggest sensations?" began a feature in Britain's *Film Weekly*

[1] Dubbing a film in a foreign language was inordinately expensive. Only the dialogue for *Oz*—not the songs—was altered.

After World War II, Italy embraced its initial 1948 release of *Il Mago di Oz* with a variety of promotional materials ranging from full-color lobby cards, advertisements, and adaptations of the film story. *Photos: Tim McGowan*

IL VARCO È FATTO: PROSEGUIAMO!
ASCOLTATE!
I RUGGITI DELLE BELVE!.. TIGRI, LEONI, PANTERE.
AD UN TRATTO ECCO SBUCAR DA UNA SIEPE UN GROSSO LEONE....

IN GUARDIA! CHI VUOL BATTERSI CON ME?
OH! NO! TI CONOSCO APPENA.
ANCH' IO!

ALLORA MI BATTERÒ CON IL CANE!

CON TOTÒ ?? BELLA FORZA LA TUA! SEI UN VIGLIACCO!

PFAFF!
IH! IH! IH! MI ESCE IL SANGUE DAL NASO!!
MACCHÈ SANGUE! SEI UN LEONE CODARDO.

NON PIANGERE! PIUTTOSTO PENSA A VENIRE CON NOI DAL GRAN MAGO DI OZ!
MI DARÀ IL CORAGGIO?

LA STREGA SCORGE NELLA "SFERA DELLA VERITÀ" I QUATTRO COMPAGNI CHE SI AVVIANO ALLA CITTÀ DI SMERALDO

AH! AH! ORA VEDRETE!
E IMMERSO UN PENNELLO NEL VELENO ROSSO, DIPINGE IL CRISTALLO.....

IL BOSCO SI È TRASFORMATO IN UN CAMPO DI PAPAVERI... TEMO SI TRATTI DI UN MALEFICIO..

CASCO DAL SONNO!
IO PURE!
NON È L'ORA DI DORMIRE: IL MAGO CI ASPETTA!

PROVIAMO A TIRARLI SU!
IMPOSSIBILE...

Il mago di OZ
NEL RACCONTO DI MARIA ROSARIA BERARDI, TRATTO DAL FILM OMONIMO

il MAGO di OZ
EDIZIONI S.A.S. TORINO

In 1945, *The Wizard of Oz* was released in Austria. Shown here is the front cover of the program for *Das Zauberhafte Land. Photo: Tim McGowan*

magazine dated September 16, 1939. "The story is a fantasy for children. . . . Though comparatively little known in Britain, some nine million copies have been sold in the U.S.A."

Between fall of 1939 and early 1940, *Oz* had already been exported to such countries as Canada, Great Britain, Mexico, Sweden, Belgium, and France. During 1938, Loew's foreign gross had reached a new all-time high, the biggest market (not surprisingly) being the rest of the English-speaking world. When Marcus Loew died, he had left a brother and two sons in Loew's Incorporated. By 1939 only one of the sons, Arthur Loew, remained with the company. Serving as the head of Loew's foreign distributing and theatre operations, Arthur would spend four to six months of the year abroad overseeing 28 foreign theatres, 126 sales offices in 47 countries, and 3 synchronization studios.

Yet amidst political unrest, many foreign countries did not receive *The Wizard of Oz* until several years after its U.S. release. The advent of World War II in 1939 had cast a shadow of gloom and despair over much of the world. While the desire for fantasy and escapism from the harsh realities of everyday life may have been at an all-time high for the people of many nations, luxuries such as an afternoon at the cinema became an infrequent commodity. Of least priority was the continued practice of releasing American-made films on the foreign market, worldwide. (Indeed, just prior to the domestic release of *The Wizard of Oz*, Loew's had lost its $1.5 million Italian market. As the Nazis infiltrated other countries, the company ultimately lost control over all of its European theatres and distribution channels.) With relations between warring countries at a standstill, the potential to recoup additional profits from foreign distributions was null and void. As a result, films released during wartime received very little international exposure; despite its Technicolor glories, *The Wizard of Oz* was no exception. It wasn't until after the war that the film enjoyed many of its original premieres abroad.

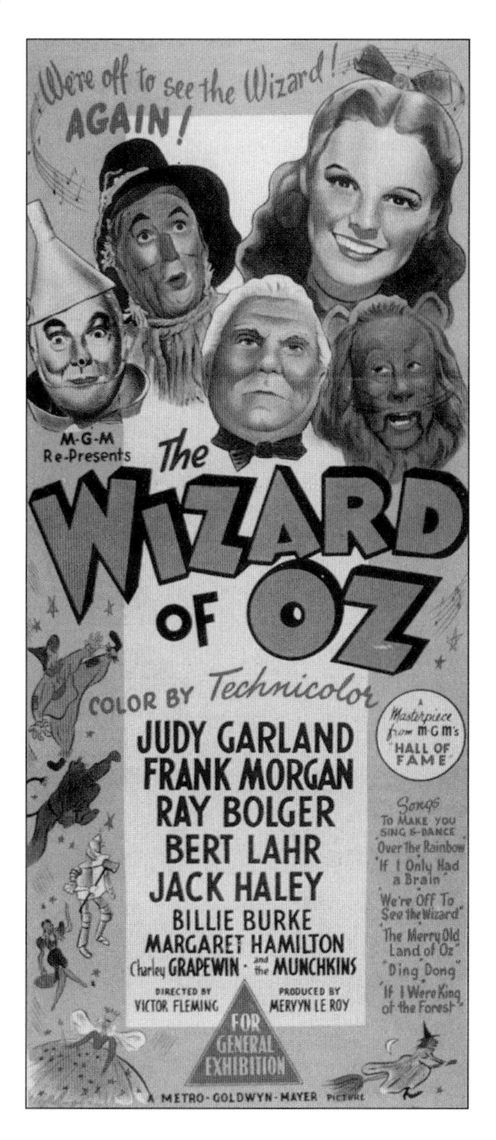

A daybill poster heralding an Australian re-release, circa 1949. ***Photo: Tim McGowan***

A publicity still for Metro's *On Borrowed Time*, 1939, uses the Witch's hourglass and stars Sir Cedric Hardwicke, Lionel Barrymore, and Bobs Watson to visually convey the film's central conflict. *Courtesy Photofest*

Epilogue

AFTEREFFECTS OF M-G-MAGIC

The Wizard of Oz is much more than a visual treat. It is a really human document, one with a lesson in it, one of the few to which grandfather can take his grandchild and both of them find entertaining . . . it is a piece of screen entertainment which can be shown every year from now on.

— *Hollywood Spectator*,
September 2, 1939

In 1941, Shirley Temple's beloved Oz-book collection still occupied the prominent first-row shelf in her bookcase. *Courtesy Rita Dubas*

Since its 1939 premiere, *The Wizard of Oz* has been a mainstay of our popular culture. At the February 29, 1940, Academy Awards ceremony, Harold Arlen and E. Y. Harburg's "Over the Rainbow" was recognized as the Best Song of 1939. Herbert Stothart was likewise honored for composing *Oz*'s original background score. *The Wizard of Oz* was also nominated in a number of other categories, including Best Picture. Cedric Gibbons and William A. Horning were nominated for Art Direction, and A. Arnold Gillespie was nominated for Special Effects, the first year for this category.[1] Judy Garland received a miniature Oscar as Outstanding Juvenile of the Screen, and she delighted the crowd with her rendition of "Over the Rainbow," which was fast becoming her signature song. During World War II, "Over the Rainbow" became an anthem of promise and hope; in postwar times, it was a sentimental standard; and in later years, it became a plaintive epitaph for the entertainer who first introduced it. *The Wizard of Oz* was revived in theatres as late as 1942. At this time, the Tams-Witmark script for stage productions of *Oz*, while loosely based on Baum's book, interpolated "music of the screen version," including "The Jitterbug." Theatrical re-releases of the film in 1949 and 1955 underscored the picture's appeal for upcoming generations, culminating in traditional showings on television beginning in 1956.

Shirley Temple makes peace between her *Blue Bird* co-stars Eddie Collins and Gale Sondergaard. *Twentieth Century-Fox; courtesy Rita Dubas*

Years of repeated *Oz* television broadcasts have dissipated any similarities with *Snow White* that may have been apparent in 1939. In fact, *The Wizard of Oz* influenced other motion pictures of its day—long before it became an everyday icon, woven into our national consciousness through film, sitcoms, editorial cartoons, and literature. The most blatant imitation to immediately follow *The Wizard of Oz* was Twentieth Century-Fox's *The Blue Bird*. Released as a theatrical roadshow in December 1939 before its general release in February 1940, *The Blue Bird* also enjoyed prior history as a classic play and silent film. Most significantly, *The Blue Bird* featured child-star phenomenon Shirley Temple.

Temple was enamored of the Oz stories. And she had previously acted with Frank Morgan, Margaret Hamilton, Buddy Ebsen, Jack Haley, Bert Lahr, and the Cairn terrier who became Toto in Metro's

[1] *Gone With the Wind* swept the awards ceremony, including the Oscar for Art Direction. The Special Effects award went to *The Rains Came*.

Oz. Rumors about Shirley Temple playing Dorothy in an Oz production circulated throughout the mid-1930s. *Screen Play* for October 1935 confided that "Darryl Zanuck, new production head of Twentieth Century-Fox, will case [Temple] for the part of Dorothy in *The Wizard of Oz*." A 1937 New York *Sunday Mirror* article about the young actress noted, "Free suggestion to Mr. Darryl Zanuck et al: How about Shirley as Dorothy in a talkie version of *The Wizard of Oz*." On February 19, 1938, the *New York Times* observed that the success of *Snow White* had generated "a wild search by producers for comparable fantasies." The article also mentioned that Fox was anxious to purchase *Oz* from Samuel Goldwyn with Shirley Temple in mind.[2] M-G-M's purchase of the story was a setback for both Fox and Temple. By April 1938, the press reported of Temple, "The greatest disappointment of her brief and eminently griefless career is that she will not be able to play Dorothy in *The Wizard of Oz*. Now and again there was talk of Mr. Zanuck buying the story from Samuel Goldwyn. . . . But it now has gone to Metro, and the role to Judy Garland."

The Blue Bird was heavily criticized for being a direct *Oz* imitation. Indeed, the similarities appear to be more than coincidental. The film begins in sepia-tone before shifting to a fantasy dream sequence in Technicolor. The story is also that of a journey, a search for the happiness that will make the home environment complete. Co-starring with Shirley Temple are Eddie Collins and Gale Sondergaard as the personifications of the family bulldog and cat, respectively. Collins's performance is a mimic of Bert Lahr's Cowardly Lion combined with the Three Stooges' Curly Howard. He quakes and guffaws throughout, particularly in a graveyard scene reminiscent of the Haunted Forest in M-G-M's *Oz*. Sondergaard's role is interesting when one considers that the year prior she had abandoned the role of the Wicked Witch in *The Wizard of Oz* when it was determined that the character would be a crone—not a sleek villainess in the Disney Evil Queen mold. Sondergaard's cat is sly and sensuous; and bits of her dialogue indicate the direction she may have taken as the *Oz* Witch.

[2] At precisely the same time, the story research department at Walt Disney Productions had drawn up synopses of the fourteen Frank Baum Oz books. An interoffice communication noted, "An analysis of our fan mail...reveals that there have been more requests for us to adapt the Oz books than for any other material...We are currently investigating the rights to these books..." One treatment for *The Wizard of Oz* served as a vehicle for Mickey Mouse in the Dorothy role, transported to Oz with Pluto and Donald Duck. Goofy and Minnie Mouse would also appear, and it was suggested that development of "The Little Humbug Wizard" might "easily surpass Dopey's excellent performance."

Other *Oz*-inspired touches in *The Blue Bird* include: Light, an ethereal starlet who hovers protectively—not unlike Glinda—in a ball of phosphorescence; individual musical themes for each character; a dramatic chase through a palace; animated trees; and a spectacular forest fire, intended to rival Metro's cyclone. Additionally, "Someday You'll Find Your Bluebird," a ballad sung by Temple but cut from the release version of *The Blue Bird*, is evocative of "Over the Rainbow."

While popular response to *Snow White and the Seven Dwarfs* and *The Wizard of Oz* paved the way for renewed interest in film fantasy, there was no great influx of like productions during the early 1940s. Reports of Jules Verne's *20,000 Leagues Under the Sea* and *Around the World in Eighty Days* following *Oz* on the screen never reached fruition. By 1939, Disney had temporarily lost interest in Oz in favor of preliminary work for *Alice in Wonderland*, *Bambi*, and *The Little Mermaid*. (Walt Disney would eventually acquire rights to the other Baum Oz books, and in 1957 began *The Rainbow Road to Oz*, another discarded feature that was to have showcased the Mouseketeers.) Competing animator Max Fleischer bore the distinction of producing the second full-length animated feature in 1939's *Gulliver's Travels*. Meanwhile, Disney's adaptation of another children's classic, *Pinocchio*, was being touted at the same time in anticipation of its early 1940 debut. *Pinocchio* was followed by Disney's controversial epic *Fantasia*. Alexander Korda's brilliant Technicolor version of *The Thief of Bagdad* also premiered in 1940.

References to *The Wizard of Oz* in other pictures of the era were more subtle than blatant. Terrytoons featured a Temperamental Lion in one of its Technicolor shorts in 1940—a character based directly on Bert Lahr's *Oz* performance. Another Terrytoons short played on the familiarity of the song "We're Off to See the Wizard" when a cartoon character falls in a trash heap and emerges looking like the Tin Man. "Over the Rainbow" can be heard in the 1941 Betty Grable picture *Hot Spot*, and the background scoring for the crystal-gazing scene in Professor Marvel's wagon can be heard in an early 1940s public-service announcement in which Joan Crawford promotes a children's charity.

Few films in postwar years acknowledged *Oz*. Abbott and Costello's musical *Jack and the Beanstalk* (1952) begins as a modern story in sepia-tone and switches to a color dream sequence (*Super*cine*color*, to be exact). The picture also reincarnates real-life characters in its fantasy portion. The Supreme Intelligence alien of

1953's science fiction nightmare, *Invaders From Mars*, resembles the Wizard's disembodied head contained in a crystal ball. Disney's *Sleeping Beauty* (1959) features a green-skinned villainess whose castle is guarded by armored goons. Like *Oz*, three characters infiltrate the castle to rescue another who has been imprisoned, but not before a chase ensues. *Snow White and the Three Stooges* (1961) was *Oz* scriptwriter Noel Langley's last screenplay. The picture features a traveling caravan (not unlike Professor Marvel's wagon); an hourglass filled with red sand, the emptiness of which signifies Snow White's death; and a broomstick-riding witch whose costume is strikingly similar to Margaret Hamilton's. The *Snow White* Witch meets her demise by plummeting from the sky to her death—as does the *Oz* Witch in an early script draft. (Even the stuffed crocodile hanging from the ceiling, which Langley designated as decor for the *Oz* Witch's castle, turned up in *Snow White*.)

Actual costumes and props from *The Wizard of Oz* could rarely be recycled because of their fantastic nature and recognizability. Still, several oversized lily pads, transplanted from Munchkinland, appear in *Tarzan Finds a Son!* (1939). A witch wearing Margaret Hamilton's *Oz* costume is among the ghouls assembled in M-G-M's 1940 short *Three Dimensional Murder*. Professor Marvel's wooded ravine was used in *Gone With the Wind* in the scene where Ashley chops kindling. The screen door to the Gale farmhouse appears in *The Philadelphia Story* (1940). Miss Gulch's basket appears on the general store counter in *Young Thomas Edison* (1940), and the Wicked Witch's basket, used to hold Toto hostage, is carried to a picnic by Robert Walker in *Till the Clouds Roll By* (1946). The outstanding footage of the cyclone resurfaced in M-G-M's *Cabin in the Sky* (1943) and *High Barbaree* (1947). (Could the *Oz* twister also have inspired the title of Republic Pictures' 1941 western, *Kansas Cyclone*?) Margaret O'Brien carries the same basket used by Judy Garland in *Oz* in Mervyn LeRoy's 1949 remake of *Little Women*. A few altered Munchkin costumes double as circus garb in *Billy Rose's Jumbo* (1962), and the Witch's hourglass can be seen in the background of scenes in *Babes on Broadway* (1941) and *Diane* (1956). Finally, the patchwork quilt that covers Judy Garland as she revives from her delirium to realize, "There's no place like home," was used again in the Wallace Beery-Marjorie Main picture, *Rationin'* (1943).

There are few events in our popular culture that Americans have experienced collectively as a people over generations. *The Wizard of*

Actress Rose Langdon donned Margaret Hamilton's Wicked Witch costume in the Pete Smith short *Three Dimensional Murder* (M-G-M, 1940).

Oz bears such distinction. *Oz* bridges generation gaps with the immediacy of instant recognition: Who among us doesn't know who Dorothy and Toto are? *Oz* is a common element in which we can all share the humor of its familiarity, whether it be a parody on *Saturday Night Live* or the punchline in a comic strip. Perhaps the closest comparable forms of popular entertainment include television reruns of *I Love Lucy*, as well as the now-classic 1960s TV comedies that have achieved cult following. If *Oz* was an exciting novelty in 1939, it is television which has firmly entrenched its status. By way of television's intimate nature, *Oz* has been invited into our homes, our living rooms, our lives.

It has been declared that every film made since *The Wizard of Oz* has contained some reference to it. This is statistically improbable, and presupposes the viability of crosswalking *Oz*'s present influence with the culture of 1939. However, each succeeding generation has experienced the annual television broadcasts of *Oz* as an indelible psychological imprint. What *is* likely is that that a growing number of creative baby boomers who became film producers and directors in the 1970s and '80s, have paid homage to *Oz* on screen, either

The basket carried by Judy Garland throughout *The Wizard of Oz* is used again by Margaret O'Brien in Mervyn LeRoy's 1949 production of *Little Women*. O'Brien's co-stars are (from left to right): June Allyson, Elizabeth Taylor, Mary Astor, Janet Leigh, and Lucile Watson.

subtly or blatantly.[3] Such examples include the futuristic *Zardoz* (1973), in which Sean Connery uncovers an *Oz*-like hoax; *Alice Doesn't Live Here Anymore* (1974); *The Phantom of Hollywood* (1974); *Annie Hall* (1977); and *20th Century Oz* (1977), an Australian musical spoof ("Follow the yellow rock road."). *Time Bandits* (1980) has some *Oz*-styled features, and was designated as "*The Wizard of Oz* of the '80s" by one critic. *Gremlins* (1984) includes a Miss Gulch-like character, and *Pee Wee's Big Adventure* (1985) features the Miss Gulch/Witch theme music. *Oz* is parodied in Robin Williams's banter in *Good Morning, Vietnam* (1986); and still more allusions occur in *Honey, I Shrunk the Kids* (1989), *Gremlins 2: The New Batch* (1990), and *Freddy's Dead: The Final Nightmare* (1991). *Oz* references litter David Lynch's violent and convoluted *Wild at Heart* (1990). By today's standards, it is indeed a rare film that *does not* reference *The Wizard of Oz*. More recent instances include *Casper* (1995); *Toy Story* (1995); *Jumanji* (1995); *A Very Brady Sequel* (1996); *The Hunchback of Notre Dame*

[3] In 1998, *Titanic* director James Cameron told *People* magazine, "To this day, I've never found a movie I like more than *The Wizard of Oz*. I loved it when I was a kid, I loved it when I was a teenager, and I still love it."

(1996); and, of course, *Twister* (1996), the thriller that follows storm chasers through the launch of their experimental data-retrieval system nicknamed Dorothy.

In 1996, a music phenomenon surfaced involving *The Wizard of Oz*, which caused the greatest controversy since disc jockeys played the Beatles' *Abbey Road* album backwards to hear the cryptic message, "Paul is dead." The furor stems from a purported synchronicity between *Oz* and Pink Floyd's rock album *The Dark Side of the Moon*. (Strange bedfellows if ever, oh ever, there was!) Proponents of the match balk at the British band's denial of the connection, and are oblivious to the fact that *Dark Side of the Moon* was released in 1973—long before home videocassettes could make such an exacting ruse feasible. Still the rumors persist, unlikely to soon fade, serving to lend sustenance to the greater Oz legend.

According to Floyd disciples, pairing the classic film and classic recording results in an uncanny series of coincidences. In fact, entire Internet websites have been devoted to such postulating. When a compact disc of *Moon* is started after the third roar of M-G-M's Leo the Lion at the beginning of *Oz*, the following (and most apparent) similarities occur.

◆ When Dorothy and Toto run away from the Kansas farm to escape Miss Gulch, lyrics from the song "Time" caution, "No one told you when to run/You missed the starting gun."

◆ The ringing cash register that begins the song "Money" goes off precisely at the switch from black and white to opulent Technicolor.

◆ As Glinda appears in Munchkinland, "Money" cynically comments, "Don't give me that do-goody good bullshit."

◆ The Wicked Witch's arrival on the scene, and Dorothy's surprise at her appearance, is a visual match for the lyrics from "Us and Them" ("Black and blue . . . and who knows which is which [witch]/And who is who.")

◆ When the brainless Scarecrow dances on the yellow brick road, the song "Brain Damage" quips, "Got to keep the loonies on the path."

◆ During the Tin Man's speech about being heartless, Dorothy puts her ear to his hollow chest as *Dark Side* closes with a pulsing heartbeat.

The skillful crafting of special effects and music combined with make-up, wardrobe, and, of course, an ensemble of talented actors make *The Wizard of Oz* truly unique in film history. It is a rare motion picture that coalesces these elements artfully, succeeds in doing so, and has the inexplicable ability to sustain its appeal across generations and cultures and over time. If *The Wizard of Oz* were to be made today, its production costs would far exceed its original $3 million. Its special effects would largely be computer generated—and likely more grandiose. And its cast would be peopled with megastars.

But the *Oz* of 1939 not only sustains but continues to influence the medium that was comparatively primitive at the time it was conceived. Its miniature farmhouse, monkeys, and witches that fly courtesy of piano wire remain acceptable if not wholly believable—sentimental reminders of a time when Hollywood created such illusions "the old-fashioned way." But believability is in the eye of the beholder. The stronghold of *Oz* has deeply psychological roots that override any hint of disbelief. The threat of a pet's demise, unwilling separation from family, and the endangerment of friends easily parallel the darkest fears of the youngest viewers, especially in today's world. Children weaned on the sophistication of modern movies and video games crammed with gratuitous special effects still shudder at the Witch, cheer Dorothy and her friends, weep at the film's conclusion—and still believe.

The men and women who created *The Wizard of Oz* still believe as well. For most, *Oz* was just another picture, another job within a studio system engineered for optimal productivity at its peak. For those individuals, the appeal of *Oz* has also evolved over time, as shared through the following observations.

> *The Wizard of Oz* was a landmark in make-up. I don't think anything has been done to exceed it. I feel that for a fantasy, it still holds up so well today—the forerunner for what's being done today.
>
> —William Tuttle, make-up man

> *The Wizard of Oz* was one of the greatest pictures ever filmed.
>
> —Jack Young, make-up man

> I never get tired of watching [*Oz*]. Make-up prosthetics have improved very much [but] for its time frame, the make-up in *The Wizard of Oz* was sensational when you realize every *idea* had to be invented because that sort of thing had never been done before.
>
> —Del Armstrong, make-up man

[*Oz*] was probably one of the greatest things I've ever done in all the years that I pursued my profession after that. . . . It's one of the few films of our time that is timeless.

—Howard Smit, make-up man

Probably one of the best productions of fantasy that's ever been produced.

—Duncan Spencer, art department

I have four grandchildren, eight to fourteen, who love running the tape of *Oz* and seeing what my part of it constituted. This really gives me a little thrill; they are obviously proud of having granddad a participant in the making of the movie.

—George Gibson, scenic art director

I would like to see it again. . . . I thought it was terrific! I still hear, "Why can't I fly over the rainbow?"

—James Roth, set designer

I can appreciate the magic of [*Oz*] and the purity of Dorothy. It's wholesome, innocent, and charming.

—Betty Ann Bruno, child actress

[*Oz*] was quite unusual at that time. It became a legend.

—Lois January, actress/singer

The picture turned out to be very good. All of us . . . we just didn't give it any thought . . . it was just a picture. I think it's wonderful for children!

—Dona Massin, assistant dance director

I made forty-nine other films, but who remembers them? But when I'm dead and gone, *The Wizard of Oz* will be on forever. I'm very happy I was a part of this picture. It's a once-in-a-lifetime role!

—Jack Haley

Long after I'm gone, I will be remembered as The Scarecrow. All the people connected with [*Oz*] will be remembered as being a part of that one beautiful moment captured on film. I'm very grateful for this!

—Ray Bolger

Oz was the most spectacular thing I've done. . . . I think it's very flattering for me and the picture that people still remember it.

—Margaret Hamilton

[*Oz*] covers all ages—little children, people my own age, and older people. It pleases them. I think Dorothy is a darling character. Just darling.

—Judy Garland

Appendix One

TOTO

A Dog's Life

Many thanks
by Carl Spitz
& Toto to
Mr. Bill Holden.

Toto strikes an obedient pose for this 1940 portrait. The still is inscribed by owner Carl Spitz and "pawtographed" by the dog as well.
Courtesy Tod Machin

Many of the actors associated with M-G-M's *The Wizard of Oz* went on to enjoy long show-business careers. Except for Margaret Hamilton, who according to her son, Hamilton Meserve, was blacklisted for being Republican during the 1940s, *Oz* brought its actors an immediate and heightened success as screen and stage favorites. On rare occasions, though, the actors would be reteamed. Margaret Hamilton proved herself meddlesome again in the Mickey Rooney-Judy Garland picture *Babes in Arms* (1939). In 1940, Frank Morgan and Billie Burke played opposite one another in Metro's *The Ghost Comes Home* and *Hullabaloo*. In a 1945 Armed Forces Radio Service musical comedy production of *Dick Tracy*, Judy Garland played Snowflake to Frank Morgan's Vitamin Flintheart (Bing Crosby was Dick Tracy). Both Garland and Morgan were cast in M-G-M's film adaptation of *Annie Get Your Gun* (1950); however, Garland's nervous exhaustion forced her out of the picture, and Morgan died during production in 1949. (The actors were replaced by Betty Hutton and Louis Calhern.) Ray Bolger would work with Garland again in *The Harvey Girls* (1946). And in 1953, Billie Burke and Margaret Hamilton appeared together in "Dear Amanda," a television production of *Summer Theatre*. But what became of Toto, the valiant little terrier so crucial to the plot of *The Wizard of Oz*?

Two budding stars: Shirley Temple and Terry in *Bright Eyes*. Of her canine co-star in the same picture, Jane Withers said, "I just loved it to pieces!" *Twentieth Century-Fox; courtesy Rita Dubas*

For the casting of Dorothy's faithful companion, producer Mervyn LeRoy apparently considered whether the part should be played by a true canine or an actor dressed like a dog. In either case, a decision was also needed as to what kind of dog Toto would be—and if the "dog" should talk. (The debate over Toto's powers of speech may be traced to the eighth Oz book, *Tik-Tok of Oz*, wherein it is revealed that Toto always had the ability to talk in Oz.) Ultimately, this important decision fell to the opinions of Oz book lovers who had written to the studio. The consensus: Toto should be a real dog, should not talk, and should be a terrier.

The part of Toto was by no means a cameo. This is evident in the finished film, but more so in various drafts of the script that further

In 1936, Terry appeared with Spencer Tracy in *Fury*.

develop the canine's heroics. A July 25, 1938, version of the script, for instance, actually has the Wicked Witch throwing the basket-encased pup into the river. (In the finished film, Toto escapes before the Witch acts on her threat.) A very suspenseful scene follows.

> [The basket] floats along, striking against jutting rocks. It is sinking gradually. Little whining noises come from inside. . . . The basket is tossed over [a waterfall]. . . . The basket has struck a rock. It has burst the catch. Toto does a Monte Cristo and pulls himself out. . . . He gasps, then shakes himself. He turns, barks a couple of times sharply, then starts leaping from rock to rock toward the bank of the river. He reaches one big rock, finds the distance to the one beyond almost too much for him. It looks for a moment as though he is not going to be able to make it, but he runs back a little way, makes a flying jump, and just barely manages to pull himself up onto the bank of the river.

The same script sees Toto's stamina through the next scene as he makes his way through the Haunted Forest to find Dorothy's companions. Here he gallops along through thorn bushes and jagged rocks, always at full speed. Upon reaching a stream, he takes a quick lap of water, then leaps the stream and goes on at renewed speed. "The whole feeling of this scene," notes the script, "should be of continuous movement, like the Northwest Mounted going to the rescue."

The dilemma that opens *The Wizard of Oz* (Toto allegedly bites Miss Gulch, trespasses in her garden, and chases her cat) was also the subject of debate in various drafts of the script. Among Toto's proposed misdoings: jumping in the butter churn and ruining "ten pounds of good butter"; biting Maggie Stoodle's hand when Dorothy brings him to school (the bite required cauterization and was feared to cause lockjaw); chewing the arithmetic papers; eating Walter Gulch's lunch; and biting Walter's leg.

Although billed in *Oz* publicity as "the wonder dog, for whom the entire country was searched," Toto was actually a female Cairn terrier named Terry. Metro contended that "the most important dog role since Rin Tin Tin was a star . . . went to Terry, a two-year-old

Cairn terrier, chosen after tests of hundreds of animals and inspection of photos of pet dogs from all over the United States, to play Toto, Judy Garland's friend and protector in *The Wizard of Oz*."[1] Terry was owned by Carl Spitz, the leading trainer of movie dogs in the 1930s and '40s. At the height of his career, Spitz also owned and operated the Hollywood Dog Training School in North Hollywood. *Oz* was far from Terry's first picture, but studio publicity would have the public believe otherwise.

> Terry came as a surprise. While the producer of the picture, Mervyn LeRoy, was searching for the dog, Carl Spitz, a San Fernando Valley dog fancier, trained Terry for two months, teaching all the tricks in the original L. Frank Baum book. . . .
>
> "Here's your dog, all up for the part," he reported, when he submitted Terry for inspection. . . .

[1] Terry was actually born in 1933, making her closer to five—not two—at the time of *Oz*.

Young Judy Garland poses with her equally charming *Oz* co-star. The official caption for poses in this series is: "*Toto—the Trick-star* . . . Judy Garland, as Dorothy, and Toto her pet go through many thrilling adventures together in Metro-Goldwyn-Mayer's all Technicolor production *The Wizard of Oz*. Here Judy and Toto brush up a bit on the tricks they do in the new film, produced by Mervyn LeRoy and directed by Victor Fleming."

A portrait of Virginia Weidler and her "little dog, too" in *Bad Little Angel*, 1939. By this time, Terry's name had been permanently changed to Toto.

> Terry could fight, chase a witch, sit up, "speak," catch an apple thrown from a tree, and took an immediate liking to Judy Garland. Frank Morgan, Ray Bolger, Bert Lahr, Jack Haley, and the rest of the cast were accepted on first acquaintance with the pup who won the role without a [screen] test.

A 1940 *American Girl* article accurately relates that Terry was left in the hands of Spitz, abandoned in lieu of an unpaid boarding bill. (The original owner was frustrated because the dog could not be housebroken.) It also describes an amusing anecdote about another film Terry appeared in.

> Once, in a movie scene, Toto's action called for pulling the end of a tablecloth so that a big ham on the table would roll to the floor. Although Toto always did her part perfectly, various other things would go wrong. The scene had to be repeated so often that she became quite an expert in this little stunt, and enjoyed it. One day, at the home of Mr. Spitz, dinner was on the table and the family was preparing to sit down. Suddenly the tablecloth began to move—and before anyone could stop her, Toto had displayed her movie stunt all over again!

Few reviewers of *The Wizard of Oz* paid notice to Toto. *Harper's Bazaar* for August 1939, noted, however: "Dorothy is played by Judy Garland, and her dog Toto—who must rescue his mistress, dance on his hind legs, and bark on signal—is *en chair et en os* a Cairn terrier named Terry." Toto's on-screen feats were described in *St. Nicholas* magazine: "Toto learned . . . to escape nonchalantly from a locked basket, like Houdini."[2] Amy H. Croughton, writing "Scanning the Screen" for the *Rochester* [New York] *Times-Union*, devoted a portion of her August 18, 1939, column to the dog.

> What we would like to know is what Toto thought about *The Wizard of Oz* as he scuttled busily through the picture. Victor Fleming . . . evidently realized that Toto was a very

[2] After *Oz* began showing on television, Carl Spitz's daughter, Annemarie, remembered her father remarked that "'trying to get Toto to stay in the basket was difficult!' I guess it was something she didn't like . . . a real feeling of insecurity."

> important member of the cast and, in the end, gave him much more prominence than he had in Baum's original story. . . . [The Oz characters] must have been somewhat amazing to a little dog like Toto at his first introduction to them, but he appears to enjoy the association . . . and proves himself a true helpful comrade when he performs that trick of pulling aside the curtain in the castle of the Wizard and revealing the old showoff for just what he is.

Terry was fondly remembered by those who had the opportunity to know her on the *Oz* set as an impeccably trained dog, silently directed by hand signals—as were all canine thespians. "Before and after filming," recalled make-up artist Charles Schram, "[the dog's] trainer would give her small tidbits of some food so that he could command the dog's attention out of camera range." Terry's attentiveness was the result of carefully regimented training sessions at the Spitz kennels. Hutzi Nickels, Carl Spitz's oldest daughter, was especially impressed with the way her father handled Terry to appear overcome by the poisonous poppies. "When Dad was teaching [Terry] in the movie for the poppy field, she had to be 'knocked out,' like she was sleeping. I just found it fascinating that a little dog who was so lively could act like she was dead almost . . . have her legs hang down on one side and her head hang down in the middle, and Dad would pick her up like that!"

On days when Carl Spitz was working on another picture, Terry was accompanied to the *Oz* set by Jack Weatherwax, an associate of Spitz. Charles Schram further remembered, "Toto would stay in her small kennel in a station wagon outside the soundstage. Jack Weatherwax would bring her in on the stage after the set was lit and rehearsals finished. After the scene was shot, out she would go again." Jack Haley recalled, "Toto was terrific to work with. [She] was trained so beautifully." Margaret Hamilton remembered feeling concern for the dog who had to cope with wind machines and charging Winkie guards: "The poor little thing almost had a nervous breakdown. It was a very confused picture for *anyone* to be around." (In later years, the actress even claimed she had asked if it wasn't possible to use another dog that wasn't so terrified.)

Little Terry shared the Spitz kennels with some notable celebrity canines. Among them Buck, the Saint Bernard from *Call of the Wild*, Prince, the Great Dane from *Wuthering Heights*, Musty, the mastiff from *Dangerous Days*, and Mr. Binkie, the Scottie from *The Light That Failed*. In a tongue-in-cheek article titled, "After

All, Why Does Screen Give All Awards to Bipedal Actors," the *New York Herald Tribune* noted that Mr. Binkie had become as much a screen "name" as his kennel mate "the Cairn terrier [who] now plays Toto to Judy Garland's Dorothy in *The Wizard of Oz*. Binkie and Toto have a lot to talk about when they get home these nights."

For *The Wizard of Oz*, Metro contended that Terry spent two weeks living with Judy Garland so that both actors could become better acquainted prior to filming. *Child Life* magazine "quoted" Garland as claiming, "They let me take Toto home with me so he'd get used to me. He slept in a little box in my bedroom. I fed him every day. . . . We all wanted to buy him from his owner." While charming, such an anecdote was borne of publicists' fabrication. Judy Garland's evenings were spent learning lines, dating, or attending parties and premieres; Terry was busy rehearsing stunts. The only time the two had available to interact was during the day, something Carl Spitz's niece, Hango Dennison, confirmed. "Movie dogs are trained to act as though they belong to the person they're with," she said. "Movie dogs have to be acclimated to people, so Terry and Mr. Binkie were both kept in the [Spitz] house." Not that Carl Spitz would have considered letting Terry out of his sight. Spitz was especially protective of his dogs, and was wary of the potential for them to become injured, or even poisoned.

At each stop of his 1940 Hollywood Motion Picture Dog Review, Carl Spitz demonstrated the silent cue technique necessary for his dogs to perform on screen. Spectators were treated to reenactments of some of the dogs' famous scenes. ***Courtesy Hutzi Nickels***

After *Oz*, the Spitz family became so accustomed to visitors wanting to see "Toto" that the family permanently changed the dog's moniker without incident. For years, Carl Spitz, Jr., believed he was responsible for causing Toto's death, circa 1943. "I turned the dog loose playing with it in the yard. It got out, ran up on the street and got hit," Spitz admitted. And while Spitz's childhood memories were murky ("I'm going on hearsay . . . that was many, many, many years ago."), his recollection of the incident was accurate; but the dog was a Pekingese belonging to his sister Hutzi. Mr. Spitz may hereafter be relieved of his burden: Toto died of natural causes sometime toward the end of World War II.[3] She was buried at Spitz's North Hollywood kennel, located at 12350 Riverside Drive in the San Fernando Valley. In 1958 the city built the Ventura freeway and made the Spitz family relocate the kennels to a new location. The original kennel property has since been supplanted by apartments.

[3] More specifically, Toto died of "some kind of kidney infection," related Beverly Allen, who was Carl Spitz's kennel man at the time of *The Wizard of Oz*. Allen explained, "She drank enormous amounts of water . . . as they get older, some [dogs] come up with that disease."

Hildegarde "Hutzi" Nickels, Carl Spitz's oldest daughter, lounges with her pals Toto and Mr. Binkie, circa 1938. Both dogs were favorite housepets of the Spitz children. Toto was especially protective of Carl Spitz, Jr., and stood vigil as he napped. ***Courtesy Hutzi Nickels***

THE FILMS OF TERRY/TOTO

Bright Eyes (Twentieth Century-Fox, 1934). James Dunn, Shirley Temple, Jane Withers; David Butler, director.

Ready For Love (Paramount, 1934). Richard Arlen, Ida Lupino; director n/a.

Dark Angel (United Artists, 1935). Fredric March, Merle Oberon; Sidney Franklin, director.

Fury (M-G-M, 1936). Spencer Tracy, Sylvia Sidney; Fritz Lang, director.

The Buccaneer (Paramount, 1938). Fredric March, Franciska Gaal, Walter Brennan; Cecil B. DeMille, director.

Barefoot Boy (Monogram, 1938). Marcia Mae Jones, Jackie Moran, Ralph Morgan (brother of "Wizard" Frank Morgan); director n/a.

The Wizard of Oz (M-G-M, 1939). Judy Garland, Frank Morgan; Victor Fleming, director.

The Women (M-G-M, 1939). Norma Shearer, Joan Crawford, Rosalind Russell; George Cukor, director.

Bad Little Angel (M-G-M, 1939). Virginia Weidler, Gene Reynolds, Guy Kibbee; William Thiele, director.

Son of the Navy (1940). James Dunn, Sarah Padden (tested for the role of Aunt Em); director n/a.

Calling Philo Vance (Warner Bros., 1940). James Stephenson; William Clemens, director.

Twin Beds (United Artists, 1942). George Brent, Joan Bennett, Margaret Hamilton ("Wicked Witch of the West"); Tim Whelan, director.

Appendix Two

CAST AND CREW

THE WIZARD OF OZ

Metro-Goldwyn-Mayer
Production #1060
(Release date: August 15, 1939)

Judy Garland amuses director Victor Fleming, actress Myrna Loy, and "Wizard" Frank Morgan on the *Oz* set. Morgan's son George reported that "Judy came over to the house a couple times to rehearse." At the time of *The Wizard of Oz*, the Morgans lived in Holmby Hills, a suburb of Beverly Hills. George believed that Judy's mother probably dropped her off, instead of staying through rehearsals. "Judy was a pretty independent kid even at a young age." But Morgan was twenty-two and didn't pay much notice to Judy given their age difference. Instead he thought to himself, "What's this precocious kid doing around here?"

Authors' Note. The on-screen listing of cast and crew members for *The Wizard of Oz* includes just forty credits. This abbreviated treatment was typical of films at the time. By today's standards, however, credits usually run long enough to accompany a complete musical overture at the end of a movie, acknowledging everyone from the payroll clerk to the caterer. In researching this book we continually came upon names of individuals who were in some way or another connected with the making of *Oz* but were not previously known for such. Although the following is by no means complete, it represents the most comprehensive and accurate list of credits to date for M-G-M's screen adaptation of *The Wizard of Oz*.[1]

JUDY GARLAND
as Dorothy

CAST

Dorothy Gale ....Judy Garland
Professor Marvel/Wizard/
Cabby/Doorman/Guard ....Frank Morgan
Hunk Andrews/Scarecrow ....Ray Bolger
Zeke/Cowardly Lion ....Bert Lahr
Hickory Twicker/Tin Woodman ....Jack Haley
Glinda, the Good Witch ....Billie Burke
Miss Gulch/Wicked Witch of the West ....Margaret Hamilton
Uncle Henry ....Charley Grapewin
Nikko ....Pat Walshe
Aunt Em ....Clara Blandick
Toto ....Toto (aka Terry)

RAY BOLGER
as The Scarecrow

THE MUNCHKINS

(Collectively billed as The Singer Midgets)

Gladys W. Allison
John Ballas
Franz "Mike" Balluck
Josefine Balluck
John T. Bambury
Charley Becker *(Mayor)*
Freda Betsky
Henry Boers
Theodore Boers
Christie Buresh
Eddie Buresh
Lida Buresh
Betty Ann Cain (child actress)
Mickey Carroll *(Second Fiddler)*

JACK HALEY
as The Tin Woodman

BERT LAHR
as The Cowardly Lion

[1] We were unable to identify positions for the following individuals but wish to acknowledge their contributions to production of *The Wizard of Oz*: Jane Harrison, Tom Held, W. E. Pohl, and Gerald F. Rocket.

JUDY GARLAND
as Dorothy

RAY BOLGER
as The Scarecrow

JACK HALEY
as The Tin Woodman

BERT LAHR
as The Cowardly Lion

Colonel Casper
Nona Cooper
Tommy Cottonaro *(Bearded Man)*
Elizabeth Coulter
"Idaho" Lewis Croft
Frank Cucksey *(Townsman #2)*
Billy Curtis *(City Father)*
Eugene S. David Jr.
Eulie H. David
Ethel W. Denis
Prince Denis *(Sergeant-at-Arms)*
Hazel I. Derthick
James D. "Major" Doyle
Carl M. "Kayo" Erickson *(Herald #2)*
Fern Formica *(Villager/Sleepyhead)*
Addie Eva Frank
Thaisa L. Gardner
Jakob "Jackie" Gerlich *(Lollipop Guild)*
William A. Giblin
Jack Glicken
Carolyn E. Granger
Joseph Herbst *(Soldier)*
Jakob Hofbauer
C. C. "Major Mite" Howerton *(Herald #3)*
Helen M. Hoy
Marguerite A. Hoy
James R. Hulse
Donna Jean Johnson (child actress)
Robert "Lord Roberts" Kanter
Eleanor Keaton (small-statured adult)
Charles E. Kelley
Jessie E. Kelley
Joan Kenmore (child actress)
Shirley Ann Kennedy (child actress)
Frank Kikel
Bernhard "Harry" Klima
Willi Koestner *(Soldier)*
Emma Koestner
Mitzi Koestner
Karl "Karchy" Kosiczky *(Herald #1/Sleepyhead)*
Adam Edwin "Eddie" Kozicki *(Fiddler)*
Joseph J. Koziel *(Townsman #1)*
Dolly F. Kramer
Emil Kranzler
Nita Krebs *(Lullaby League)*
"Little Jeane" LaBarbera
Hilda Lange
Johnny Leal
Ann Rice Leslie
Charles Ludwig
Dominick Magro
Carlos Manzo
Howard Marco
Gerard Marenghi *(Lollipop Guild)*
Bela Matina
Lajos "Leo" Matina
Matjus Matina
Patsy May (child actress)
Walter M.B. Miller *(Bespectacled Munchkin)*
George Ministeri *(Coach Driver)*
Priscilla Montgomery (child actress)
Harry Monty
Yvonne Moray Bistany *(Lullaby League)*
Olga C. Nardone *(Lullaby League)*
Nels P. Nelson
Margaret C.H. Nickloy
Franklin H. O'Baugh
William H. O'Docharty
Hildred C. Olson
Frank Packard
Nicholas "Nicky" Page *(Soldier)*
Leona M. Parks
Johnny Pizo

"Prince Leon" Polinsky
Lillian Porter
Eva Lee Quiney (child actress)
Meinhardt Raabe *(Coroner)*
Margaret "Margie" Raia
Matthew Raia *(City Father)*
"Little Billy" Rhodes *(Barrister)*
Gertrude H. Rice
Hazel Rice
Fredreich "Freddie" Retter *(Fiddler)*
Ruth L. Robinson
Sandor Roka
Jimmie Rosen
Charles F. Royale
Helen J. Royale
Stella A. Royale
Albert Ruddinger
Elly A. "Tiny Doll" Schneider
Frieda "Gracie Doll" Schneider
Hilda E. "Daisy Doll" Schneider
Kurt "Harry Doll" Schneider *(Lollipop Guild)*
Valerie Shepard (child actress)
Elsie R. Schultz
Charles Silvern
Garland "Earl" Slatten
Ruth E. Smith
Elmer Spangler
Parnell Elmer St.Aubin *(Soldier)*
Carl Stephan
Alta M. Stevens
George Suchsie
Charlotte V. Sullivan
August Clarence Swensen *(Soldier)*
Betty Tanner
Arnold Vierling
Gus Wayne *(Soldier)*
Victor Wetter *(Army Captain)*
Viola White (child actress)
Gracie G. Williams
Harvey B. Williams
Margaret Williams *(Villager/Sleepyhead)*
Johnny Winters *(Navy Commander)*
Marie Winters
Gladys V. Wolff
Murray Wood *(Soldier)*

WINGED MONKEYS

Buster Brody
Harry Cogg
Sid Dawson
Walter Miller
Harry Monty
Lee Murray
George Noison

WINKIES

Philip Harron
Mitchell Lewis *(Leader)*
Ambrose Schindler
Bob Steangelo
Harry Wilson

MARGARET HAMILTON
as the Wicked Witch

BILLIE BURKE
as The Good Witch

FRANK MORGAN
as The Wizard

NIKKO
Aide to The Wicked Witch

JUDY GARLAND
as Dorothy

EMERALD CITY CITIZENS

Lorraine Bridges
Tyler Brook
Charles Irwin
Lois January
Dona Massin
Elivda Rizzo
Oliver Smith
Ralph Sudam
Bobby Watson

DOUBLES

For Judy Garland . . . . Bobbie Koshay
For Frank Morgan . . . . Paul Adams
For Ray Bolger . . . . Stafford Campbell
For Bert Lahr . . . . Jim Jawcett, Pat Moran
For Jack Haley . . . . Harry Masters
For Margaret Hamilton . . . . Betty Danko
For Pat Walshe . . . . Freddie Retter

RAY BOLGER
as The Scarecrow

SPECIAL VOICES

Nick Angelo *(Munchkin)*
Billy Bletcher *(Mayor/Lollipop Guild/Munchkin)*
Robert Bradford *(Munchkin)*
Lorraine Bridges *(Lullaby League)*
Adriana Caselotti *(Juliet)*
Lois Clements *(Munchkin)*
Pinto Colvig *(Munchkin/Lollipop Guild)*
Ken Darby *(Winkie Leader)*
The Debutantes *(Optimistic Voices/Munchkins)*
Abe Dinovitch *(Apple Trees/Munchkin)*
Buddy Ebsen *(group Tin Man choruses)*
Zari Elmassian *(Munchkin)*
J.D. Jewkes *(Munchkin)*
Lois Johansen *(Munchkin)*
Virgil Johansen *(Munchkin)*
The King's Men Octet *(Munchkins)*
Betty Rome *(Lullaby League)*
The Rhythmettes *(Optimistic Voices)*
The St. Joseph's Choir *(Munchkins)*
Harry Stanton *(Lollipop Guild/Coroner/Munchkin)*
Georgia Stark *(deleted "King of Forest" tag)*

JACK HALEY
as The Tin Woodman

BERT LAHR
as The Cowardly Lion

George Stoll *(Munchkin)*
Carol Tevis *(Lullaby League)*

PRODUCER

Mervyn LeRoy
Assistants:
William Cannon
Barron Polan
Production Assistant:
Arthur Freed

DIRECTOR

Victor Fleming
Assistant:
Al Shoenberg
Uncredited:
George Cukor
Norman Taurog
Richard Thorpe
King Vidor

SCREENPLAY

Noel Langley
Florence Ryerson
Edgar Allan Woolf
Uncredited:
Irving Brecher
William Cannon
Herbert Fields
Arthur Freed
E. Y. Harburg
Samuel Hoffenstein
John Lee Mahin
Herman Mankiewicz
Jack Mintz
Ogden Nash
Sid Silvers

MARGARET HAMILTON
as the Wicked Witch

BILLIE BURKE
as The Good Witch

FRANK MORGAN
as The Wizard

NIKKO
Aide to The Wicked Witch

SCRIPT MANAGER

Wallace Worsley
Assistant:
Dave Marks

UNIT PRODUCTION

Charlie Chic (Department Head)
Joe Cook (Assistant)
Ulrich Busch (Unit Production Manager)
Keith Weeks (Unit Production Manager)

CASTING

W. L. Gordon (Assistant Casting Director)
Leonard Murphy

MUSICAL SCORE

Lyrics . . . . .E. Y. Harburg
Music . . . . .Harold Arlen
Musical Adaptation/Conductor . . . . .Herbert Stothart
Associate Conductor . . . . .George Stoll

Musical score incorporates the works of Felix Mendelssohn and Modest Moussorgsky

ORCHESTRAL AND VOCAL ARRANGEMENTS

Leo Arnaud
George Bassman
Murray Cutter
Ken Darby
Paul Marquardt
Conrad Salinger
Bob Stringer

JUDY GARLAND
as Dorothy

RAY BOLGER
as The Scarecrow

JACK HALEY
as The Tin Woodman

BERT LAHR
as The Cowardly Lion

PIANO ACCOMPANIST

Eddie Becker
Roger Edens (deleted "Over the Rainbow" reprise)

VIOLIN SOLOS

Toscha Seidel

DANCE DIRECTOR

Bobby Connolly
Assistants:
Arthur "Cowboy" Appell
Dona Massin
Busby Berkeley (deleted Scarecrow dance)

ART DEPARTMENT

Cedric Gibbons (Department Head)
William A. Horning (Associate/Unit Art Director)
Wade Rubottom (Associate/Unit Art Director)
Jack Martin Smith (Lead Sketch Artist)
Hugo Ballin
Malcolm Brown
Draftsmen:
Preston Ames
Ed Carfagno
Conklin
Marvin Connell
Harvey Gillett
William Hellen
K. Johnson
Ted Rich
James Roth
Russ Spencer
Steffgen
Marvin Summerfield
John Thompson
Leo Vasian
"Woody" Woodward

MARGARET HAMILTON
as the Wicked Witch

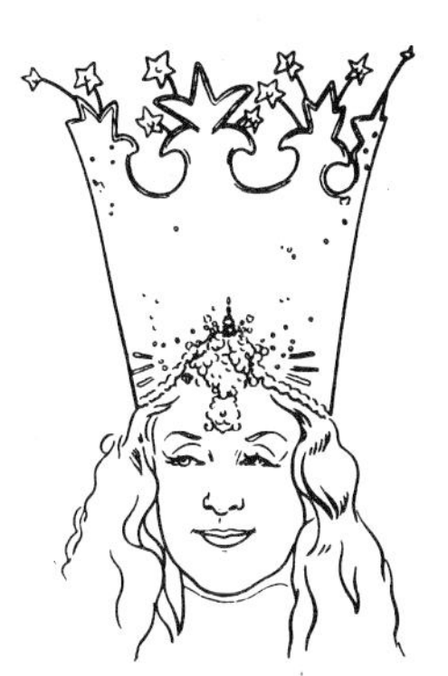

BILLIE BURKE
as The Good Witch

FRANK MORGAN
as The Wizard

NIKKO
Aide to The Wicked Witch

JUDY GARLAND
as Dorothy

RAY BOLGER
as The Scarecrow

JACK HALEY
as The Tin Woodman

BERT LAHR
as The Cowardly Lion

Grauman's Chinese Theatre decorations:
Elmer Sheeley
Backdrops:
George Gibson (Scenic Art Director)
Leo F. Atkinson (clouds)
John Coakley
Randall Duell
William Gibson
Clem Hall
F. Wayne Hill
Roy Perry
Clark M. Provins
Arthur Grover Rider
Duncan Spencer

PROPERTY SHOP

Special Effects:
A. Arnold Gillespie (Department Head)
Jack Gaylord (Assistant)
Marcel Delgado (miniature monkeys)
Mack Johnson
Jack McMaster
Hal Millar
Franklin Milton
Glenn E. Robinson

SET DECORATION

Edwin B. Willis (Department Head)
Ray O' Brien (Assistant)
Company Props:
Harry Edwards
Billy H. Scott
Charles B. Steiner

STAFF SHOP

Henry Greutert (Chief Plaster Sculptor)

CAMERA

John Arnold, A.S.C. (Department Head)
Harold Rosson, A.S.C. (First Cameraman)
Allen Davey, A.S.C. (cameraman provided by Technicolor)
Ray Ramsey
Sam Cohen
Max Fabian (special effects)

TECHNICOLOR

Color Director . . . . Natalie Kalmus
Associate . . . . Henri Jaffa
Technician . . . . George Cave
Technician . . . . Nelson Crodes
Technician . . . . Fred Detmers
Technician . . . . Henry Imus
Assistant . . . . Clifford Shirpser

RECORDING DIRECTOR

Douglas Shearer

SOUND

Gavin Burns
Chip Gaither (sound boom [microphone])

ELECTRICIANS

A. W. Brown
Chris Bergswich
Raymond Griffith
Shug Keeler

HEAD CAMERA GRIP

Pop Arnold

MARGARET HAMILTON
as the Wicked Witch

BILLIE BURKE
as The Good Witch

FRANK MORGAN
as The Wizard

NIKKO
Aide to The Wicked Witch

FILM EDITOR

Blanche Sewell
Ernie Grooney (Assistant)
Margaret Booth

MATTE PAINTINGS

Warren Newcombe

WARDROBE DEPARTMENT

Sam Kress (Department Head)
Costumes by Adrian
Jack Rohan (Dresser: Men)
Sheila O'Brien (Dresser: Women)
Rose Meltzer
Vera Mordaunt
Marian Parker
Marie Rose
John B. Scura
Marie Wharton

MAKE-UP DEPARTMENT

Character make-ups created by Jack Dawn (Department Head)
For Judy Garland . . . . .Webb Overlander
For Frank Morgan . . . . .Jack Dawn
For Ray Bolger . . . . .Norbert Miles
For Bert Lahr . . . . .Charles Schram
For Jack Haley .Lee Stanfield/Emile LaVigne
For Billie Burke . . . . .Lyle Wesley Dawn
For Margaret Hamilton . . . . .Jack Young
Josef Norin (Sculptor)
Gustaf Norin (Sculptor/Lab Technician)
Del Armstrong
Holly Bane
Don Cash
Jack Kevan
Louis LaCava
George Lane

JUDY GARLAND
as Dorothy

RAY BOLGER
as The Scarecrow

JACK HALEY
as The Tin Woodman

BERT LAHR
as The Cowardly Lion

Eddie Polo
Howard Smit
William Tuttle
Betty Masure (body make-up)
Edith Wilson (body make-up)

WIGS

Max Factor
Fred Frederick (Designer)
Bob Roberts (Designer)

HAIRDRESSER

Beth Langston

STILL PHOTOGRAPHERS

Virgil Apger
George Hommel
Eric Carpenter (portrait gallery)
Clarence Sinclair Bull (Billie Burke)

ANIMAL TRAINERS

Carl Spitz (Owner/Trainer of Toto/Terry)
Jack Weatherwax (Toto Trainer)
Freddy Gilman (Trainer of Munchkinland ponies; Horse of a Different Color [impersonated by two horses named Mike and Ike])
Curly Twifard (Trainer of Jim, the raven)
Bill Richards (exotic birds)

PUBLICITY

Howard Dietz
Andy Hervey
Mary Mayer (Unit Publicist)
Si Seadler
Howard Strickling
Frank Whitbeck

MARGARET HAMILTON
as the Wicked Witch

BILLIE BURKE
as The Good Witch

FRANK MORGAN
as The Wizard

NIKKO
Aide to The Wicked Witch

JUDY GARLAND
as Dorothy

RAY BOLGER
as The Scarecrow

JACK HALEY
as The Tin Woodman

BERT LAHR
as The Cowardly Lion

MUSICAL SCORE CONTRACTS AND PERMISSIONS

Nat Finston

M-G-M COMMISSARY

Frances Edwards (Manager), special accommodations for the *Oz* unit

CATERER FOR THE SINGER MIDGETS

Brittingham Commissary, Inc.

BIBLIOGRAPHY

Abbott, Peter. “Inside Stuff” department. *Movie Mirror*, vol. 14, no. 5, April 1939.

Arnold, John, A.S.C. “Hollywood Color Problems.” *Minicam*, vol. 2, no. 12, August 1939.

Baum, L. Frank. *The Wonderful Wizard of Oz*. Chicago: George M. Hill, 1900.

——. *The Patchwork Girl of Oz*. Chicago: Reilly and Britton, 1913.

Benjamin, George. “Setting You Straight on Judy.” *Modern Screen*, vol. 19, no. 6, November 1939.

Bolger, Ray. “*The Wizard of Oz* and the Golden Era of the American Musical Film.” *American Cinematographer*, vol. 59, no. 2, February 1978.

Bolger, Ray. Written questionnaire conducted by Tod Machin, 1983.

Buxton, Teresa. “’Round New York Town” department. *Movie Mirror*, vol. 15, no. 2, July 1939.

Caine, Denise. “A Garland For Beauty.” *Motion Picture*, vol. 58, no. 2, September 1939.

Catsos, Gregory J. M. “That Wonderful Wicked Witch: A Lost Interview with Margaret Hamilton.” *Filmfax*, no. 41, October/November 1993.

——. “An In-Depth Interview with Margaret Hamilton, Jack Haley, and Ray Bolger!” *Hollywood Studio Magazine*, vol. 22, no. 4, April 1989.

Clark, Sue. “How Make-up Made Me into an Emerald Empress.” *Modern Woman*, August 1939.

Collura, Joe. “Lois January: Covering All the Bases.” *Classic Images*, no. 250, April 1996.

Cox, Steve. *The Munchkins of Oz*. Nashville: Cumberland House, 1996.

Croughton, Amy H. “Scanning the Screen.” *Rochester Times-Union*, August 18, 1939.

Crowther, Bosley. “A Lahr unto Himself.” *New York Times*, July 30, 1939.

Dawn, Jack. “Glamour and the Modern Girl.” *Picturegoer*, vol. 9, no. 421, June 17, 1939.

del Valle, John. “After All, Why Does Screen Give All Awards to Bipedal Actors.” *New York Herald Tribune*, August 13, 1939.

Early, Dudley. "*The Wizard of Oz.*" *The Family Circle*, vol. 15, no. 3, July 21, 1939.

Eustis, Morton. "Designing for the Movies: Gibbons of M-G-M." *Theatre Arts Monthly*, vol. 21, no. 10, October 1937.

"Foyer and Greenroom Gossip" column, "Drama and Music" section. *Boston Globe*, September 11, 1904.

Finch, Christopher. *The Art of Walt Disney: From Mickey Mouse to the Magic Kingdoms*. New York: Harry N. Abrams, 1973.

Garland, Judy. "I've Been to the Land of Oz!" as told to Gladys Hall. *Child Life*, vol. 17, no. 9, September, 1939.

Grigsby Doss, Helen. "Dog Stars of the Movies." *The American Girl*, vol. 23, no. 3, March 1940.

Hamilton, Margaret. Written questionnaire conducted by Tod Machin, 1983.

Harmetz, Aljean. *The Making of The Wizard of Oz*. New York: Alfred A. Knopf, 1977.

Harrison, Paul. "Shirley Temple Is Getting to Be a Big Girl Now." Newspaper clipping, circa April 1938.

Hay, Peter. *M-G-M: When the Lion Roars*. Atlanta: Turner Publishing, 1991.

Hollis, Richard, and Brian Sibley. *Walt Disney's Snow White and the Seven Dwarfs and the Making of the Classic Film*. New York: Simon and Schuster, 1987.

"Hollywood Wizards in the Land of Oz." *Baltimore Sun*, August 27, 1939.

Holmes, Anna. "*Oz* in the Pink?" *Entertainment Weekly*, May 30, 1997.

Hope, Bob, with Melville Shavelson. *Don't Shoot, It's Only Me*. New York: Putnam, 1990.

Howe, Anne. "This is Hollywood." *Screen Play*, October 1935.

Kobal, John. *The Art of the Great Hollywood Portrait Photographers*. New York: Alfred A. Knopf, 1980.

"Loew's Inc." *Fortune*, vol. 20, no. 2, August 1939.

"Marvels of Make-up." *Silver Screen*, vol. 9, no. 10, August 1939.

McCaleb, Kenneth. "I Visit Shirley Temple." *New York Sunday Mirror*, April 25, 1937.

McClelland, Doug. *Down the Yellow Brick Road: The Making of The Wizard of Oz*. New York: Pyramid Books, 1976.

McIlwaine, Robert. "Sweet Sixteen." *Modern Screen*, vol. 19, no. 3, August 1939.

McGinnis, Edith. "Pictures You'll Like." *St. Nicholas*, August 1939.

"M-G-M Risks $3,000,000 on *Wizard of Oz*." *Des Moines Sunday Register*, July 2, 1939.

Nugent, Frank. "Fantasy on Strings: *The Wizard of Oz* Is Gay Make-Believe If You Don't Mind Piano Wires." *New York Times*, August 20, 1939.

Othman, Frederick C. "*Wizard of Oz* Replete with Oddities." *Rochester Democrat and Chronicle*, August 14, 1939.

Photoplay Studies. New York: Educational and Recreational Guides, vol. 5, no. 12, series of 1939.

"Portrait of a Woman in Love." *Film Weekly*, September 16, 1939.

Rebello, Stephen, and Richard Allen. *Reel Art: Great Posters from the Golden Age of the Silver Screen*. New York: Abbeville Press, 1988.

Stillwell, Miriam. "The Story Behind Snow White's $10,000,000 Surprise Party." *Liberty*, April 9, 1938.

Sullivan, Ed. "Looking at Hollywood with Ed Sullivan." Newspaper clipping, September 3, 1939.

Surmelian, Leon. "Studio Make-up Artist Confesses." *Motion Picture*, vol. 57, no. 2, March 1939.

Taylor, Al, and Sue Roy. *Making a Monster*. New York: Crown, 1980.

Turner, George. "Behind the Curtain." *American Cinematographer*, vol. 79, no. 12, December 1998.

Underhill, Duncan. "Bert Lahr: Hamlet of Burleycue." *Screen Book*, vol. 22, no. 1, August 1939.

Ussher, Bruno David. "Film Music and Its Makers." *Hollywood Spectator*, May 27, 1939.

Walters, Gwenn. "Fantasy in Fashion." *Photoplay*, vol. 53, no. 8, August 1939.

"*Wizard of Oz*." *Harper's Bazaar*, August 1939.

"*The Wizard of Oz* Now Makes Magic on Screen." *Young America*, September 15, 1939.

Young, Jack. *From the Files of a Hollywood Make-up Artist*. Manuscript, authors' collection.

INDEX

Dedicated to Bill and Dorothy Jansky who have taught us when snapping our own personal ruby slippers all we have and need in life (courage, wisdom and love) has always been there!

by the Audubon Road Social Society

July 2000